A CULTURAL HISTORY OF THE SEA

VOLUME 6

A Cultural History of the Sea
General Editor: Margaret Cohen

Volume 1
A Cultural History of the Sea in Antiquity
Edited by Marie-Claire Beaulieu

Volume 2
A Cultural History of the Sea in the Medieval Age
Edited by Elizabeth Lambourn

Volume 3
A Cultural History of the Sea in the Early Modern Age
Edited by Steven Mentz

Volume 4
A Cultural History of the Sea in the Age of Enlightenment
Edited by Jonathan Lamb

Volume 5
A Cultural History of the Sea in the Age of Empire
Edited by Margaret Cohen

Volume 6
A Cultural History of the Sea in the Global Age
Edited by Franziska Torma

A CULTURAL HISTORY OF THE SEA

IN THE GLOBAL AGE

VOLUME 6

Edited by Franziska Torma

BLOOMSBURY ACADEMIC
LONDON • NEW YORK • OXFORD • NEW DELHI • SYDNEY

BLOOMSBURY ACADEMIC
Bloomsbury Publishing Plc
50 Bedford Square, London, WC1B 3DP, UK
1385 Broadway, New York, NY 10018, USA

BLOOMSBURY, BLOOMSBURY ACADEMIC and the Diana logo are
trademarks of Bloomsbury Publishing Plc

First published in Great Britain 2021
This edition published in Great Britain 2024
Reprinted 2024

Copyright © Bloomsbury Publishing, 2021

Franziska Torma has asserted her right under the Copyright,
Designs and Patents Act, 1988, to be identified as Editor of this work.

Cover image © View of the Earth seen by the Apollo 17 crew traveling
toward the moon (NASA).

All rights reserved. No part of this publication may be reproduced or
transmitted in any form or by any means, electronic or mechanical, including
photocopying, recording, or any information storage or retrieval system,
without prior permission in writing from the publishers.

Bloomsbury Publishing Plc does not have any control over, or responsibility for,
any third-party websites referred to or in this book. All internet addresses given in
this book were correct at the time of going to press. The author and publisher
regret any inconvenience caused if addresses have changed or sites have
ceased to exist, but can accept no responsibility for any such changes.

Every effort has been made to trace copyright holders and to obtain their permissions
for the use of copyright material. The publisher apologizes for any errors or
omissions and would be grateful if notified of any corrections that should be
incorporated in future reprints or editions of this book.

A catalogue record for this book is available from the British Library.

A catalog record for this book is available from the Library of Congress.

ISBN: HB: 978-1-4742-9909-1
       Set: 978-1-4742-9910-7
       PB: 978-1-3504-5129-2
       Set: 978-1-3504-5130-8

Series: The Cultural Histories Series

Typeset by Integra Software Services Pvt. Ltd.
Printed and bound in Great Britain

To find out more about our authors and books visit www.bloomsbury.com
and sign up for our newsletters.

CONTENTS

LIST OF ILLUSTRATIONS   vii

GENERAL EDITOR'S PREFACE
Margaret Cohen   x

Introduction
Franziska Torma   1

1   Knowledges
    Sabine Höhler   21

2   Practices
    Colin Dewey   45

3   Networks
    Johanna Sackel and Anna-Katharina Wöbse   71

4   Conflicts
    Simone M. Müller   95

5   Islands and Shores
    Rebecca Hofmann   117

6   Travelers
    Helen M. Rozwadowski   139

7	Representations *Jon Crylen*	161
8	Imaginary Worlds *Ariane Tanner*	181
NOTES		204
BIBLIOGRAPHY		209
NOTES ON CONTRIBUTORS		239
INDEX		242

ILLUSTRATIONS

FIGURES

0.1	Harbor seal and a plastic bottle	2
0.2	Coral reefs with a school of fish	5
0.3	Map of the world made of garbage	7
0.4	"Earthrise"	9
0.5	The *Titanic*	11
0.6	A humpback whale	20
1.1	Blue Planet: View of the Pacific Ocean by GOES-11 satellite, 2009	22
1.2	"The Principle of Direct Echo Measurement," 1926	27
1.3	"Route and Stations of the *Meteor*, 1925–1927," 1933	29
1.4	"Morphological West-East Profile of the North Atlantic Ocean," 1933	32
1.5	Heezen-Tharp Map of the World Ocean, 1977	36
1.6	Topex-Poseidon Measurement System	39
1.7	View of the Pacific Ocean by TOPEX-Poseidon satellite, 1997	41
2.1	Exterior of Panamanian freighter	50

2.2 Bales of wool being loaded at Victoria Docks in Melbourne   52

2.3 Lascar (Indian or Southeast Asian) stokers in the engine room of
     a P&O steamer shoveling coal to keep the fires burning   54

2.4 A Wessex helicopter owned by the Bristow Helicopter Group flies
     over the Shell supertanker *Melania*   57

2.5 A navigation error led to the grounding of the Liberian flagged
     MV *Rena*, 2011   67

2.6 An employee of a Philippine marine staffing agency for seafarers,
     2008   68

3.1 Onlookers visit the carcass of a slaughtered baleen whale,
     England, 1900   76

3.2 Walther Schücking and José Suárez in the League of Nations'
     committee on the codification of international law   77

3.3 Participants at Pacem in Maribus in Malta, 1971   86

3.4 Presentation to Ambassador Hamilton S. Amerasinghe, 1973   86

3.5 Greenpeace's *Arctic Sunrise* in the harbor of Halifax/Nova
     Scotia, 2016   90

4.1 Members of the Royal Army Ordnance Corps place shells on
     gravity rollers that take the ammunition over the side of the
     ship and into the sea   99

4.2 Barge on its way to the ammunition dumping ground Beaufort's
     Dyke off Cairnryan, Scotland   100

4.3 J.M.W. Turner, *Seascape*, 1828   104

4.4 Barge loaded with ashes on its way to ocean dump, 1973   108

5.1 Islands of Oceania   119

5.2 Japanese Second World War Gun in Chuuk Lagoon   122

5.3 Bow Gun on the *San Francisco Maru*   126

5.4 Nuclear Weapon Test at Bikini Atoll, Micronesia, July 25, 1946   129

5.5 Flood event at Chukiyénú, Toon, Chuuk, November and December 2011 — 135

6.1 *Popular Science* cover from July 1953 — 143

6.2 Scuba diving training at a pool in Madison, Wisconsin, 1961 — 145

6.3 Irving and Exy Johnson at the wheel of the schooner *Yankee* with their son in 1938 — 150

6.4 *Hōkūle`a*, a double-hulled Hawaiian voyaging canoe, arriving in Honolulu from Tahiti in 1976 — 152

6.5 Endangered southern right whale sighted by a whale watcher off Patagonia — 157

7.1 Cartoon announcing undersea photography — 164

7.2 Esther Williams with Tom and Jerry in *Dangerous When Wet*, 1953 — 168

7.3 Filming of a scene from Disney's *20,000 Leagues Under the Sea*, 1954 — 169

7.4 Extreme close-up of coral polyps in Tubbataha, Phillipines — 171

8.1 Rachel Carson standing seaside, examining specimen in jar — 182

8.2 Antique illustration of life in a water drop — 186

8.3 Melvin Calvin inspects *Chlorella* tanks in his laboratory, Berkeley, 1961 — 189

8.4 *Soylent Green* (1973), film still — 192

8.5 NASA ocean data shows "climate dance" of plankton, 2014 — 197

8.6 NASA NEEMO 22, aquanaut crew, 2017 — 200

TABLE

4.1 Existing International and Regional Ocean Dumping Conventions — 114

GENERAL EDITOR'S PREFACE

MARGARET COHEN

Over the past thirty years, oceanic studies has emerged in the humanities as a leading interdisciplinary field. It owes its importance to its capacity to give an account of globalization spanning millenia that is robustly cross-cultural. As this new field has taken shape, it has both incorporated and revised an earlier generation of scholarship, which attended to maritime transport, naval warfare, and global exploration, often within a framework of national history. Contributions of oceanic studies range across scales: from showing how maritime transport and marine resources join separated lands into water-based regions to resurrecting how a meeting on a beach between societies never before in contact could create intractable structures of domination to revealing the impact of a single photograph from outer space of the earth as a blue planet. Today, oceanic studies aims to tell the stories of all who have traveled the seas: professionals, adventurers, passengers, forced migrants—and animals.

Further, this emerging field recognizes that the seas are a rich realm for the imagination, all the more so given the paradoxical tension between their remoteness for many people and yet their life-sustaining importance. It is telling that a poet, the Nobel prize-winning Derek Walcott, has penned the memorable phrase, "The Sea is History."[1] At the same time, the imagination of the seas is not purely fanciful but rather takes shape in relation to located marine environments and how humans practice them, leading humanists to engage the reality of the physical world. When modern oceanography and marine biology took shape in the nineteenth century, these sciences established the oceans as nonhuman natural realms, despite their prehistory in mixed, practical knowledge conjoining environmental curiosity with the pursuit of power and wealth. Since this disciplinary cleavage, the sea has time and time again shown us the need to recognize its existence for and with humans, as well as in itself.

GENERAL EDITOR'S PREFACE

In the twenty-first century, the importance of the sea in world-defining developments, including second-wave globalization, postcolonial conflict, and climate change, has become so evident that its social and cultural reality cannot be ignored. In the words of Franziska Torma, volume editor of *The Global Age*, such developments have "forced us to 'think science and humanities' together, because science provides data and humanities 'translate' them into social and academic interpretation; this opens up historical perspective on the oceans from antiquity to the present" (Franziska Torma, personal communication, May 2020). Whether drawing on nautical archaeology resurrecting sunken cities and shipwrecks, or using scientific research about the impact of climate change on coastal communities, oceanic studies is taking the lead among humanities fields in pursuing this urgent, if vexed, disciplinary crossing.

In editing *A Cultural History of the Sea*, I have been fortunate to work with volume editors who have made major contributions to setting the agenda of oceanic studies in its twenty-first-century form. Taken together, their expertise encompasses the oceans of the globe, notably the Mediterranean, the Indian Ocean, the Atlantic, and the Pacific and includes the history of science and the environment as well. We have launched our project from our institutional homes in transatlantic universities, even as we mark our starting point at once to acknowledge and brush against the grain of Western-oriented perspectives. Further, readers will see that the abstraction Western itself fractures when subjected to the pressure of water-based movement and seafaring practices. Thus, maritime travel creates far-flung contact zones across thousands of kilometers, which cannot be reduced to the orientation of the West, even if Western Europe may have been a point of departure. These contact zones are characterized by extreme social complexity, which modify those whom they involve, and the importance of the physical environment in such contact zones creates yet another set of considerations. The demands of sea-oriented life, moreover, unmoor those who work on ships to the point where they may be a culture unto themselves, unnervingly apart for their societies, due to such factors as the rigors of shipboard living and the multicultural *habitus* even on vessels enforcing the routes of empire.

Our interest in conveying the heterogeneous histories that meet on the sea extends to the themes we have chosen for our series' organization. A unique feature of the Bloomsbury *Cultural History* series is to devise eight chapter headings for each volume that can run from antiquity to the present. These headings address culture understood in its expansive, anthropological sense: as designating the diverse realms of practices organizing the structures of a society. In the case of the seas, important aspects include but are not limited to war, technology, and trade at sea, scientific knowledge, as well as myth and imagination. We defined our themes in a fashion that would enable contributors to present a democratic history. Thus, for example, we framed histories of "War and Empire," at sea as "Conflicts," to take account of the many scales of violent struggles at sea, including frames of state-supported navies, non-state actors, and the violence of shipboard life, ranging from mutinies to treatment of passengers and transport of the enslaved. Or thus, we reframed the theme "Science and Technology," as "Knowledges," to provide an opportunity to include knowledge beyond the strict boundary of science. Such knowledge ranges from philosophical speculation in classical antiquity to sea knowledge and practice outside Western paradigms.

In organizing the chapters, we have respected conventional Western historical periodization, which has been shaped by events on land. At the same time, readers will find within the volumes chapters that take up the question of whether such periodization stops at shore, due to the previously mentioned pressures of a sea perspective on concepts whose operations are focused toward the land. Thus, the history of Egyptian seafaring and contacts with other cultures of the Mediterranean basin traverses the land-based periodization of this particular culture, traditionally understood in terms of its ruling dynasties, from Greek prehistory through the classical period and into Roman times, roughly the second millennium BCE to the first century CE. Within the modern era, to take the example of a single technology, the years from 1769 to 1989 form one period in the history of navigation, although this epoch runs across three volumes in the series. In 1769, British engineer John Harrison perfected a chronometer that would keep accurate time over a long traverse. With the ability to compare noon during a ship's traverse and noon at an arbitrarily defined starting point—it became the Greenwich Meridian by convention—navigators could finally establish their longitude while a ship was sailing, a development that would vastly improve safety at sea, even if it took decades to expand beyond naval circles. Celestial navigation would remain the best practice for establishing a ship's location until the invention of the global positioning system (GPS) in the third quarter of the twentieth century, which could be dated to 1989, when the US Department of Defense launched a satellite system that would become GPS, replacing with the touch of a few buttons the arduous calculations needed for celestial navigation.

Another dimension to the specificity of sea-based periodization is the timescale of the oceans as a physical environment. For eons marine history moved at a geological pace, but in the age of the Anthropocene we are learning about the human impact on a realm of the planet long considered an inexhaustible resource and a vast power beyond human reach. Such an impact can occur within a person's lifetime, as is the case, for example, with melting ice caps at the poles, which have drastically diminished in satellite visualizations, dating back to 1979 (Starr 2016). This impact in turn is affecting societies, from Indigenous inhabitants of the Arctic to farmers around the world, who depend on weather patterns disrupted by global warming. Yet further entangling human and geological timescales at sea, melting ice caps open up new shipping routes through the Arctic, which present potential for a greater human footprint there.

The global consequences of polar ice melt exemplify how a sea perspective reorients terrestrial units of geographical analysis, which is the case not only for the oceans as an environment but also for the oceans as an arena of human practice. Chapters across the series reveal how state-drawn borders may be less important for cultures at sea than fluid spaces defined by natural features, and how islands or coasts eccentric from the perspective of land-based history may play an outsized, formative role in a nation's oceanic ambitions. Further, sea transport produces states that are at once joined under the same flag yet are also territorially disconnected, with unique and uniquely difficult administrative features. Yet another challenge, at the lexical level, is that when we try to express oceanic phenomena with language from the land, we reach to unsatisfactory imagery that impedes understanding. A good example today is the great "garbage patch" of pollution in the Pacific Ocean. The figure of a "patch" misleadingly limits its reach and does not capture the microscopic pervasion of plastic in sea water.

The seas are vast expanses, whose study drives home the point that any research is necessarily fragmentary and located. Contributors to these volumes include established and emerging voices, who have written chapters that are original research around our central themes rather than summaries of secondary literature. Volume editors have encouraged their contributors to present their insights in whatever way they thought would best bring out the originality of their topic and suit their disciplinary expertise. Some have used the narrative of a survey. Other have taken a single event as their canvas, whether the event is exemplary or tellingly anomalous. Yet others have spun out their questions at the scale of one marine environment.

Such flexibility is also important because "the sea" of our series' title is not one thing. Rather, the saltwater element is culturally constructed and imagined in widely different ways, depending on who is engaging with it and to what ends. This range is evident as well in the rich imagery accompanying the chapters, which is another feature of the *Cultural History* series. Thus, readers will see how in antiquity, the sea was never represented directly but rather suggested metonymically on frescoes and vases, with depictions of fish, ships, or mythological sea creatures. Grand seascapes, exhibiting the ocean as a theatre of awe, in contrast, compelled audiences in Enlightenment and Romantic eras. One constant across centuries are practical charts, which have used a variety of methods, shaped by different epistemes and environments, to find and mark paths across the waters, all nonetheless sharing an aim of safety. To draw a parallel between navigating vast, and in many cases, untracked waters and emergent areas of scholarship: as readers constellate the diverse subjects and approaches collected in this series, I hope they will gain a better understanding of the abiding, pervasive human interface with the seas as well as recognize new and future directions for oceanic studies.

Introduction

The Sea as Culture in the Global Age

FRANZISKA TORMA

What is the difference between the cultural history of the sea and "the unnatural history of sea," as the professor of marine conservation Callum Roberts (2007) has put it? This question can be addressed by looking at the relationship between nature and culture in the twentieth and twenty-first centuries. In the global age, ideas of untouched nature, of virgin land- and seascapes, have become phantoms: thirty years ago, the *New York Times* journalist Bill McKibben (1989) announced the end of nature. Bill McKibben's swansong of wilderness and the Garden of Eden came along with the rising awareness in the Western world that human culture and society have left deep footprints on the earth's surface. Biologists and conservation societies talk of the "sixth wave of extinction" (Wikipedia 2020). The earth has lost half of its wildlife according to the World Wildlife Fund (Carrington 2014). Human footprints on nature can be found everywhere: in waste and pollution, in melting polar icescapes, and in plastic remains in the water (see Figure 0.1).

Political, economic, and social history considers the global age as the "Age of Extremes" (Hobsbawn 1994), but the cultural footprints on nature have also become part of scholarship in recent times. Environmental history and the history of science contemplate the global age as the "Anthropocene." Bringing culture and the environment together, the Anthropocene appears as one of these extremes.

FIGURE 0.1 Harbor seal with a plastic bottle. © Cliff Nietvelt/Getty Images.

Although the wide public and academic use of the term "Anthropocene" is relatively new, the idea itself dates back to the nineteenth century. Geologist Antonio Stoppani, for example, observed the effects how modern modes of production, communication, and transportation had changed the earth. He acknowledged a new "anthropozoic era" as early as the 1870s. Scientists in the Soviet Union used "the Anthropocene" in the 1960s, to describe the most recent geological epoch. Limnologist Eugene Stoermer talked informally of the "anthropocene" in the 1970s and 1980s, but it was atmospheric chemist Paul J. Crutzen who popularized it from the year 2000 onwards (Crutzen 2002; Trischler 2016). In recent times, the "Anthropocene" has received public attention as a way to describe the intensified human impacts on Earth since the Industrial Revolution. Journals, newspapers, academic articles, talks, and exhibitions present humanity as a geological agent. In 2008, the Stratigraphy Commission of the Geological Society of London first attempted to formalize the Anthropocene as a geological epoch (Zalasiewicz 2008) and created the "Anthropocene Working Group." This interdisciplinary group has been making strong arguments for the Anthropocene as new geological epoch.[1] Drilling cores show the layers of human impact on Earth.

Human footprints cannot only be found in the earth's strata, but the Anthropocene has changed the meaning of culture. Culture is no longer restricted to the realm of human civilization and the fine arts. Human culture is intertwined with nature, humans either appear as a threat to the planet or as its hope. In both cases, cultural practices entangle the natural and the human worlds. In the years of global environmental extremes, the stories that have unfolded in between gain in importance (LeCain 2016). History can be considered as one way of giving cultural meaning to the Anthropocene.

In this history, the oceans are a predominant space, because water makes the materiality of planet Earth and is the precondition of human life. Histories of the oceans can make sense of the current situation by looking at stories from the past. The sea connects the past with our present and future (see Tanner in this volume). The oceans are a culturally framed environment, where human actors and global natures meet. On shores and islands, underwater and on land, humans and the sea have interacted over centuries. The twentieth and twenty-first centuries are the years of intensified contacts, when the sea was rediscovered as an integral part of system Earth.[2]

TRACES: LAYERS AND MOVEMENTS

The Anthropocene is a concept of deep time and deep space. It takes its legitimation from geology. The fossil record has preserved the human impact on Earth. Technofossils, human debris, and litter have become part of the stratigraphy. The last two hundred years have brought most of the planetary changes associated with the Anthropocene. Accelerated industrialization has left visible traces on Earth and in its atmosphere, such as the increase of carbon dioxide, global warming, and the loss of biodiversity. Drilling cores display the strata of human technological progress as well as the resulting pollution (Ellis 2018; Möllers, Schwägerl, and Trischler 2015; Steffen et al. 2011). This industrial output can be seen in terrestrial geology, but how did the Anthropocene impact the water? Oceans are the opposite of solid rocks. They are fluid and move in currents and waves. Water cannot preserve human traces as the compact layers of the land do. The sea has its own hydrographical structure, a coastline and a shore, a surface and a floor. The water is layered in five distinct zones: the photic zone extends from the surface to approximately 200 meters deep. It is the part of the ocean that sunlight reaches. Coral reefs grow in this part, and photosynthesis takes place there. Humans use this zone for leisure activities (swimming, diving), for fishing and travel (oceanic transport). The mesopelagic zone (twilight or midwater zone) is beneath it. It reaches from 200 to 700–1,000 meters below the surface. Only a little sunlight penetrates. Animals such as swordfish live here. The bathyal is between 1,000 and 4,000 meters deep. It is the midnight zone of the ocean. Immense pressure reigns and influences the physiognomy and appearance of the deep sea fish. Most mammals could not exist there, but sperm whales are adapted to search for food in this zone for a limited time. The next zone, the abyssal, lies between 4,000 and 6,000 meters deep; temperatures are near zero, and there is no natural light. Invertebrates such as squids and sea stars exist here. The hadal zone corresponds to the trenches of the ocean basin, between 6,000 meters and the bottom of the ocean. Natural light does not come through, but some fish are able to live there. Humans would need specialized equipment (diving vessels or remote sensing devices) to enter and get insights into this part of the ocean. These five zones are distinct but interconnected by the flow of the water.[3] Although humans can only reach the first zone without great efforts, they have influenced the other parts of the oceans as well—but how can we keep and read the traces of human culture in this fluid environment?

We can think of two ways of considering the human connections to the sea: the environmentalist and the romantic approach (see as well Rozwadowski 2018: 148–51, 210–13).[4] Both follow human traces through the different zones of the sea. The environmentalist approach emphasizes how climate change has influenced the ocean. The rise in sea temperature and in sea levels, as well as the melting of the polar icescapes, has changed the movement of the water. The system of global ocean streams is likely to change its direction and pace in the near future. Due to the rise in global temperature, the oceans' ecologies have already been changing. Coral bleaching is leading to the death of coral reefs and so-called "invasive species" (classics on "terrestrial" debates on the topic are Crosby 1986, 1994) are altering the global seascapes. Bio "invaders" have arrived in new locations via trade ships, battle ships, passenger ships, and cargo ships, either as stowaways attached to the vessel or with the ballast water that ships drain off in ports of call (Bergstrom and Chown 1999; Carlton 2019; Williams et al. 1988). In addition, overfishing has changed the biology of the sea (Jackson et al. 2001). Whales and polar bears roaming in their natural habitat could soon become memories on picture postcards. When one species disappears from a niche, another one settles in. In the twentieth and twenty-first centuries, humans appear as invasive species. They have started to move through almost every layer and zone of the ocean, starting with the discovery of the deep and open sea in the beginning of the nineteenth century, and evident in the diving industry of the present day. The mechanization of fisheries and the expansion of fishing grounds all over the globe have led to new cultures of exploitation, such as deep sea fisheries. In the 1950s, the idea of the "living resources" came into being, to differentiate between two ways of deploying the sea (United Nations 1955). The mineral resources on the ocean floor, manganese nodules, promised new sources of energy, fueling the rapid industrialization that followed the Second World War on a global scale (Jonsson 2012; Ruppenthal 2018). Developing nations discovered the animals in their coastal waters as riches of the sea and their path to modernity and wealth. The living resources are on the way to extinction. Although fisheries sciences calculated "sustainability" as the exact amount of fish that could be extracted to keep the ocean profitable on a global scale (Finley 2011), overfishing changed the equilibrium of ecology and economy in such a way that animals disappeared from the coastlines of the Global South. Recent environmentalist efforts to manage fisheries have restricted certain industrial fishery techniques.

Developing states needed (and need) new sources of income and discovered tourism: the European shores became leisure spots for aristocrats in the late eighteenth and early nineteenth century (Corbin 1994). In the twentieth century, tourists stepped into the eco-cultural niche that was opened up by the disappearing fish and fishing industry in Asia and Australia (Biggs et al. 2015; Miller 1993).

In the second half of the twentieth century, ocean travel expanded horizontally and vertically. Voyagers, who had formerly traveled to the beaches in Europe and North America, became attracted by the touristic development of the Asian shores. Travelers, who used to swim, started to dive. Tourism led to new challenges for marine ecologies but also brought landlubbers into contact with the sea. Fathoming, plumbing, and dredging had emerged as human practices of engaging with the deep and open sea in the last decades of the nineteenth century, but scientists and navy officers saw and experienced the open sea only from a distance. They either collected specimens at the shore or investigated the water from the ship's deck. Diving brought people into underwater worlds they might have already known from the colorful movies of Jacques-Yves Cousteau. Movies reframed the romantic approach: looking on cinema screens at the last coral reefs that were (still) alive could awake human appreciation of the oceans' beauty (see Figure 0.2 and Crylen in this volume).

FIGURE 0.2 Coral reefs with a school of fish. © Csaba Tökölyi/Getty Images.

The romantic approach emphasizes the bonds of humans with the oceans. One special branch of romantic biology was inspired by Darwin's work, but also by romantic natural philosophy. Holistic thought connected science and the appreciation of the oceans (Esposito 2013): the sea has been discovered as a living organism in the twentieth century. Ocean expeditions, and the research on microorganisms and deep-sea creatures, created the awareness of the deep as an animated environment, or "biosphere" (Höhler 2015b). Analogies with the human body emerged. Like the human body, the ocean has, or even is, a metabolism that the stress of climate change affects (Thompson 2015).

Starting with Darwin's theory of evolution, the oceans have been considered the origin of global life. According to Darwin's terracentric view, however, homo sapiens emerged from the land. In 1972, Elaine Morgan formulated the aquatic ape theory that gave evolution an oceanic and feministic turn: humanity did not descend from the plains of Africa, but from a female water creature, the aquatic ape (Hardy 1960; Morgan 1972, 1982; Westenhöfer 1942). On the one hand, this theory melded older myths of sirens and mermaids with (apparently) marine biological evidence. On the other hand, it reinvented the ocean as an evolutionary continuum: the pure possibility of becoming aquatic (again) allowed imaginations of new relationships between sea creatures and the human world (see Rozwadowski and Tanner in this volume). One could ask: if humanity came from the sea, are not whales and dolphins the nearest relatives of homo sapiens?

The (imagined) evolutionary bonds and biological fascination made whales and dolphins the most prominent examples of charismatic megafauna in the ocean. In most parts of the Western world, whales were heraldic animals of marine conservation, and at the center of the first conservation laws (Wöbse 2012). In the ocean, conservation was not static but instead moved from these individual life-forms to the three-dimensional ocean space. Marine national parks can be seen as a romantic answer to human traces that became visible in the sea. Putting stretches of water under protection, from the surface to the floor, was an attempt to minimize human impact on these areas, where the oceans' stress was most measurable. These marine reserves, however, follow the nostalgic idea that runaway climate change can be stopped by defining water bodies as protected (Gerber and Hooker 2004; Pollnac et al. 2010). Time cannot be stopped by encircling space. Feelings of nearness with warm-blooded sea mammals or the appreciation of beautiful seascapes are the flipsides of the heavy exploitation of fish stocks, of pollution, and of the material changes of the ocean as biosphere. Seen from below the waves, the whale and the cod are antipodes within the oceanic imagination. The whale is the emblematic figure of romantic conservation; the cod stands for the crash of the fishing industry (Walters and Maguire 1996; Harris 1999; Kurlansky 1998). Both animals were

FIGURE 0.3 Map of the world made of garbage. © Benjamin Shearn/Getty Images.

parts of the material world. Culture and history mediate the tensions between the imagined and the material worlds.

We can see that the water as very substance has been changed and is changing. Plastic particles and garbage are flowing as a new biological category into oceanic life cycles (see Figure 0.3). Microplastics have the potential to dissolve the boundaries between culture and nature substantially, by entering the food chain and the human body.

INTERPRETATION: PICTURES AND STORIES

Three master narratives frame today's academic and media trains of thoughts on the sea: declensionist history, the narration of the "eternal sea," and the eco-romantic narrative. They either emerged from the environmentalist approach or are variants of romantic appreciation.

1. Environmental history started with land-based topics in the years between the 1950s and the 1970s. The sea joined in with a certain time lag. It was not cultural interpretation but the materiality of resource exploitation that linked the sea with the planetary "Limits to Growth" (Meadows et al. 1974). In 1990, the New England cod fishery collapsed and failed to recover in the following years (Rozwadowski 2018: 217–18). The environmentalist view of the ocean brought a declensionist history to the fore: the oceans have been and are dying. This narrative culminated in Jeffrey Bolster's book *The Mortal Sea* (2012).

2. Before anthropogenic change had become visible, the narration of the eternal sea was a single master narrative. The oceans have been considered as timeless entities, a notion that was connected to the mythical realm of the Bible or the fables of antiquity. Between the 1970s and the twenty-first century, the sea came to be seen as endangered. This interpretation challenged the notion of the sea as chaos, wilderness, and a realm beyond history, a space that human intervention cannot affect or change (Bolster 2006).

3. This tale of the eternal sea is still one undertone of modern eco-romantic notions, a subtle longing for what and how nature *could* be, if humanity would not destroy it. Modern romantics search for an earthly paradise. They emphasize the sublimity of the oceans as a special place on planet Earth.

In the Anthropocene, however, humans have entered "Eden." The romantic approach of the twenty-first century connects notions of sublimity and human practices. The sea reemerged as a special place on the globe that can be destroyed or protected by humans. Within this eco-romantic narrative, the sea appears as the "other world" of planet Earth, as a sunken space, where strange creatures live and unfamiliar natural laws reign, and into which humans can only enter if they are prepared and well equipped (Helmreich 2009). The ocean, however, is also considered in an environmentalist way, as the "sea around us," the world we live with, as Rachel Carson (1951) put it as early as the 1950s.

THE GLOBE: "BLUE PLANET"

Carson popularized the intrinsic value of the ocean with a perspective from within, but the image that made water visible as the main component of the earth's surface, was a view from the outside. The photograph of the earth as seen from outer space gave rise to the term "Blue Planet." It was taken on the Apollo 17 lunar mission from a distance of about 45,000 kilometers, on December 7, 1972. The globe appeared as the size of a glass marble, covered with clouds. The "Blue Marble" had a predecessor, the picture "Earthrise" taken by the astronaut during the Apollo 8 mission, on December, 24, 1968 (see Figure 0.4).

"Earthrise" and "Blue Marble" were released in the years of emerging environmentalism. For the cultural history of the sea, these pictures are more than mere environmental icons. They are iconic for the sea as culture in the global age. They bridge the temporal gap to previous centuries (Cohen and Elkins-Tanton 2017). They play with tensions of the oceanic and the satellite sublime (Sörlin and Wormbs 2018; Wormbs 2017). "Earthrise" and "Blue Marble" suggest a view from above and the outside, while the viewer is summoned to live with the earth that is depicted from above. The sublimity of the earth opens space for an interplay of proximity and distance. Feelings of nearness (with the whale, for example) and alienation (from the cod) were

FIGURE 0.4 "Earthrise." © Wikimedia Commons (public domain).

framed by spatial abstraction (seen from outer space). The Anthropocene picks up on themes sparked by "Earthrise" and "Blue Marble." They appear as visions of wholeness and fragility that are constructed by human technology. They point to the future, to humanity's common destiny on the water-covered planet, traveling through space.

In addition, they meld with particular eras: "Blue Marble" was taken during the last crewed lunar mission, and henceforth this picture, like no other, links the end of heroic frontier exploration with the future. Cold War politics triggered the exploration of the planet's final frontiers, outer space, and inner space (Rozwadowski 2012). During the Cold War years, ocean and outer-space research were in competition. Could either the moon or the ocean floor serve as living space for humans? This question stood at the threshold of older colonial fantasies, claiming "empty" spaces on a global scale and doomsday visions of where humanity could go when the surface of the earth was destroyed. The successful moon landing and the sheer possibility of going there, like Neil Armstrong did, finally shifted public fascination and the state funding machine from the ocean to space (Hamblin 2005). This shift speaks to a special kind of remoteness of the oceans from humans' everyday lives. The moon seemed to be more accessible than the deepest trench on planet Earth! Due to the biological constraints of the human body, and the opaque nature of water, the ocean stayed the "other world" of the planet. The sea, however, created new, even more contradictory utopias in the Cold War years. As soon as the possibility of material conquest was dissolved, other ways of appropriating the sea were invented. The ocean emerged as a "common heritage of mankind," but also as a potentially inexhaustible and self-regenerating reservoir of resources. This later focus on resources has still a legacy and legitimation in its humanistic version. Techno-cultural fantasies speak of energy generation from the sea, developmentalist visions of fighting world hunger by utilizing the ocean's biomass.

In the depths of the ocean, narratives from the past are never gone. The currents of the sea do not follow simple structures; they show disturbances and unexpected temperature patterns, the waters sometimes even glow. Nor do the temporal layers of ocean history follow a simple linear movement (Bolster 2006: 581). The sea connects the past and future of human cultures on planet Earth—in waves and currents, sometimes in circles and vertical and horizontal movements. Past and present narratives and images form an oceanic repertoire. In that repertoire, apparently older and seemingly outdated words and images can come to the surface again, since they were not simply replaced by newer layers of meaning but framed in new ways. Older romantic ideas converged with environmentalism, economic interests with conservation. Stories are part of the human traces on the hydrographical record. The cultural history of the sea in the global age is confronted with the simultaneousness of these oceanic layers of meaning.

THE VOLUME: THE LONG TWENTIETH CENTURY AS VIEWED FROM THE OCEAN

Multiple stories, of multiple oceans, told in various ways, from different standpoints build the narrative structure of this volume. The experiences of different actors unveil the extent to which human contact with the sea is mediated by technologies, imaginations, and representations (Rozwadowski 2012: 583). Media and transport technologies gave voyagers, divers, scientists, and filmmakers new opportunities to enter and represent the ocean.

The chapters in this volume encompass what is known as the "long twentieth century" (Arrighi 2010). They start in the years of European nationalism and high imperialism and end in the present. Nationalism and imperialism were political but also cultural phenomena. Within the spheres of international cultural competition, national prestige could be demonstrated by technological devices that would become the Anthropocene's techno-fossils. At the beginning of the twentieth century, however, they were not debris but "Modern Wonders": "technologies occupied a prominent place in British and German public life" (Rieger 2003: 53). The introduction of steel into ship design "gave birth to luxurious 'floating palaces'" (153). Even in these times, passenger ships displayed sociocultural ambiguities in the face of technological innovations. The fear of technology's failure melded with the enthusiasm for mastering the elements: the air and the waves. The media played a crucial role in communicating modernity's victory over nature. One of the marvelous sea-going vessels was the liner *Titanic* (Figure 0.5).

Picture postcards stylized the ship as a symbol of "Western civilization." From an oceanic viewpoint, it was not only the First World War, with the advent of submarine warfare that was the seminal catastrophe of the young twentieth century. The first key event at sea was the sinking of the *Titanic*. This event was one of the greatest maritime disasters in the world. About 1,500 people died. It had far-reaching legal consequences. *Titanic*'s primary message

FIGURE 0.5 The *Titanic*. © Wikimedia commons (public domain).

was that human hybrids cannot fully master oceanic nature. The question of guilt, who exactly was responsible for the accident, led to governmental investigations; the lessons learned influenced safety regulations at sea. In January 1914, the first Convention on Safety of Life at Sea (SOLAS) in London took decisions on life-saving equipment, ship construction, signaling processes, and protocols (see Dewey in this volume). Strategies to avoid similar disasters included the improvement of radiotelegraphy and precise acoustic navigation (see Höhler in this volume). The First World War continued these efforts to improve marine technologies. Warfare triggered research in acoustic measurement, as a technology to locate hostile submarines and ships. Maritime technologies floated between the military and civilian sphere. In the interwar period, the echo depth sounder emerged as a scientific technology to measure the depth and structure of the ocean floor for scientific purposes (see Höhler in this volume).

After the First World War, colonial and multinational empires collapsed on land, and the ideas of self-determination triggered demands for independence in the colonies. The First World War changed global seascapes as well: Germany lost its former Pacific colonies; Japan and the United States formalized their claims on the South Pacific (see Hofmann in this volume). The League of Nations emerged as a new political power. It watched over the new territorial and oceanic regimes. In the interwar period, the League of Nations structured new cultures of environmental diplomacy. Based on early concepts of the sea as shared human heritage, a network of advocates for protecting the sea came into being. The topics anticipated today's debates: the ocean's beauty and fragility, as well as its endangerment through pollution, stood on their agendas. These early concepts of a global marine management regime remained vague (see Wöbse and Sackel in this volume). Simultaneously, technology gave birth to new ways of imagining and visualizing the underwater world. Film made the world beneath the waves accessible for the viewer (see Crylen in this volume). High-performance microscopes and microphotography made plankton visible, one of the tiniest fragments of oceanic life. These microbial animals and plants became the basis of the concept of biomass that fueled utopias of controlling (and exploiting) the oceanic metabolism (see Tanner in this volume).

The Second World War brought destruction and violence on the surface of the globe, but its effects could and can be found beneath the waves as well. The weapons of the war, for example, were dumped into the ocean, in the hope that its waters would wash the evils away (see Müller in this volume). Being under the waves was equated with being out of sight. Dumping and movies are different practices and cultural products, but share a similar ontology. The oceanic world cannot be seen in everyday life, and for many people the invisible is beyond knowledge. "Viewing" created a form of pictorial knowledge (see Crylen in this volume, on the case of the movies). "Hiding" hazardous items caused the opposite: the hope that their disappearance from human sight would dissolve the problems themselves. Dumping, furthermore, tells a story of conflicts in the long twentieth century. It shows that some oceanic wars were silent ones. The ocean's currents, however, brought the waste from the ground to the surface again. The bits and pieces of poisonous and explosive materials reappeared in the 1960s and 1970s (see Müller in this volume). They reemerged at a time when society became susceptible to the idea that pollution was an environmental problem, and modern environmental activism gained shape. Yet the predominant focus of scholarship on the emergence of environmentalism on land overlooks the oceanic currents that paved the way for it. People learned about the environment through reading, listening to, and watching stories of an ecosystem that they cannot see (see Crylen in this volume; Rozwadowski 2018: 202–4).

Hence, the oceans became places for scientific research, romantic visions, and environmental concerns as well as laboratories for new regimes of governance. In the years when modern environmentalism emerged, international agencies (such as the United Nations and its multiple subdivisions) inaugurated an era of global governance. Political cooperation on an inter- or transnational level was intended to help in solving problems that affected the world beyond a regional or national scope. Governance created a new notion of globalization. It reacts to interdependencies between different societies, the political, the economic, and the cultural sector, as well as between humans and the biosphere.

The sea was one of the first environments that unified global governance and diverse diplomatic networks. These networks became most influential in the years when public concerns about the health of the oceans gained shape (see Wöbse and Sackel in this volume). Between 1956 und 1982, the United Nations hosted several conferences on the Law of the Sea (UNCLOS I, II, III). The UNCLOS III convention stated that the marine environment should be protected from human exploitation (United Nations 1982). In fact, this ideal principle was codified only for the ocean floor and its resources. The open sea remained untouched by legal restrictions. In the years of postcolonial participation, UNCLOS III's agenda was to secure the equal sharing of the oceans' mineral resources and to restrict the exclusive access of the industrialized countries. Fish, the living resources, were part of a different global vision. The Food and Agricultural Organization (FAO) aimed at closing the protein gap in the Global South. Contradictions between claim and reality expressed itself plainest in the ideal of the sea as a "common heritage of mankind" (Amstutz 2018).

The concept of the global commons predated the long twentieth century, and originally described international, supranational, and global domains, where resources could be found (Neeson 1995). The term comes from patterns of using "common land" in the British Isles. In the 1970s, it was expanded to describe the earth as the heritage of every human. The deep ocean, the atmosphere, outer space, and the Polar regions cannot be claimed by one state or society.

Recently, the United Nations Environment Programme (UNEP) has identified new strategies for managing the marine commons. Building national capacities for actions in developing countries, as well as the improvement of fisheries management, of trans-regional cooperation, and of the control of nuclear and hazardous waste, should be strengthened to protect the oceans for future generations. A recent program identified a worldwide system of large, strictly protected marine reserves (Thorpe, Failler, and Bavinck 2011; see also UN Environmental Programme; International Union for Conservation). The question, however, of who defines the pattern of use and limits access to the sea still remains in the hands of diplomats and lobby groups, mainly with backgrounds in industrialized nations (see Wöbse and Sackel in this volume; see Müller in this volume for the special case of dumping conflicts).

The cultural history of the sea displays the frictions within the colonized/decolonized world that continued into recent times. Especially in the Anthropocene, people in the Global North suffer less from climate change, sea-level rise, and global warming than people in the Global South. The distribution of cause and consequence are uneven on a global scale. Whereas the industrialized nations produce most of the problems, people in the Global South bear most of the consequences. Islands drown and seascapes change rapidly, tremendously, and irreversibly (see Hofmann in this volume).

Taking developments and contradictions, as well as continuities and breaks, into account, this volume suggests a certain periodization. The first phase started with the emergence of marine science and the fascination of technology in the era of imperialism. Legacies of imperialism still influence the postcolonial situation up to the present, but the First World War and the *Titanic* disaster also led to the loss of (Western) confidence in the human mastery of the waves. The second period encompasses the interwar period. During this time, the first schemes of international governance emerged within the League of Nations, together with new ways of making the sea visible on the movie screen. Ocean travel expanded, horizontally and vertically (see Rozwadowski in this volume). First visions of the oceans' beauty and fragility began to circulate in politics and the public. The third period started in the 1940s/1950s, with the broad success of Rachel Carson's ocean books *Under the Sea Wind* (1941) and *The Sea Around Us* (1951) as a prequel to (terrestrial) environmentalism. Movies and visions of the oceans' beauty and fragility began to influence politics and the public. In the 1970s, the new awareness of the health of the sea was connected with environmental activism. Campaigns did not put the sea as an entity on central stage but rather focused on the topics of marine mammals and oil pollution. These debates had their roots in the 1920s (see Wöbse and Sackel in this volume). The emerging awareness did not change practices of exploitation, which continue today, but the environmental years culminated in the new extreme of the Anthropocene. A different strand of *longue durée* than cultural history draws our attention to long-term phenomena in the oceanic environments, such as the El Niño effect (see Höhler in this volume). These affect the world on a global scale.

Looking at the oceans in the age of the Anthropocene shifts the common interpretation of the twentieth century. The "Age of Extremes" starts with the rise and ends with the decline of communisms in a "short twentieth century." The narrative highlights the world wars, the Cold War, the processes of decolonization, the end of communism, and (if we wish to complete the list with respects to recent extremisms) new forms of terrorism, mass migration, and right-wing movements. Terrestrial views of globalization emphasize the movement of commodities, people, and information. Seen from the islands, shores, and underwater worlds, the "long twentieth century" looks different. The metaphoric dimension emphasizes "flows," "circulation," and "fluidity."[5] The fluid way of looking at history gives key events of the twentieth century new meaning. The world wars, for example, are only traceable in their legacies, or as effects on society and culture. They informed social practices in the Pacific (see Hofmann in this volume) or made new technologies available for civilian use in the Western world. Diving gear was improved for military use before it became a leisure device in the 1950s (see Rozwadowski in this volume). The process of decolonization gave people in the Global South confidence and political voices with which to set climate change onto the international agenda (see Hofmann in this volume). Networks of activists in this region also started to articulate their interests in using and protecting the sea.

Oceanic history offers an array of actors and individuals who often stay out of sight in terracentric historical narratives: scientists, workers, novelists, diplomats, activists, people from industries and politics, the military and journalists, islanders, divers, seafarers, animals (small and big), filmmakers, and visionaries of different kinds. This group of living beings was diverse, but in their engagement with the sea they developed certain common patterns and themes. Resources (living and mineral ones), became key topics of the cultural history of the sea. With the expansion of human mobility came regulation, conventions, and laws (see Dewey in this volume). Mobility, horizontally on ships as well as vertically in diving vessels or as fish, was crucial to the invention of the ocean's depth as part of planet Earth.

THE CONTRIBUTIONS

The contributions follow these protagonists, practices, and stories through the oceans' layers: Sabine Höhler explores in the first chapter ("Knowledges: Creating the Blue Planet from Modern Oceanography") how the sea emerged as a comprehensible and communicable object of knowledge. She centers her argument on the idea of (scientific) ocean literacy, the question of how physical oceanography acquired an opaque and materially inaccessible environment. Höhler shows how national endeavors of ocean sounding and mapping in the years of European imperialism created the conditions and demands for international collaboration in the following years. Scientific data became central after 1945 as physical oceanography reemerged as climate science. The chapter highlights the fact that ocean literacy led to nationalist claims on the sea as well as to modes of inter- and transnational cooperation.

Colin Dewey ("Practices: Robots, Memories, Autonomy, and the Future") examines the material practices of seafaring as well as their representations. He considers the changes within shipping fleets as a result of the twentieth century's broader historical developments: mechanized wars, decolonization, and the transformation of empire to global capitalism. Traditional shipping lines became fleets of multinational flag-of-convenience freighters, tankers, and bulks. These shifts changed the culture and ethos of seafaring. The novels of Joseph Conrad, Malcom Lowry, and Francisco Goldman are windows into the changing twentieth-century maritime practices. They demonstrate how the material experiences of seafarers lost the traditional heroic ethos of "autonomy." The expression "autonomy" refers today to technologically driven robotic ships that can operate without human intervention, but the novels show how tales of victimization created collective resistances, as a new form of autonomy.

Johanna Sackel and Anna-Katharina Wöbse investigate the networks of ocean diplomacy ("Networks: The Fluid Culture of Maritime Diplomacy"). They analyze how maritime networks created the all-encompassing concept of a shared and fragile global ocean, the idea of the "global commons." For networks, the sea served as a projection surface for worldviews and interests, for resource dreams and ecological concepts of wholeness. Wöbse and Sackel reconstruct how maritime networks diversified during the twentieth century, alongside with maritime usage categories. Some actors even generated competing concepts that concurred with the construction of the ocean as common space. They analyze diverse groups of people, follow ocean advocates of the late nineteenth century, analyze the discourses in the League of Nations as well as processes of institutionalizing, introduce activists such as Elisabeth Mann Borgese and consider new patterns of non-governmental organization (NGO) networking. This array of examples puts the broad variety of networks and their opposing interests into concrete terms.

Simone M. Müller concentrates on marine and maritime conflicts ("Conflicts: Underneath the Quiet Waves"). Over the course of the twentieth century, myriad conflicts have erupted on as well as over ocean space. In the face of the dramatic Cod Wars, the territorial struggle over the South China Sea, or the battles of the world wars, the quieter and slower conflicts over ocean uses are overseen. For centuries, the ocean has provided humans not only with resources but also an apparently limitless capacity to assimilate an ever-growing amount of waste, ranging from sewage sludge to dredge spoils or chemical weapons. The waters' flowing quality and opaque nature made the ocean the perfect receptacle. Müller foregrounds the quiet conflicts on the practice of ocean dumping. She shows how all around the world the sea has served as the ultimate sink for all sorts of waste, how different nations and the international community have found ways to regulate ocean dumping, how remediation efforts were undertaken to clean the oceans, and why the topic of ocean dumping still has currency until today.

Rebecca Hofmann takes a Pacific perspective on oceans and their wars ("Islands and Shores: War in the Pacific"). She argues that the role of Pacific shores and islands remain at the edge of global history, since they became important only when they gained strategic value. The internal wars on the Pacific islands, if at all, are brushed aside as premodern barbarism or confined to a mere footnote, but war played an important role for Pacific societies. Especially the effects of the Second World War continue to shape people's identity, their collective memory and cultural heritage as well as their life practices and environmental assets to this day. Hofmann shows how colonial and Second World War legacies continue to inform postwar island societies and civil conflicts. She additionally highlights that some of the most tragic chapters of recent history were nuclear tests, which were part of Cold War geopolitics. In the course of history, Pacific Islanders gained new confidence in protesting against outsider's claims on their homes. They use metaphors of "war" to stir global attention to fights for their interests, most recently against the effects that climate change has on their home islands.

Helen M. Rozwadowski ("Travelers: Vertical and Horizontal Voyaging On and In the Nonhuman Ocean") examines three groups of voyagers: She investigates voyagers who explored the ocean's third dimension—from the relatively shallow waters visited by early divers to the vast depths reachable with submersibles. Travelers also embarked on restored or replica "tall ships" to teach historical maritime skills and knowledge through activities that respect history and imbibe in nostalgia. The third group consists of nonhuman ocean travelers, fish, whales, and dolphins. Rozwadowski considers them in light of recent scientific studies that document culture in groups of whales and fish. For the analysis of these travelers, Rozwadowski recognizes the binaries that characterize their relationship with the sea: play joins work as the occasion for experiencing the ocean; technology and imagination are important mediators for (non)human engagement with the ocean; and both exaction and addition characterize the direction and flow of material resources, of knowledge, and of imaginative constructions.

Jon Crylen ("Representations: On Undersea Filmmaking") focuses on film as one specific form of representing the oceans. The chapter proceeds from the assumption that most representations of the marine world have, from a cultural standpoint, been predominantly cinematic. Motion pictures were the dominant popular medium of the twentieth century, a time increasingly suffused with mediated images. Within the industrialized world, moving images of ocean exploration and marine life have played a greater role than any other facet of culture in shaping the common understanding of the sea. Crylen focuses on three conceptual frames of "reading" ocean films: (1) the careful aesthetic-technical constructedness of the underwater world as "the cinematic aquarium" (see also Crylen 2015) refashions the ocean for display; (2) particularly documentaries bear out, through a variety of visual techniques, a negotiation of reason and wonder, of science and spectacle film; and (3) deep-sea filmmaking relies on large-scale exploratory apparatuses that enable ocean cinema to be made. These movies are products of the material environment, the circumstances of film production, and artistic expressions. All in all, they shape imaginary underwater worlds.

These imaginary worlds, in a broader sense, are the last chapter's topic ("Imaginary Worlds: The Human–Ocean Relation in Fantastic Futures of Affluence and Formidable Visions of Unsettledness"). The author, Ariane Tanner, focuses on ocean imaginaries, especially how the human relationship to the sea was imagined. She argues that the concept of "biomass" fostered the first set of imaginaries from the 1920s onwards. During the 1970s, new repertoires emerged: the oceans became a target of postcolonial geopolitics. Finally, the discourse of planetary boundaries created the awareness of the oceans' vulnerability and fragility. These imaginary worlds converge in the years of the Anthropocene. Human perceptions shaped visions from escapism and geoengineering to aesthetic and ontological ideas of a new thinking of the human–ocean relation beyond simple anthropomorphization. Furthermore, the history of the human–ocean relation displays the historical interrelatedness between humans and nature whose distinction has become obsolete.

NAVIGATING THE BLIND SPOTS: NON-WESTERN VIEWS AND ANIMALS

The contributions try to be as comprehensive as possible, but the volume has blind spots. The volume cover depicts "Blue Marble" as the unique icon of planet Earth. It shows the original picture from outer space. Africa was in daylight, Antarctica was illuminated. A cyclone is caught in the top right. The

Tamil Nadu cyclone brought flooding and high winds to India in December 1972. Most remarkably, the image is "upside down." It shows Antarctica on top, which went against cartographic conventions. The picture credits Eugene Cernan, Ronald Evans, and Harrison Schmitt. NASA flipped the snapshot for public circulation and public campaigns used the picture with the North on top, adjusted to (Western) cartographic conventions.

If the volume is imagined to be a flight over the "Blue Marble," only parts of the earth and its oceans would be visible. Although the picture suggests an objective view from above, its history raises questions on the constructions of global views. How comprehensive can a global view of the sea be? The global gaze, as NASA's decision to flip the image shows, can be constructed and changed by certain interests and decisions. Who makes global views of the ocean, for whom, and with what intentions?

Our book navigates the seven seas from certain perspectives and leaves blind spots. The authors (and the introduction) follow the traces that people from industrialized nations have left in the world's oceans. One exception is the chapter on the Pacific Islands that shows how Indigenous peoples experienced the sea (see Hofmann in this volume). This perspective flips the Western, terracentric view: for people living on the industrialized continents, the land is the space of everyday experience. For Pacific Islanders, water influences society in everyday life. What would a Pacific Islander's "Blue Marble" look like? This question cannot be answered in this volume. Perspectives from subaltern studies and social anthropology might help to give people a voice beyond the Western gaze.[6] We can imagine that they had and have a different perspective on the sea, not from above, but from within. The ocean would be the sea around them, as Rachel Carson has put it, the environment that defines and structures their lives. For them, the ocean is more than a cultural abstraction that can be experienced through the media, through technologies and representation. Cultural similarities between these peoples and maritime workers occur. For both groups, the sea is experienced not with the brain and the eyes, but with the body, the skin, and the nose (Tuan 2010, 2013; see Dewey in this volume).

Humanity's largest blind spots are not the people but the animals that live in the sea. "Culture" is defined as set of habits, traditions, and practices that makes a living being human. Culture is language, art, social behavior, and communication in a broader sense. Whales, for example, do not write diaries, draw pictures, or produce movies, but does this mean that they do not have a culture? This volume includes animals in the cultural history of the sea in a twofold way: they inhabit human science and imagination of the underwater world (see Tanner in this volume). People all over the world visit public aquaria to admire sea life. In film, sea mammals, such as Flipper, became movie stars. Biological sciences have recognized the fact that cetaceans have a certain culture (Mann 2001; Norris 2002; Tyack 2001), but what about the fish?

FIGURE 0.6 A humpback whale. © Chase Dekker Wild-Life Images/Getty Images.

Although we know about swarm behavior and the schooling of fish, fish exist beyond our cultural radar. Fish, as behavioral studies is beginning to teach us, feel pain and joy, can solve problems and learn (see Rozwadowski in this volume). They are intelligent, but if they do have "culture," what does the overexploitation of this species say about human culture?[7] An ethical thinking with fish would include their lives as part of the "Blue Marble," lives that needed to be treated with respect. This would again shift the perspective from the abstract view from above, to a notion of the sea as around us and them. We cannot (yet) tell what the "Blue Marble" would look like through fish eyes. We can imagine, however, that animals would wish it to be the common heritage of all living beings.

CHAPTER ONE

Knowledges

Creating the Blue Planet from Modern Oceanography

SABINE HÖHLER

"OCEAN LITERACY," PRESENT AND PAST: AN INTRODUCTION

"The ocean is the defining feature of our planet." Based on this central insight from the earth sciences, a number of renowned US national organizations published a programmatic list of principles in October 2005 to promote the concept of "Ocean Literacy."[1] The institutional network of governmental organizations, environmental foundations, learned societies, educational institutions, and conservation organizations campaigns for a national standard of ocean science education that shifts the focus from the earth's landmasses to the earth's water bodies. In the aim to render the sea intelligible in the same way that the land became "legible" through modern surveying and mapping techniques (Scott 1998) the network strives to raise attention to the circumstance that the sea covers about 70 percent of the earth's surface. Planet Earth is a Planet Ocean; it literally is the Blue Marble that was perceived first from outer space in the 1960s and continues to attract our attention (Figure 1.1). The iconic display of blue and white, brown and green was perceived as signifying intricate processes of life on earth that were held to be unique in the known universe. Meanwhile the color blue has moved to center-stage. The network's seven essential principles highlight this contemporary understanding of the earth's "one big ocean" and its climate and ecosystem functions; its wealth of nutrient, mineral, and energy resources; and its increasing exploitation as the planet's largest dumping site.

FIGURE 1.1 Blue Planet: View of the Pacific Ocean by GOES-11 satellite, 2009. © NASA.

The Ocean Literacy network's call for a deeper ocean knowledge and mastery connects to the rising fields of "Blue Ecology" on the ocean as an environmentally critical infrastructure and "Blue Economy" on the ocean as economic resource (Armitage, Bashford, and Sivasundaram 2018; Holm, Smith, and Starkey 2001; Rozwadowski 2018). Recently, also the "Blue Humanities" have formed to address ways of knowing the sea through the arts and literature and through historicizing the ocean (Gillis 2013; Gillis and Torma 2015; Mentz 2015). Evidently, the significance of the sea in culture and society has not diminished but increased over time. Yet, Ocean Literacy Principle #7 acknowledges that "the ocean is largely unexplored." Ocean-going expeditions have been surveying the sea in breadth and depth since the mid-nineteenth century. Nevertheless, human access to the oceans has remained so limited that until the present, ships and planes can disappear in abysmal depths without a trace. When Malaysia Airlines flight MH370 vanished on March 8, 2014, on its way from Kuala Lumpur to Beijing, there were good reasons to assume that the aircraft had disappeared in the Southern Ocean region southwest of Australia. As it were, this region continues to be one of the deepest and least explored ocean regions in the world. To the present day the aircraft has not been found.

Despite accumulated rich ocean knowledge, the sea is anything but clear and transparent. Until the modern age a main approach to the sea has been to cross its surface as fast as possible to reach safe haven. Humans are terrestrially bound creatures. The sea remained literally superficial even to local fishing communities whose livelihood has depended on the sea for centuries. Furthermore, to a large extent, the sea remains literally opaque also to oceanographers and their scientific instruments. Water absorbs not only visible light but also radio waves, microwaves, and X-rays. It is impermeable to electromagnetic radiation, which forms the basis of modern radar, GPS, and telecommunication technologies. At depths of one hundred meters, the sea is pitch black. In the search for flight MH370 an autonomous underwater vehicle (AUV) was deployed. In a course of three weeks the unmanned mini-submarine scanned an area of roughly four hundred square kilometers of the Southern Ocean in depths of nearly five thousand meters. It would take two hours to descend before it could scan the sea floor for sixteen hours. It took another two hours to return to the surface. An area of some five by eight kilometers could be searched in a day. Reading out and analyzing the data from the device took another four hours. According to Dutch physical oceanographer Erik van Sebille (2014) from the University of New South Wales, Australia, the search became "a game of blind man's bluff." In many regards, ocean exploration is a venture undertaken by blindfolded scientists groping around in a vast dark expanse of which less than 5 percent has been explored.

This chapter sets out to explain how despite these conditions of opaqueness the sea has emerged as a comprehensible and communicable object of knowledge in the long twentieth century. It expands the notion of the "short" century of 1914 to 1991 (Hobsbawm 1994), which bracketed historical developments by a series of world wars. To understand how the earth's "one big ocean" became evident the politics of the ocean need to be studied and also the modern ocean sciences and their practices of measuring, scaling, visualizing, and legitimizing ocean knowledge. The long twentieth century takes into consideration that major developments in modern oceanography were instigated with national ocean-going expeditions in the late nineteenth century. It also acknowledges that the ripples of "high-modern" (Scott 1998) oceanography, which built up at the turn of the century and reached its peak during the Cold War, have expanded into the twenty-first century and inform current environmental ocean sensing and monitoring. The chapter will explore how national endeavors of ocean sounding and charting at the heights of European imperialism created the conditions and the demands for international collaboration that developed well before the First World War. The internationalization of ocean research in turn made scientific data the basis of both ocean territorialization and commoning strategies. As marine resources of oil and ore became technologically accessible, these conflicting views culminated in the UN Law of the Sea conventions and regulations of the oceans after the Second World War. In the latter part of the twentieth century, the ocean became the object of environmental surveillance and the subject of moderating and regulating the earth's climate systems. Physical oceanography was refashioned as a climate science that researched ocean-atmosphere interactions.

Much like oceanographic research itself, the chapter combines in-depth and surface accounts to span time and space. To sketch this global knowledge of the sea I will tap into the history of physical oceanography, the sciences of the non-living sea. I will focus on practices of ocean depth measuring, data processing routines, and visual tools of ocean knowledge such as graphs, maps, and images. Inspired by science studies scholar Stefan Helmreich's (2011) notion of the "sensory trajectory" I trace processes of making a sea legible that had been marvelous and alien for centuries. The trajectory leads from the tactile sense of probing to the auditory sense and the soundscapes of echo sounding to the visual sense of translating tactile and auditory information into text and image. As versatile data became decipherable ocean landscapes, or seascapes, this "architecture for perception" (Goodwin 1995: 254) fostered imagined ocean futures based on modeling and forecasting practices. While the oceanographic perspectives discussed in this chapter are largely based on the credibility and dominance of (Western) science, their interactions and frictions with other forms of ocean knowledge were historically pervasive. Nonscientific ocean knowledges will come to the fore by situating scientific knowledge in its geographical, political, and cultural contexts.

Taking a multidisciplinary approach inspired by historical science and technology studies as well as by the environmental humanities, the chapter attempts to shift perspective from the national frameworks of knowing the sea to the inter-, trans-, and supranational oceans, ocean sciences, and modes of ocean governance. The sections revolve around three related aspects of ocean knowledge that place the qualities of the sea in the center: depth, resourcefulness, and power. As the sea changed from an unfathomable and treacherous immensity to traverse to a deep volume to gauge and lay bare, the deep sea became imagined as a space complementary to the land. It became a source and a sink of extractive industries, an arena for legal regulations, and a potent climate moderator that could be modeled and forecasted but that continues to resist its categorizations and predictions.

THE DEEP SEA

When Malaysia Airlines flight MH370 disappeared from the global flight monitoring screens in 2014, a Swedish journalist contemplated the unlikely possibility of disappearing for good in our present time of allegedly seamless satellite monitoring, national intelligence, and global surveillance systems (Wahllöf 2014). In this residue of remoteness, he found not only grief but also consolation and dream-inspiring hope. The intimacy of rigorous scientific precision and mythical vagueness, of enlightenment and obscurity could be observed already in the nineteenth century when physical oceanography was just about to form into a scientific discipline. Jules Verne's novel *20,000 Leagues Under the Sea* from 1870 mediated well between different images of the sea prevalent in his time. In a short passage on the Atlantic Ocean, Verne praised the sea's immense spatial and temporal span with mathematical exactness: "The Atlantic! A vast expanse of water whose surface covers 25 million square miles, 9,000 miles long, with an average width of 2,700" (Verne [1870] 2001: 284). The modern sciences of the sea did not replace but reclaimed the marvelous and fantastic views on the nature of the sea, and they did so by applying precise figures and vast data sets. Like the science fiction genre he established, Verne presented two closely related narratives of the ocean spaces to be outlined, the spectacular and the scientific.

The oceans were deep well before the founding of the ocean sciences in the mid-nineteenth century. What lay beneath the waves out on the sea, however, had hardly ever been tangibly experienced. Far into the modern era the world's oceans were perceived mainly as transit spaces dividing the continental landmasses. Fishermen and whalers were well experienced with their fishing and hunting grounds. Largely, however, ocean knowledge concerned sea surface matters of marine trade, naval wars, and colonial expansion. Shipping routes relied on astronomical knowledge, nautical skills, navigational tools as well as on detailed coastal charts. This section explores how the oceans became deep as scientific tools of depth sounding and depth representation were developed in systematic ocean-going expeditions, which I will study in relation to national and imperial ambitions of the European states in the time period between 1870 and 1945.

To gauge the deep ocean, a groping and probing tactile approach prevailed until the turn to the twentieth century. Measurements with a lead weight attached to a line to fathom ocean depths of several kilometers could take several hours and involve the entire ship's crew. The leadsman would take the line toward the bow of the ship. The sailors took up the line in coils and arranged themselves along the side of the ship from bow to stern. Upon releasing the line, the crewmen counted the knots in the line passing their hands and memorized their succession collectively in the form of a song, then to enter the depth in fathoms into a chart. Ocean literacy at this time was built on digits. While sailors were often illiterate, they were generally numerate (Rozwadowski 2005).

Instruments, theories, skills, and routines needed to come together to perceive underwater features clearly. The operational knowledge-generating device at this time was the research vessel itself: the ship was a scientific instrument, a probe, a collecting and ordering device, and a field laboratory in which hierarchy and discipline ruled. The emerging ocean depths were the results of organized collective practices and they served not only scientific but also commercial interests. The telegraph industry was a late-nineteenth century endeavor that depended heavily on accurate depth measurements. The effort of laying a transatlantic submarine telegraph cable across the so-called Telegraphic Plateau in the 1850s, a submarine expanse between Newfoundland and the British Islands in the North Atlantic Ocean, motivated further development of sounding techniques (Hanlon 2016). In the late nineteenth century, when national survey missions of land and sea were underway, the techniques of line-and-lead sounding were systematically refined. Rope was replaced by wire, sinkers detaching mechanically from the sounding line were introduced, and the steam-powered winch replaced the tremendous manual labor of hauling up miles of heavy line. Such changes made large national ocean charting projects more efficient and attractive for governmental funding.

The British *Challenger* expedition of the early 1870s illustrates how the newly formed science of oceanography proved itself worthy of national support by symbolically appropriating the earth's ocean floors. The *Challenger* was the first expedition equipped solely for the purpose of deep-sea research. Its deep-sea soundings accounted for hitherto abyssal oceanic depth in the language of precise scientific measurements (Hsü 1992). Traveling nearly seventy thousand nautical miles (130,000 kilometers) across the globe between 1872 and 1876, the *Challenger* cataloged about four thousand new species and took about four hundred deep-sea soundings. The circa forty nautical charts resulting from the expedition were the coproduction of an evolving and specializing deep-sea research and a national investment to appropriate the sea as an expression and a means of imperial power. In 1875 the crew sounded the Mariana Trench in the western Pacific Ocean, the deepest part of the world's oceans. The estimated deepest point of more than eight thousand kilometers at the trench's southern end was named the *Challenger* Deep. Utopian sites persisted as ocean science moved across the earth's surface, meticulously fathoming its remotest places and crevices to part with curiosity and wonder.

Ocean sounding devices remained unreliable and tedious until the early twentieth century when acoustic sounding technology put observations into practice that sea water was an almost perfect sound medium. Sound waves traveled much faster in water than in air and they propagated practically without loss with a velocity of approximately 1.5 kilometers per second that increased with pressure and salinity, echoing an acoustic signal off the ocean floor in a matter of seconds (Figure 1.2). The AUV searching for the remains of

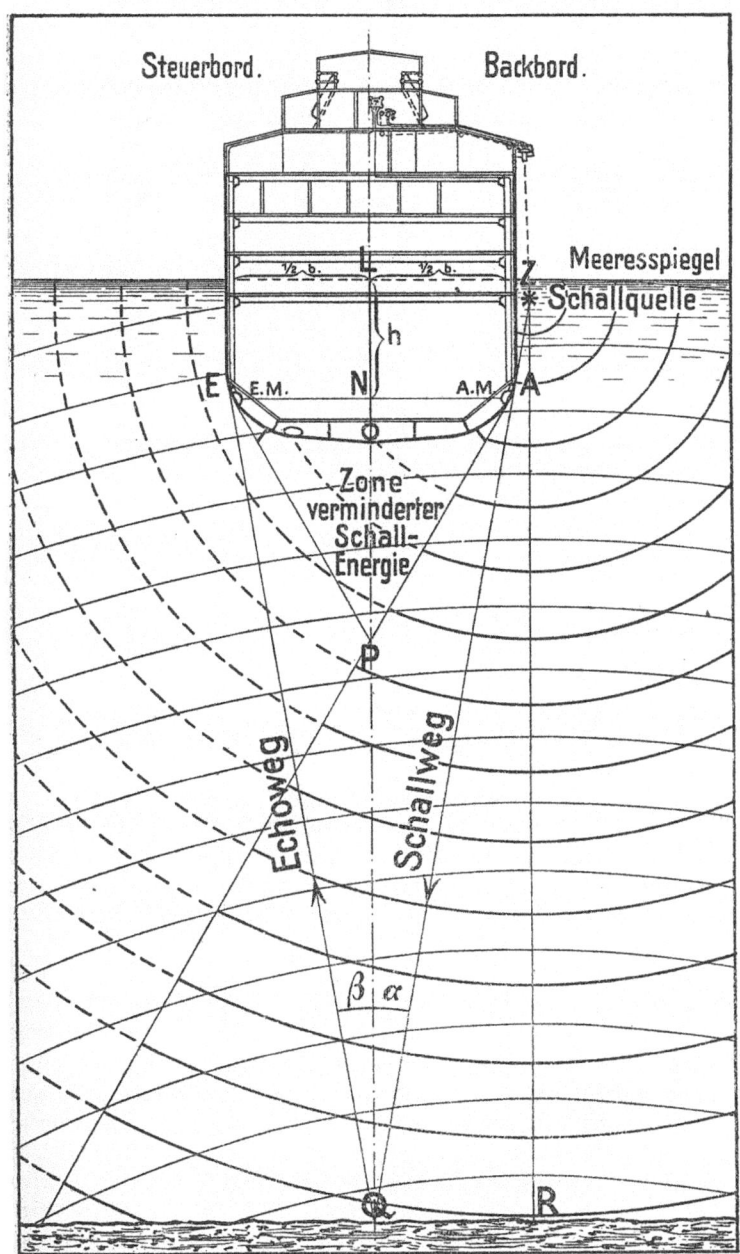

FIGURE 1.2 "The Principle of Direct Echo Measurement," from Gerhard Schott, "Messung der Meerestiefen durch Echolot," in *Wissenschaftliche Abhandlungen des 21. Deutschen Geographentages zu Breslau vom 2. bis 4. Juni 1925*, 140–50 (Berlin: Dietrich Reimer, 1926), 141. © Public domain.

flight MH370 could map dozens of square kilometers per day because it carried a "side-scan sonar," an acoustic device that could create a much wider sound image of the sea floor than any onboard optical camera, let alone pointwise measurements with line and lead. The technological shift from sounding with slow and heavy winches and weights to swift and comparatively precise acoustic and electroacoustic sounders around 1900 also meant a shift in the medium and in the sensory arrangement of approaching ocean depths: sound waves are material waves; they propagate by the medium of water itself. The ocean became a sounding body.

The first acoustic sounding experiments involved simple sound sources such as underwater gunshots, and the first receivers were human listeners who picked up the signals with their bare ears or with earphones. The German physicist Alexander Behm secured a patent on an "echo sounder" in 1913 which employed a siren as sound emitter and a mechanical "sonometer" as receiver determining depth based on signal strength (Behm 1913). At the same time, acoustic sounding devices were developed in the United States that used electric underwater sound emitters and receivers. All devices had in common that complicated manual conversions of measurements had to be performed *ex-post*, to translate measures of time into units of distance and to derive the actual depth at a certain position (Höhler 2002a).

The question of precision of acoustic navigation and positioning became urgent "as a result of two modern catastrophes – the sinking of the *Titanic* in 1912 and the onset of World War I in 1914" (Beyer 1999: 197). Acoustic depth measurement benefited enormously from the sound transmitter and receiver technology developed for submarine communication and for the localization of ships and submarines, especially in the UK, France, Germany, and the United States. The echo depth sounder was the first peaceful application of the new technology. With the increasing automation of acoustic depth measurement confidence in the method grew. The procedure of humans audio-monitoring great depths was considered imperfect since "the subjective moment of human listening to the echo" had not yet been "eliminated," as Gerhard Schott from the Deutsche Seewarte, the German Sea Observatory, admitted in 1926 (Schott 1926: 142). But Schott was confident and assured that "the purely mechanical registration also at the end of the process, i.e. of the echo, is likely to be achieved" (142). Self-registering echo sounders that actively sent out and recorded sound pulses to determine the distance of a ship or submarine to the seabed were developed in the 1920s but did not come into use before the 1930s.

The "German Atlantic Expedition" conducted onboard the survey vessel *Meteor* between 1925 and 1927 was the first expedition to apply the new technology of acoustic sounding to a systematic deep-sea survey. Traveling the South Atlantic Ocean, the *Meteor* scientists made use of all hydrographic observations of the Atlantic since the British *Challenger* expedition by ordering them into a "Kartothek," a register of maps that upon departure in 1925 contained about ten thousand sheets (Merz 1925). Alfred Merz, the scientific head of the expedition, set up research "stations" in advance, creating a dense sampling grid of fixed, equidistant points spanning the terrain under oceanographic investigation (Figure 1.3). Merz arranged stations in fourteen cross-sections, narrowly spaced in intervals of five degrees in latitude. Twenty

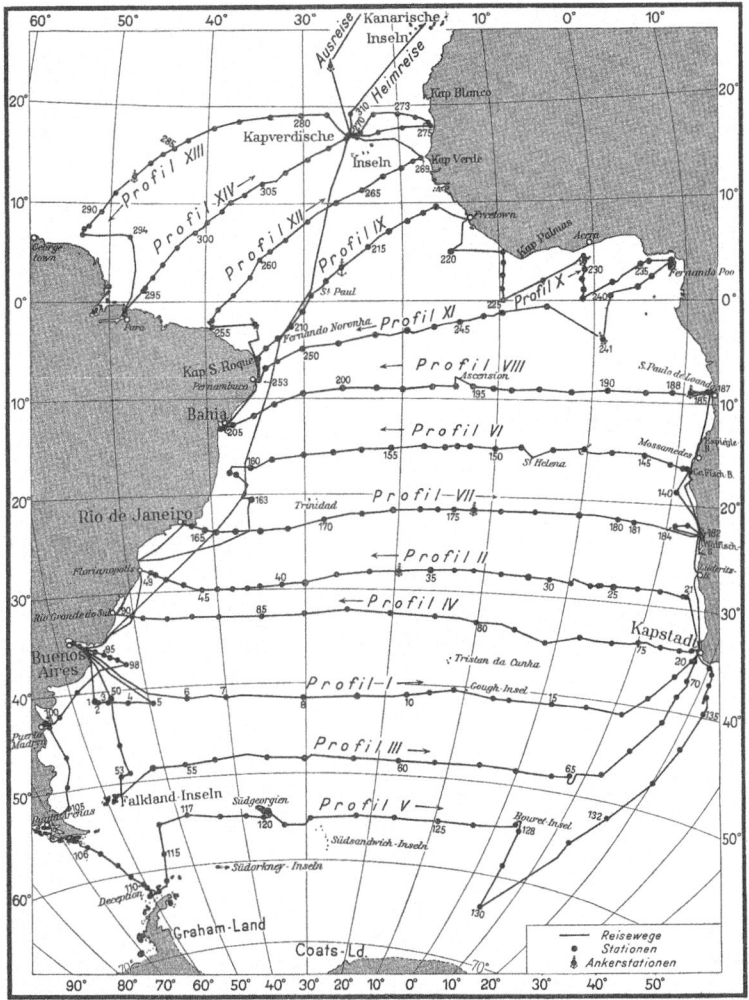

FIGURE 1.3 "Route and Stations of the *Meteor*, 1925–7," from *Deutsche Atlantische Expedition auf dem Forschungs- und Vermessungsschiff "Meteor," ausgeführt unter der Leitung von Professor Dr. A. Merz † und Kapitän z. S. F. Spiess, 1925–1927. Wissenschaftliche Ergebnisse herausgegeben im Auftrage der Notgemeinschaft der Deutschen Wissenschaft von Dr. A. Defant*, vol. 2, *Die Echolotungen des "Meteor,"* ed. Hans Maurer (Berlin: De Gruyter, 1933), 300. © Public domain.

to thirty stations, 150 to 350 kilometers apart, were aligned on each cross-section, adding up to a total of 310 stations between the coasts of South America and Africa. The total length of the voyage of the *Meteor* proceeding from station to station encompassed about 130,000 kilometers. At each station hydrographic series were run, including deep-sea soundings with line and lead to check the three different acoustic sounding devices aboard. Deep-sea measurements during the voyage amounted to roughly 60,000 soundings at 30,000 spots no more than twenty minutes apart. According to Hans Maurer, the scientist concerned with the *Meteor*'s soundings, 67,388 soundings were taken during the expedition (Maurer 1933: 24), a precision that recalls Jules Verne's scientific spirit and a survey density that would have been science fiction in Verne's time. This sounding enterprise would have taken seven years of sounding day and night, had it been conducted with line-and-lead sounding.

Measuring separate physical ocean qualities along the water column at each station, the "German Atlantic Expedition" analyzed the ocean into a large array of physical information in three dimensions. The physical oceanographers onboard the *Meteor* worked with a model of the "Atlantic Circulation," which had first been theoretically outlined by the Norwegian physicist Vilhelm Bjerknes in the early years of the 1900s in his circulation theorem of atmospheric and oceanic motion (Bjerknes et al. 1910/11). The *Meteor* oceanographers set out to compare the theory and corresponding calculations of ocean drifts and ocean circulation to a range of new measurements in which quantitative methods replaced former qualitative approaches. Their extensive instrumental gear included deep-sea thermometers, current meters, water samplers, closing nets, bottom samplers, and coring tubes. To determine the direction and velocity of Atlantic sea water, current measurements were obtained directly and indirectly through observation and determination of water temperature, salinity, and density. Chemical investigations concerned sea water qualities such as alkalinity (the water's capacity to resist acidity) and contents of oxygen, nitrogen, and minerals. By relating their station work on the water columns to their depth measurements, the oceanographers onboard the *Meteor* combined the emerging depth charts of the Atlantic Ocean and the more abstract isoline-charts that displayed the contents and distributions of different measured quantities. They arranged the (same) data visually in all conceivable ways intelligible to conventional three-dimensional spatial imagination: into cross sections, longitudinal sections, and horizontal sections, representing different strata of ocean depth. In doing so, they supplemented the existing maps of ocean coastlines and depths with a picture of the ocean water body. The seemingly empty space between the sea's surface and its bottom was filled by an ocean of data.

Mapping, as James Corner has argued, "*unfolds* potential: it re-makes territory over and over again, each time with new and diverse consequences" (1999: 213, emphasis in original). Following Corner, maps are constructed from sets of techniques, instruments, and conventions that make the spaces they describe derive from those aspects of "reality" that are susceptible to the techniques. Corner identifies three mapping operations that can describe the *Meteor*'s framing and knowing of the Atlantic Ocean (231). First, the oceanographers created a field, set rules, and established a system, including a graphic system encompassing the frame, orientation, coordinates, scale, units of measurement, and graphic projection. Second, they extracted parts, isolated or "de-territorialized" as data. And third, they plotted relationships between the parts and "re-territorialized" these parts into a whole. From the complex fabric of single data, the Atlantic Ocean was reterritorialized as a scientific volume.

Among the numerous charts and maps the *Meteor* returned to Germany were fourteen spectacular morphological profiles of the South Atlantic Ocean (Figure 1.4). These depth charts were intended to give evidence of Germany's unbroken scientific excellence after the First World War. They also acquired substantial meaning within German after-war struggles to regain lost colonial authority and military strength in symbolic fashion. The unprecedented comprehensiveness of the expedition framed the South Atlantic Ocean and ocean floor as territory under (national) control. The "German Atlantic Expedition" was a prestigious project of the Notgemeinschaft der Deutschen Wissenschaft, the German association promoting the continuance of the sciences, strong before the war, after the reparation payments, disarmament requirements, and territorial concessions imposed by the Allied Powers. The Notgemeinschaft contributed to the prevalent postwar rhetoric of (spatial) deprivation, economic impoverishment, and exhausted resources brought upon the Germans through the reparation demands and the military restrictions by the Treaty of Versailles (Höhler 2002b). The German geographer Albrecht Penck, at the time the director of the Institute of Geography at the University of Berlin and of the Berlin Institute of Maritime Research, explicitly connected oceanic space to lost scientific and colonial territory. "The field of work of the German colonies was lost, the largest part of the country in the possession of powers that had been hostilely confronting Germany during the war, so that only few areas stood open to the German scientist" (Penck 1925: 243). This situation, according to Penck, was "different on the seas." Penck projected the open sea as a "field Germans could engage on unobstructed" (243). The *Meteor* itself was a decommissioned battleship provided by the German Navy and refurbished as a research vessel, which saved it from being demolished according to the terms of the Versailles Treaty.

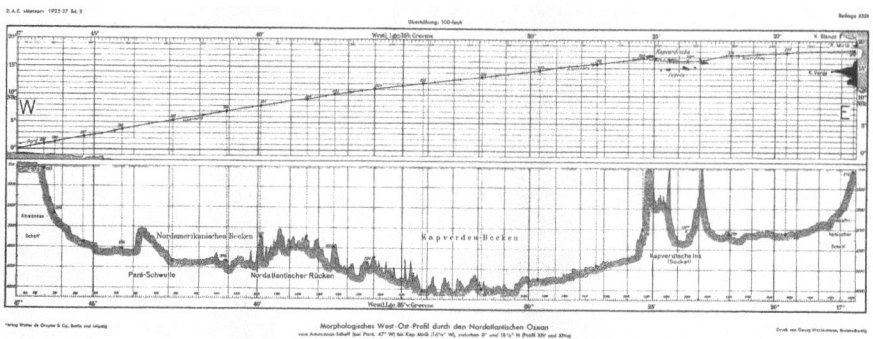

FIGURE 1.4 "Morphological West-East Profile of the North Atlantic Ocean," from *Deutsche Atlantische Expedition auf dem Forschungs- und Vermessungsschiff "Meteor", ausgeführt unter der Leitung von Professor Dr. A. Merz † und Kapitän z. S. F. Spiess, 1925–1927. Wissenschaftliche Ergebnisse herausgegeben im Auftrage der Notgemeinschaft der Deutschen Wissenschaft von Dr. A. Defant*, vol. 2, *Die Echolotungen des "Meteor,"* ed. Hans Maurer (Berlin: De Gruyter, 1933), supplement 29. © Public domain.

Indicative of the close relations of ocean scientific and military purposes, acoustic sounding became an important application of ocean knowledge in the Second World War. Promoted by the *Meteor* expedition, echo sounding was refined and put into practice in German and British submarine warfare. While the German Navy brought the technology of passive underwater hearing by sound receivers, or "hydrophones," to perfection, the British Navy worked on more refined active echo search systems. The acoustic echo location system ASDIC (an acronym that resolved to Anti-Submarine Detection Investigation Committee[2]) held a once-established acoustic contact and fixed the object as if caught in a search beam. The technology of active echolocation also materialized in the technology of SONAR (sound navigation and ranging). The US Sonar system was the auditory equivalent to the better-known RADAR (radio detection and ranging), which locates objects with radio waves. In the second half of the twentieth century, "sonar" became the collective term for all sound-based remote sensing techniques, whether horizontal or vertical, active or passive. The oceanographic success story of "seeing in depth" was dampened, however, when global campaigns by animal and environmental organizations drew attention to the fact that underwater noise acoustically tortures and misleads whales, dolphins, and other marine mammals. To conclude this section, it is not without irony that the increasing probing of the oceans since the late 1800s and their insetting acoustic penetration since the early 1900s revitalized the emptied sea of physical oceanography precisely by disturbing oceanic life.

THE RESOURCEFUL SEA

At the turn to the twentieth century, the imperial scramble for space reached the very few remote areas that were left to be charted on earth: the heart of Africa, the extremes of the polar regions, and the depths of the oceans. For the fledgling European nation-states, "to rule the waves" had everything to do with military dominance. At the same time, national control of the seas was associated with scientific ambitions and with access to ocean spaces and resources at the peak of imperialism. Ocean nationalism created a volatile constellation on the eve of the First World War that spilled over to the Second World War and its severe marine and submarine battles. While national competition remained strong in the postwar years, international collaboration became equally powerful in shaping the world oceans. This section explores ocean internationalization as the flip side of ocean nationalism following the Second World War. Opening with an outline of the first international oceanographic efforts at the turn to the twentieth century, the section's main focus will be on the Cold War period between 1945 and 1990, when international regulations became increasingly important to govern access to oceanic resources. The section discusses the role of physical oceanography in providing the parameters and the tools both for ocean internationalization and ocean territorialization.

The national formation of the earth and ocean sciences depended on international communication and exchange. The growing numbers of international scientific organizations at the end of the nineteenth century illustrate the difficulties of nationally operating sciences to observe atmospheric, oceanic, and tectonic phenomena that frequently transgressed national boundaries. The First International Polar Year (IPY) launched by the International Meteorological Congress and the International Polar Commission in the early 1880s presents a vivid example of the need and desire for collaboration within the professionalizing earth sciences. The earth-spanning observation effort carried out between August 1882 and 1883 provided the technological and metrological infrastructure to the growing scientific internationalism (Lüdecke 2004). This infrastructure allowed for the concerted collation of measurements and a common metrics, calibrated instruments, and the coordination and processing of measurements following international conventions. In 1899 the International Congress of Geography commissioned a general map of the earth's ocean basins and standardized the terminology of the deep sea. By the early twentieth century, maps of all ocean basins existed, based on some 18,000 soundings (Rozwadowski 2002).

The "mechanics of internationalism" (Geyer and Paulmann 2001) in marine research were fraught with friction, however. Firstly, the new ocean observation regimes rested heavily on military, economic, and technological structures that enabled and constrained collaborative research. Observation infrastructure development followed the dominant European shipping transport and communication routes and the imperial gradients of military and economic power by sea. The topologies of ocean knowledge emanating from the infrastructural networks were all but global. These networks operated from the European centers, and they entailed governance structures that were predicated on political power relations. Secondly, international scientific coordination did not necessarily imply cooperation. Global oceanographic surveys mostly collected information from arrays of single national contributors. Under the umbrella of the International Council for the Exploration of the Seas (ICES), founded in 2002, national institutions were able to obtain vessels dedicated to marine research. Unlike other international scientific organizations of this time, ICES was composed not of individual scientists but of eight founding states in Northern Europe. ICES was concerned primarily with the North and Baltic Seas, including Norwegian and Barents Seas, in its stated aim to promote and coordinate scientific work among its member countries (Rozwadowski 2002). In many regards, ICES was the first intergovernmental marine science organization and presented a model for international scientific coordination. Yet, ICES also displayed the frictions of internationalism in marine research by exposing the inadequacies of ocean governance structures beyond the immediate national shorelines.

Further need for political negotiation and regulation became particularly apparent when, thirdly, new technologies of marine resource extraction made new large-scale extractive operations possible and profitable for commercial purposes. The advent of industrial-scale trawl fisheries in the first decades of the twentieth century and of seabed mining prospects in the 1960s contested century-old traditions and agreements about access and property rights in the high seas. One of the oldest attempts of sea regulation was the "freedom of the sea" principle, *mare liberum*. In the colonial dispute about trade routes between the Netherlands and Portugal Hugo Grotius resolved in 1609 that the high sea, according to the Roman concept of *ius naturale* or natural law, was "common to all and proper to none": "The sea therefore is in the number of those things which are not in merchandise and trading, that is to say, which cannot be made proper. Whence it followeth, if we speak properly, no part of the sea can be accompted in the territory of any people" (Grotius [1609] 2004). In the nineteenth century, the widely accepted international law of the seas recognized the principle of limited national rights to a coastal zone of three nautical miles (5.6 kilometers). This definition of territorial waters corresponded to the range of cannons at the time and answered to the contemporary technical possibilities and needs of national defense. The law of the seas also regulated deep-sea fishing and merchant shipping. The seabed and the subsoil played no role, neither in economic nor in military terms. Like the high sea, the deep sea remained "free" in Grotius's sense.

The twentieth century challenged these centuries-old arrangements technologically and scientifically. The sheer number of marine activities during the second large international earth survey event, the International Geophysical Year (IGY) of 1957 and 1958, can be read as a strategy of making the oceans "legible for geopolitical reasons" (Barr and Lüdecke 2010; Dodds 2010: 65). Ocean literacy and ocean access were closely related and they became increasingly important in the 1960s when undersea oil and gas production increased and manganese finds in the deep sea promised a rich new source of ore. By the 1970s, the problem of regulating access to the seafloor and subsoil moved onto the agenda of the United Nations, which had been founded in 1945 as an international and intergovernmental organization to reestablish and maintain peace and security after the Second World War. Offshore oil and gas operations, at the time only projected in the negotiations, would take off in the 1980s (Avango and Högselius 2013). Moreover, in the face of a rapidly growing world population, experiments with underwater habitations and laboratories and new techniques for extracting plankton and krill from the seas heightened the hopes for the oceans as a protein storage and a supplementary human living space (Hamblin 2005; Kehrt and Torma 2014). Plans for military applications as well as the increasingly apparent flip side of postwar affluence, the sea as a growing landfill (or rather, seafill), further fueled the struggle over the world's oceans in the international arena, between highly technologized and "developing" states, between coastal states—those states that had a coastline— and those states with no access to territorial waters.

All of these disputes were settled in the form of property regulations. As legal scholar Scott Shackelford has observed, in the Western world the establishment of property rights was not seen as the problem, but as the (only) rational solution for managing resources outside of national jurisdiction. As soon as the harvesting or extraction of a resource was in sight, property rights seemed to be necessary to catalyze resource "development" (Shackelford 2008). It is not coincidental that the discussions over a new international maritime law fell into the decades of the 1950s to the 1980s. Three major United Nations conferences held in 1956, 1960, and again in 1973 discussed the reorganization of ocean ownership and use rights. At their preliminary end stood the United Nations Convention on the Law of the Sea (UNCLOS), agreed on in 1982 and ratified in 1994. The convention newly defined territorial waters and established the system of Exclusive Economic Zones (EEZs). This new zoning system granted a coastal country sovereign rights of offshore fishing and resource extraction measured from the sea surface to the seabed up to an extent of two hundred nautical miles (370 kilometers) from the coastline, or up to the limits of the "continental shelf," the edge of the continental landmass that was submerged under water but geologically attributed to the land (Miles 1998). The system concluded the question of whether to expand territorial waters or preserve the sea as a commons in a management scheme that was both protective and expansive. For one, the international agreements on economic zones practically invited further efforts of national fishing and trawling, probing and drilling of hydrocarbon resources, both within and beyond the territorial waters. Moreover, the legal frameworks were not independent of scientific definitions. The definition and legal concept of "continental shelf" itself changed over the decades, as both measurement and extraction technologies advanced. The determination of the extent of a continental shelf to demarcate an economic zone rested entirely on the perception of subsea geomorphological features, which in turn invited further oceanographic research to corroborate a country's claims.

The increasingly dense and versatile plot sheets of physical oceanography became powerful scientific evidence in the controversies about continental shelf extents. Accurate gathering and analyzing of data were required to determine the outer edges of continental margins, and physical oceanographers could provide the necessary set of tools to determine depths and slopes, mineral composition and sediment thickness to differentiate continental crusts from oceanic crusts and ridges. In 1977, American geologists and oceanographic cartographers Bruce Heezen and Marie Tharp at the US Lamont-Doherty Geological Observatory published a topographical map of the world ocean floor (Doel, Levin, and Marker 2006) (Figure 1.5). This map became famous because it exposed a vast undersea landscape that had hitherto been "invisible." The map also exhibited the enormous expansion oceanography and other earth sciences saw during the

FIGURE 1.5 Heezen-Tharp Map of the World Ocean, produced by the US Navy, 1977. © NOAA National Oceanic and Atmospheric Administration.

Cold War, primarily for military motives (Doel 2003). In the 1950s Heezen and Tharp had begun to assemble a map of the Mid-Atlantic Ridge, an undersea mountain range in the middle of the Atlantic Ocean formed by the boundary of two continental plates, the North American and the Eurasian plate. The Mid-Atlantic ridge had been mapped first as part of the *Challenger* expedition in the 1870s with the aim of sounding the ocean floor for the optimal position of the planned transatlantic telegraph cable. The subsequent *Meteor* expedition had confirmed the existence and detailed the extent of the ridge by acoustic sounding measurements in the 1920s. Based on this elaborate data archive of the earth's ocean floors from line-and-lead and sonar soundings, Heezen and Tharp found that the ridge formed a part of an extensive system of seismologically active ocean ridges across the earth's surface. Their topographical map of the world ocean floor clearly displayed these undersea features. Additionally, the map gained reputation from supporting the theory of seafloor spreading and of the continental drift that had been proposed decades earlier—unsuccessfully—by the German geophysicist Alfred Wegener.[3]

Despite the rich archive of depth measurements, Heezen and Tharp had to compile their map by extrapolating depths across vast data voids. Nevertheless, their map was visually impressive; it carried the topographical sensation of an emerging underwater space. It presented an ocean floor panorama perceived as "continuous" while technically the data continued to reflect single measurements. The map was a result of several steps of translation, from painstakingly plotting available depth soundings manually to the polished relief painting (Höhler and Wormbs 2017). "Optical consistency" is Bruno Latour's (1986) term for a synopsis created from single measurements drawn together into a stable visual form. The topographical map became an operational device to move further along the sensory trajectory of knowing the sea, from the tactile to the auditory to the visual sense. Optical consistency highlights more than the unity and integrity of a map made from an abstraction of single data points. It stresses its stability in translation and transport. Such "immutable mobiles" (Latour 1990) reconciled the scientific-technical representation of the abstract object of the ocean floor with its new visual reality. Heezen and Tharp's ocean map did not remain with the community of physical oceanographers but found entrance into geographical textbooks and popular atlases where it reflected the US oceanographic institutions' dominance and territorial coverage at the time of the Cold War.

The Heezen-Tharp topographical map of the world ocean floor exhibited the geological features that shifted scientific assumptions about plate tectonics and about shelf extent at one glance. Thereby, the map literally opened up the space for technoscientific prospecting and projecting of the resourceful sea. Outlining the continental shelf regulations in UNCLOS in such a way that access claims could be made (only) on scientific grounds resulted in a proliferation of scientific demarcation attempts. Coastal countries continue submitting their claims to the

UN Commission on the Limits of the Continental Shelf (CLCS), which was established at the third UNCLOS conference in 1982 to decide on shelf extent on the basis of oceanographic measurements. Currently, we can watch a genuine race for oceanic resources by shelf measurement. Especially in the Arctic, melting ice caps have opened up new shipping routes and resource fields to tap into that have attracted state and private investors. Paradoxically, under UNCLOS, established to safeguard the fair use and management of marine resources, very little of the Arctic Ocean is left unclaimed. In summary, scientific surveys were and are neither politically neutral nor objective. Assigning an oceanic area to a country has never been a strictly geological process but happens in the context of scientific definitions, political conventions, and economic or military motives. International oceanic coordination has not only supported ocean protection but also aggravated the problem of ocean exploitation. Legitimating international institutions such as the United Nations became indispensable for the regulation of growing claims on the sea in the second half of the twentieth century, but they were hardly sufficient to settle territorial disputes once and for all.

THE POWERFUL SEA

Oceanographic probing and observing the sea in breadth and depth in the second half of the twentieth century provided global overviews that in their geographic and scientific scope increasingly diverged from other established local experiences of the sea. This discrepancy became even more pronounced with the formation of earth system science in the 1980s. Among a range of fields, earth system science took a systems approach to the planet's hydrosphere and atmosphere and their interactions as a climate indicator, a climate regulator, and a climate generator (Edwards 2010, 2017). The new technology of satellite remote sensing spurred oceanography's turn into a subfield of the climate sciences by combining physical oceanography and space technology. This section explores how "satellite oceanography" and its observational techniques, measurements, imagery, and forecasting efforts collected distant local measurements into wholly new data fabrics from which, so the contemporary expectation, the texture of the earth's climatic cycles became visible. Since the 1990s and until the present, as this section will show, satellite oceanography has fed high hopes of climate modeling, weather forecasting and disaster management through ocean data storage and processing facilities.

Satellite oceanography gained ground at the end of the Space Race between the two superpowers, which had absorbed much of early Cold War military investment and scientific attention. When the last Apollo flight returned from its trip to the moon in December 1972, public interest and governmental funding in space flight had already waned. American and European space programs had to refashion themselves as earth programs, "changing the mission," as Naomi Oreskes (2014a) so aptly termed it. In the 1980s, NASA, the US National Aeronautics and Space Administration, launched its "Mission to Planet Earth" program. Mission to Planet Earth was designed as a long-term international research project in the earth sciences, and it marked NASA's change from a space agency to an environmental agency. Its second major satellite mission was the joint US-French project "TOPEX/Poseidon" (Conway 2006; Krige 2014). TOPEX stood for "Ocean Topography Experiment." Radar technology was employed to monitor ocean current and wave patterns as well as sea-level increase. Active self-registering satellite sensors provided altimetric (altitude) and gravimetric (gravity) data that were read out in digital form as the satellite was downlinked to receiver stations on the ground. In August 1992 the orbital satellite TOPEX/Poseidon was launched with the aim of taking sea surface height measures as indicators of the oceans' heat content (Figure 1.6). The mission's overall goal was to understand global ocean dynamics. A more specific goal was to improve the scientific knowledge of upper-ocean circulation in the tropical Pacific that was deemed essential for the reliable prediction of El Niño events (Höhler 2017a).

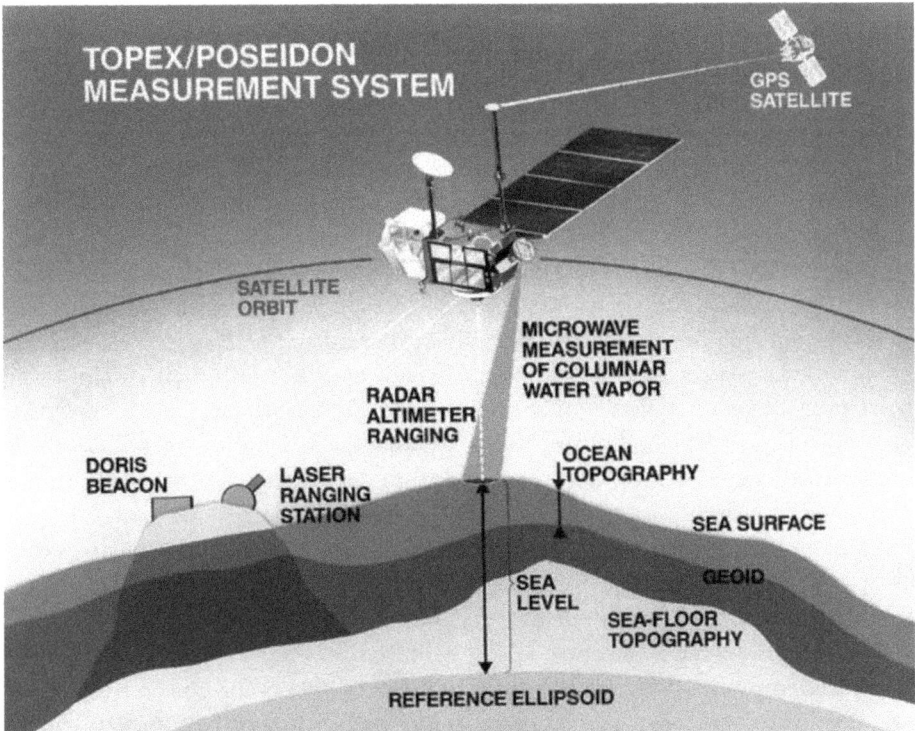

FIGURE 1.6 Topex-Poseidon Measurement System. © NASA Jet Propulsion Laboratory.

El Niño is the expression for a recurring warm-water period in the Pacific Ocean region. El Niño had been locally awaited and dreaded for centuries for the extreme weather events these warm-water streams triggered. In the coastal states of South America, Indonesia, and Southeast Asia, memories and stories of El Niño's arrivals are cultivated to convey both the bliss of rich harvests and the catch of fish and the disasters of tropical winter storms and floods, droughts, and famines (Philander 2004; Schwartz 2015). To the earth sciences El Niño arrived in the form of observed differences in Pacific Ocean surface temperatures. Oceanographic records of ocean warming go back to the eighteenth century. From this time, however, only single temperature readings from sporadic ships and merchant ships exist. As outlined in the first section of this chapter, the formation of physical oceanography as a disciplinary field in the second half of the nineteenth century did not instantaneously fill the vast measurements gaps. Oceanographic records provided no immediately intelligible story. Well into the twentieth century, temperature recordings were interpreted as indicators of El Niño events in hindsight only. An encompassing international oceanographic research network was in place first by the late 1950s. This close scientific ocean observation program was established in relation to the IGY 1957–8, as mentioned in the previous section. Partly also, the program was as a result of the strong El Niño year of 1957–8, which happened to coincide with the IGY.

The increasing measurement density of the twentieth century was complemented by ocean circulation theory. In the 1960s the Norwegian-American meteorologist Jacob Bjerknes attended to the phenomenon of El Niño in the tropical Pacific. Jacob was son to the Norwegian physicist Vilhelm Bjerknes who had first outlined the "Atlantic Circulation." Based on oceanographic sea-surface temperature readings and long-term weather recordings Jacob Bjerknes connected the atmospheric pattern of temperature, pressure, and rainfall variations in the Indian and Pacific Oceans, as identified by the British meteorologist Gilbert Walker in the 1920s, with data from the strong El Niño episodes of the 1950s and 1960s. By relating the El Niño phenomenon to Walker's "Southern Oscillation" Bjerknes could establish a pattern of ocean-atmosphere interaction in the Pacific Ocean that became known as "Southern Oscillation El Niño" (Mills 2009).

Satellite oceanography provided ocean circulation models with vast geographical coverage and proliferation of ocean temperature measurements. Satellites could not "see" in depth, to echo Charles Goodwin's (1995: 254) reflections on the technoscientific "architecture for perception," the specific set of research interests, conceptual assumptions, instruments and research activities that needed to be in place to render oceanic and atmospheric phenomena visible to the human eye. Since sea water proved opaque to electromagnetic radiation satellites skimmed sea surfaces; they took their readings off the near-surface layers of the sea. In return they covered enormous ocean regions, as becomes visible in the TOPEX/Poseidon satellite image from 1997 with its terrific view of the planet and its focus on the Southern Pacific Ocean (Figure 1.7). The process of weaving satellite data into a comprehensive fabric and view of the Blue Planet was by no means self-evident, however. The satellite image does not display the intricate routines that enabled its fabrication. Several steps of conversion were required to compute sea surface temperatures from satellite readings. Measurements of time had to be converted to distances and translated to units of temperature. The measurement principle of TOPEX/Poseidon's radar worked similar to the sonar technology explained in the first section of this chapter. The time of the reflected radio signal to travel to the sea surface and back translated

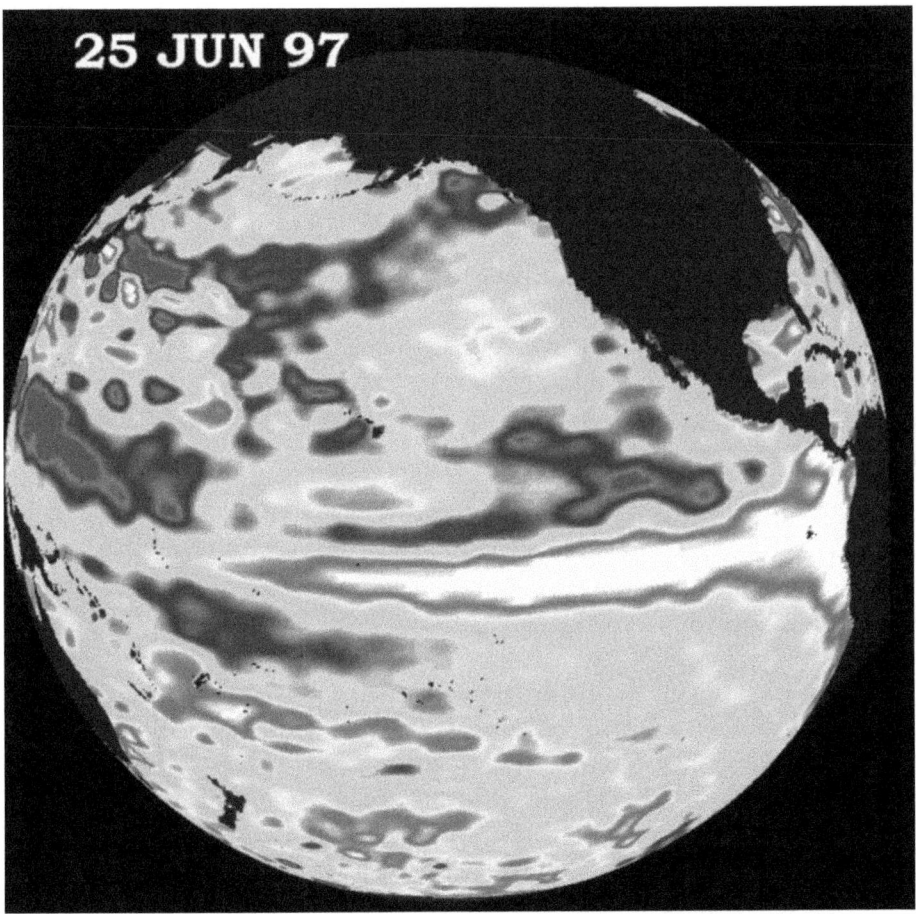

FIGURE 1.7 View of the Pacific Ocean by TOPEX-Poseidon satellite, 1997. © NASA Jet Propulsion Laboratory.

to a distance that in turn translated to the sea surface temperature based on empirical knowledge about the expansion of water bodies with temperature.

The TOPEX/Poseidon image does not give away that data were gathered not in one moment but in separate satellite orbits. Data points had to be interpolated across large time spans. Like earlier ocean charts relying on single-spot measurements, synopsis was created retrospectively. Single data points had to be arranged into the hemispherical form to represent the planet. The coloring scheme was designed to follow the contemporary conventions of temperature coloring and coding. Together, these practices created the impressive satellite view that indicated that an El Niño situation was approaching. By delivering such images satellite oceanographers could promise to provide early warnings of natural weather disasters such as storms and floods from an early discovery of a developing El Niño episode. Optical consistency made the images legible and plausible. To speak with Latour again, they presented "a new way of accumulating time and space" in a transportable and stable form (Latour 1990: 31).

Satellite imagery, made openly accessible by NASA, seems to present the preliminary end of the sensory trajectory of knowing the sea that I began this chapter with. Charts, maps, and satellite data images were visual devices to understand and communicate the sea. In the increasingly digital cultures of the late twentieth century, the visual sense superseded tactile and auditory perceptions. The power of ocean literacy, however, lay not in the data images but in the data archives. The standardized and centralized satellite data held much greater authority and power than the satellite images. Driven by remote sensing technology and by the availability of ever larger computing capacity, a new operational device changed physical oceanography: the digital database. Its power resided in data versatility. Satellite information and computer power invited the infinite conversion, aggregation, and recombination of data to operationalize ocean-atmosphere forecasting. More data would allow for more extensive information processing, so the optimistic hopes of oceanographers. Better information and better simulation tools would enable oceanography to convert and recombine oceanographic data to make El Niño predictions based on probabilistic models.

The sea surface temperature databases entailed another crucial shift in ocean knowledge, the shift toward future ocean projections and predictions. Satellite oceanography entangled formerly distant events into a new analytic fabric, which far exceeded the "global synoptic descriptions" of the ocean-atmosphere circulation that oceanographers had envisioned in the mid-1980s (Revelle 1985). NOAA, the US National Oceanic and Atmospheric Administration, hosted the aggregated comprehensive collections of El Niño-related data gathered in a huge database on ocean-atmosphere circulation. From these data sets, El Niño emerged not as the catastrophic exception but as part of a quasi-periodic, regular climate pattern. El Niño turned into a veritable climate engine that today drives the earth's global climate system. Invented by the World Climate Research Program (WCRP) in the 1980s and in close reference to Jacob Bjerknes, this climate engine was called ENSO—El Niño Southern Oscillation (Reeves and Gemmill 2004). ENSO became a major reference in the emerging discourse on the earth's climate cycles. ENSO also fundamentally reoriented the understanding of rising world ocean temperatures and more generally of current global climate change.

The record-breaking El Niño winter of 1997–8, which has been termed the "climate event of the century" (Changnon 2000), was hardly apparent neither in the images provided by TOPEX/Poseidon nor in the cautious forecasts the satellite data entailed. Only in retrospect did the world experience one of the most violent winters in recorded weather history with floodings and droughts, tornados and ice storms in the Pacific region but also globally, natural disasters that widely changed public perceptions of weather and climate. While ENSO has become the dominant scientific signature of the global climate pattern, devastating weather incidents have impressed themselves on local communities ever since and will most likely continue to do so as the oceans are heating up and the atmosphere carries more water. To summarize, physical oceanography since the late twentieth century has supported an understanding of the earth's climate through remote-sensing tools enabled by the earth and ocean sciences as well as by space technology. Satellite oceanography contributed to shifting the focus to ocean modeling and forecasting based on continuously augmented digital databases that in their practical power have by and large replaced previous tools of ocean probing and perception. The scientific regularity of ocean-atmosphere interaction as a climate factor, however, is in a peculiar incongruence to the powerful interventions of the oceans that seem to belittle any managerial or engineering thought of ocean control.

CONCLUSION

In the course of the twentieth century, physical oceanography compiled data records and edited an ever more encompassing and complex ocean volume. The sea, formerly a vast realm filled with imagination but largely opaque to humans, turned into a seemingly transparent three-dimensional physical space that meets the eye in the form of ocean charts, maps, and satellite images. To return to the contemporary network and project of Ocean Literacy I began this chapter with, physical oceanography helped turn the sea into a legible environment. The scientific tools of oceanographers employed the human senses from the tactile to the auditory to the ultimately privileged visual sense. Surveying techniques and synoptic images created ocean knowledge that began with digits and ultimately resided in digital data sets and the potentials of data recombination.

Oceanographers never worked in isolation. They worked in close alliance with national, military, technological and commercial endeavors. They hooked into developments in other fields of modern science and technology, from electroacoustics to space technology to information technology. Furthermore, they helped to create the networks and frameworks in which the sea shifted from a national object of prestige to an international object of juridification to a global object of environmental governance. Oceanographical data sets formed the fundament for disputing claims on the oceans as national or corporate territories. Databases also enabled and faciliated ocean access, extraction, modeling, and, in recent climate mitigation strategies for carbon removal, also ocean engineering. The shifting architectures for perception, this chapter has attempted to demonstrate, stabilized the legibility both of scientific knowledge and of the sea as a scientific object.

Do we know the sea? Today's AUVs can store sonar information of hundreds of square kilometers of sea floor topography on a small hard drive that can be downloaded and utilized for scientific, commercial, or military uses. Yet, large ocean areas remain unexplored. Humans know more about the surface of the moon than about the ocean depths. If there is something to conclude at this point it would be that the place and significance of the sea in science, culture, and society has not diminished but increased. At the turn to the twenty-first century, the sea has lost its status of ungovernable forceful nature to be admired and feared and passive resource to be annexed, exploited, and managed. The sea has turned into a powerful actor that itself intervenes on the global scale and governs the global water cycles and global climates. While current geoengineering schemes continue to take a managerial perspective to the sea with the idea to harness the oceans as carbon storage facilities, the sea of today in many ways is not less but more powerful than the abysmal sea of our ancestors.

CHAPTER TWO

Practices

Robots, Memories, Autonomy, and the Future

COLIN DEWEY

INTRODUCTION

A cultural history of seafaring technologies is crucial to understanding the significance of the ocean in modern Western culture. To do this suggests examining the material practices as well as their representation, their value, who has performed them in the past, and who performs them now.[1] By far the most significant oceanic material practice is that which constitutes the infrastructure of commerce, capitalism, and empire, and gives rise to the term "maritime." But the global marine transportation system, like other infrastructures, has been constructed "in relation to historically specific social imaginations" (Starosielski 2015: 30). With nostalgic hindsight, the seafarer and novelist Joseph Conrad remembered his rugged world of harsh discipline and men mastering the elements and themselves as "the laborious absorbing practice of an art whose ultimate result remains on the knees of the gods" (1988: 31). However, beginning with the universal adoption of mechanized propulsion in the early twentieth century, commercial seafaring matured into an avatar of globalized capitalism—part of a logistics network operating within a dense commercial and international infrastructure, within which Conrad's romanticized ocean is one curiously persistent part. Writing about the internet infrastructure of undersea fiber-optic cables that revisit, topographically, marine trade routes pioneered centuries earlier and which in turn gave shape to imperial telegraph networks, Nicole Starosielski notes that "new infrastructures are often layered over existing [...] systems and rarely develop in isolation" (2015: 31). Maritime culture is a web of practice that carries an uncanny sense of its own never-disappearing past. To many, seafaring continues to be performed as it always has been—for them the sea is the same—but the cultural experience of seafaring is not.[2]

The twentieth century saw two global mechanized wars, uneven decolonization, and the eventual supplanting of empire by regimes of globalized capital. As part of that transformation, networks of seasonal shipping routes developed by local agents and served by tramp freighters were consolidated under centralized management into more efficient liner services. Further economic efficiencies came with the deployment of specialized multinational flag-of-convenience container carriers, tankers, and bulkers. These changes were partly realized through developments in shipbuilding technology that allowed operators to achieve economies of scale and reduced labor costs, partly through the rise of petroleum over coal as both a major bulk cargo and energy source, and partly through changes in finance and corporate business practice. Many innovations in maritime practice were conceived during the crises of the World Wars but only fully articulated, and "capitalized," after them. International labor and safety regulations have been formulated by advisory bodies such as the International Maritime Organization (IMO) in reaction to catastrophic failures and the public discovery of dreadful conditions aboard ships or visible environmental damage, but enforcement by individual nation-states impedes uniform application. Sometimes the internationalist goals of the regulators have conflicted with member (or nonmember) states' assertions of sovereignty and their perceived economic interests.

As these monumental changes progressed, the ideal maritime subject, the embodiment of seafaring's historically specific social imagination, has seen the cultural value of this work shift. This idealized subject is characterized by self-sufficiency in a hostile and demanding environment and represents a shifting relation to the history and practice of the sea that I refer to as "autonomy." The ideal of individual action and heroism was praised by Conrad and remains potent in cultural memory. Yet existing vessels at sea carry crew and machinery that are monitored and managed 24/7 by people ashore who perform the role of Olympian gods, electronically directing human activities from "the cloud." Technology has reduced crew size in engine rooms and on navigation bridges to the point that some seafarers now complain that the skills honed over a lifetime are being lost—they feel they have been reduced to pushing brooms, watching for alarms, and completing never-ending paperwork. Once, the autonomous subject seemed essential to the seafaring experience that Conrad called a "a single-handed struggle with something much greater than yourself" (1988: 31) but in the twenty-first century the logistics industry looks forward to the "Maritime Autonomous Surface Ship," or MASS. MASS is a proposed category of vessel that, "to a varying degree, can operate independently of human interaction" (IMO 2018). Autonomy, in this brave new world, means progressively larger, remotely operated ships—or even ships commanded by artificial intelligence (AI)—carrying consumer cargo as part of a global logistics chain that, in the dreams of its designers, operates without human intervention at all. This tension—palpable to maritime workers as growing demands for efficiency and regulatory scrutiny arrive under conditions of increased isolation and threats of redundancy—structures the contested "social imagination" of twenty-first-century globalized transport as did the "wooden ships and iron men" of the storied past.

JOSEPH CONRAD: *LORD JIM*

Joseph Conrad was born Józef Teodor Konrad Korzeniowski in 1857 to Polish parents in Ukraine. Orphaned at age eleven, as a young man Conrad made his way to the port of Marseilles. Although he first sailed from France, Conrad decided early on that if he was to become "a seaman, then a British seaman and no other" (Conrad 1988: 119). During his nearly nineteen-year career in the British merchant navy, Conrad worked as able-bodied seaman, steward, third, second, chief mate, and master. He sailed in barques, schooners, clipper ships, and steamers on British and European routes, across the Atlantic, and around the Cape of Good Hope to Australia and South East Asia. In 1894, Conrad received a modest inheritance that helped him to retire from the sea and begin seriously developing his meditative, philosophical, style of sea fiction. Conrad's *Lord Jim* (first published 1900), only partly a sea novel, charts an ordinary British merchant officer who began his career with dreams "of the sea in the distance, and the hope of a stirring life in the world of adventure" (1996: 9). Jim's unexceptional but respectable career ends, however, when as first mate of the SS *Patna*, believing that his ship is sinking, he unaccountably—even to himself—abandons his sleeping passengers, eight hundred Muslim pilgrims bound from Singapore to Mecca.[3]

Lord Jim, straddling the transition between Victorian and modernist aesthetics, inaugurates an era in which adventure narratives of the "sea-life of light literature" (1996: 9) with their ethos of individual, heroic autonomy became problematic. Instead, as Frederic Jameson (1994) argues, the melodrama of the anti-hero, Jim, splits in a "bifurcation" characteristic of modernist literature. Meanwhile, the novel illustrates the efficiency with which a colonial commercial network collected and distributed information. In the early twentieth century, a network of local agents in colonial ports and brokers in the metropoles connected distant ports and knit different nationalities, shipping lines, and trades into an efficient commercial web with tremendous social and cultural consequences.

At the beginning of the novel, Jim's fall is already complete. He is introduced performing his new "beautiful and humane occupation" as "water clerk"—a ship agent in an eastern colonial port. Conrad's narrator, Captain Marlow, explains the importance of a good water clerk to the industry: "to the captain he is faithful like a friend and attentive like a son" (7). Marlow is representative of his maritime community, a traditional, even nostalgic, brotherhood of the sea. The bulk of the novel focuses on how Captain Marlow tries to piece together the circumstances of Jim's disgraceful performance. After all, he reasons, Jim "was of the right sort; he was one of us" (50). For Marlow and his circle (and perhaps Conrad), the shared trauma resulting from Jim's experience aboard the *Patna* represents a line between an idealized and vanishing sense of duty and honor, and modernity's encroaching uncertainties. Marlow speaks with the hegemonic voice of ideologically traditional seamanship that he calls "craft" and, more ambiguously, seems to want to preserve: "I was aggrieved against [Jim], as though he had cheated me—me!—of a splendid opportunity to keep up the illusion of my beginnings, as though he had robbed our common life of the last spark of its glamour" (81). Marlow's frustration, and some reader's, dramatizes how the text—without warning—abandons the valorization of manly endeavor, adventure, and the notion that, as Jameson (1994: 214) puts it, "the 'subject' of [the] book is courage and cowardice [...] which we are meant to interpret in ethical" terms. Instead, the "tale" becomes a case of collective misunderstanding by characters who don't see that the ideological position they have occupied no longer requires their service, even if their trade does.

In *The Novel and the Sea*, Margaret Cohen (2010) writes about "craft" as an "*ethos*," represented by an accumulation of practical knowledge and attitudes that she convincingly distills out of records of early modern voyages of commerce and exploration.[4] Cohen reads Jim's obscurity as ratification of Conrad's grim pronouncements on his former industry. She writes, "there is no spark of glamour illuminating Jim because craft has disappeared," but she also recognizes the emergence of conditions that, I argue, do not herald the historical or material "loss" of craft at sea but rather a foretaste of the actual position of the maritime worker following the emergence of logistics and information-based economics; she writes, "Marlow's search [...] makes the struggles of the protagonist, like that of the reader, only about coordinating information" (207). Coordinating information or coordinates *and* information are one important way that an early twentieth-century network of shipping agents connected by telegraph became, in later decades, a model for the internet-driven logistical network of modern capitalist commerce. Considered this way, Frederic Jameson's argument makes more sense. Jameson writes that as a "tale of courage and cowardice, a moral story" (even one about the "loss" of traditional seafaring ways), the "ostensible or manifest 'theme' of the novel is no more to be taken at face value than is the dreamer's immediate waking sense of what the dream was about" (1994: 217). Therefore, to "estrange" the anti-heroic theme of Jim's failure—instead of being confused along with Marlow and his cronies—is to ask why we "assume, in the midst of capitalism, that the aesthetic rehearsal of the problematics of [...] honor—should need no justification and should [...] be of interest to us" (217). Like Marlow, Conrad, by his own later testimony, resisted changes to maritime practice he knew were already well underway. Jim's murder at the end of the novel is portrayed as a senseless, absurdly meaningless event. Conrad foresaw the secularization of craft required by capitalism as it replaced his aestheticized ideal of seafaring as an art, with the rigorous, but meaningless, exactitude of the engineer:

> I think I can lay my finger upon the difference between the seamen of yesterday, who are still with us, and the seamen of to-morrow, already entered upon the possession of their inheritance... The taking of a modern steamship about the world (though one would not minimize its responsibilities) has not the same quality [...]. It is less personal and a more exact calling; less arduous, but also less gratifying [...]. Its effects are measured exactly in time and space as no effect of an art can be.
>
> (1988: 30)

STEAMSHIPS

For Conrad, the masts and spars of a sailing vessel were "the towering structure of her machinery," above the "insignificant, tiny speck of her hull" (1988: 36). Aesthetics aside, the outsized rig of the sailing ship limited cargo-carrying space and obstructed the decks below. For the benefit of cargo, steamship hulls were subdivided into several holds, and since each hold had its own hatch, it was possible to simultaneously access more than one at a time in port (Figure 2.1). Furthermore, steamers were capable of quickly loading and unloading themselves using deck mounted and steam-powered derricks, or booms, two to four installed at each hatch (Woodman 2010: 147). Although the speed at which new developments in marine engineering and technology emerged accelerated astonishingly by the mid-twentieth century, the material foundations were largely in place before 1900. In the early 1800s, steamships had appeared alongside sailing ships, the two for decades sharing seaways and competing for trade. Telegraph cables soon connected colonial ports with the major markets in Europe (150). However, the Suez Canal, opened in 1869, along with railroads and the steam-driven tramp ship definitively ended the commercial practicality of sailing vessels in the early 1900s (Miller 2012: 69). As the volume of world trade increased nearly tenfold through the beginning of the twentieth century, these new technologies opened world markets to "regular, safer, all-weather, rapid, and increasingly lower-cost transport" (69–70).

FIGURE 2.1 Exterior of Panamanian freighter. © Sam Shere The LIFE Picture Collection/Getty Images.

Twentieth-century steamships were built to accommodate cargo, whatever the cost in traditional beauty or crew comfort: sailors complained that "steam-vessels were wet and uncomfortable with no thought given for the working of the vessel or the basic needs of the crew" (Woodman 2010: 148). Conrad objected: "the machinery, the steel, the fire, the steam have stepped in between the man and the sea" (1988: 72), an opinion shared by sailing ship Captain Charles W. Brown who, writing in 1925, criticized young sailors who only knew steamships. Captain Brown, among many who resented steamships and the men willing to work below decks in their engine rooms, remembered the sailing ship officers and the crews he had sailed with as a boy: "*men*—bold, brave, adventurous—*men*" (quoted in Grider 2014: 110–11, emphasis in original). Engineers were a threat to traditional shipboard authority from the start as "deck officers saw […] that engineers had 'the potential to appropriate that area of competence which custom and tradition had ordained as peculiarly their own'" (H. Campbell McMurray, "Technology and Social Change at Sea: The Status and Position on Board of the Ship's Engineer, circa 1830–60," quoted in Dixon 1996: 232–3).

Engineering officers arrived on ships in two classes: "one 'raised from the shovel,' the other supplied with the engines by the makers and having a background as boiler-makers, millwrights, turners, and mechanics" (Dixon 1996: 231). The latter, especially, were treated as though they were part of the equipment; they were taken almost as engine parts themselves, and not immediately accepted as members of the crew. Before steam, a ship carried officers, petty officers, both able and ordinary seamen, plus carpenters, sailmakers, cooks, etc., but steamships required engineers—and the previously all-around seamen were divided into firemen, coal-passers, deck crew (responsible for the outside of the vessel), engine crew (responsible for the engines), and steward's crew, who waited on officers and passengers. "Ordinary" deck seamen became less necessary, and their skills became less valuable. By the beginning of the twentieth century "seamen made up only about 25 percent of steamship crews. In short, the true 'sailor' was being replaced by the engineer and fireman, and sailing men had reason to worry about their future on the seas" (Grider 2014: 119). Adding to the prejudices of tradition, firemen and coal-passers sometimes earned greater pay and better shore liberty than did their colleagues on deck. Working in the engine room often "paid better but it forced men used to working in the fresh air inside the stale hull of the ship where they had to learn how to perform new tasks" such as managing coal furnaces to keep them burning evenly and cleanly, and keeping coal bunkers from sliding around in a rolling and pitching ship (125).

The great advantages of steamships—their ability to travel in any direction and their ease and efficiency of cargo handling—were exploited by new business models. Steamships' quick and efficient cargo handling abilities with smaller crews cut down time in port, saving berthing costs and increasing profit margins. Gangs of longshoremen muscling loads of bags or pallets full of goods seem labor intensive and inefficient today compared to the rapidity of containerized cargo, but steam-powered break-bulk ships, with their practical design and the economies of scale achieved by larger capacity, were a significant advantage (Figure 2.2). Steamships and their operating companies influenced the development of economies worldwide. Enormous quantities of grain grown in North America or Argentina could be shipped quickly and reliably to European ports, and rice grown in Burma and Indochina was transported in bulk to markets in India, Europe, and the Americas. Yet liner companies made heavy demands on ports and their infrastructure, often at public expense. For ports to be able to serve the high-volume rapid service that scheduled liners required meant significant investment in port facilities and inland transport, including river or rail connections, availability of local labor, and sufficient amounts of the right kinds of berthing and cargo handling space. Major liner companies therefore gravitated to ports that met these needs. Adequate ports with the ability to

FIGURE 2.2 Bales of wool being loaded at Victoria Docks in Melbourne. © Universal History Archive Universal Images Group/Getty Images.

serve high-volume ships on a schedule were often cities with long histories of waterborne commerce. In some cases, new ports developed to link hinterland systems with the global grids of deep-sea transport, but in many trades, modern shipping infrastructure only solidified long-standing colonial trading networks (Miller 2012: 71).

MALCOLM LOWRY: *ULTRAMARINE*

Life aboard an ordinary coal-powered freighter in the post-First World War Far East trade is the setting for Malcolm Lowry's semi-autobiographical novel *Ultramarine* (first published 1933). Lowry's text shares some of the formal experimentation found in other novels published at the time, but aboard his transnational multilingual tramp ship, a world away from pristine luxury passenger liners, daily practice dispenses with the sleek smoothness of modernist (and globalist) fantasy, revealing the squalor and semi-organized chaos at the heart of global capital. Lowry was heavily influenced by Nordahl Greig (1927) and Conrad Aiken (1927), both of whom had written sea novels featuring young male protagonists in the 1920s. After graduating from public school in Cambridge, England, in 1927, Lowry, inspired by his reading of Eugene O'Neill and Joseph Conrad, convinced his father to allow him to take a gap year voyage at sea. His father arranged the voyage and almost disastrously had Malcolm driven to the ship in the family limousine. This event appears in the novel, where it amuses the experienced seamen in the crew but exacerbates the "outsider" status of *Ultramarine*'s young protagonist (Lowry 2005: 5). Lowry's maritime *bildungsroman* starts from a post-Conradian position accepting the ambiguity of craft and the seductiveness of industrial machinery. The novel narrates a ship's arrival and brief stay in an obscure port, but the route or location of ship or harbor matters little. The nineteen-year-old English protagonist on his first trip to sea is called Dana Hilliot, after Richard Henry Dana, author of the American marine *bildungsroman*, *Two Years Before the Mast* (1840). Dana's inexperience and "posh" upbringing increase the amusement of the more experienced hands aboard the portentously named *Oedipus Tyrannus* who mock him as a "toff." The multilingual, although mainly European, crew taunts Dana as "useless, we don't know what sort of a bloody man you are at all. Just a nancy," and scoffing, "a man who would go to sea for fun would go to hell for a pastime" (Lowry 2005: 16, 20–1). The transnational history of the ship is revealed by the signs and engraved placards left over from previous registries: "First she was registered in Tvedestrand, then bought by an English firm, who re-registered her [...] then she was bought back by Norway; after which she was rebought by England, and after her reconditioning was completed, received a charter. She sailed out an exile, an expatriate; with *Seamen* scarcely substituted for *Matroser*, or *Firemen* for *Fyrbötere*" (53).

Dana feels the physical burden of his labor acutely; there is no romance or "glamour" in his dirty, grubby work nor any honor of craft:

> Sweating rust and coal dust, I made my bunk, which was full of chippings shaken from my dungarees. Then I had to chip the bed of a winch [...]. The sack I was lying on seemed to be searing my stomach; there was no room to

work with my wrists, which were bruised every time they came into contact with the reverse gear. Paint and burning oil dropped off the winch on to my face, mingling with my sweat.

(Lowry 2005: 81)

In a more reflective moment, Dana's observation of the ship and sea is laconic but far from picturesque or sublime: "beyond, the bow did whatever a bow did, lolled back, then did it again." The monotonous roll of the ship is contrasted by the reciprocating engine, which "throbbed away cheerfully somewhere down below" (22). The engine's "Cloom—cloom—cloom—cloom" punctuates the entire text. Notwithstanding the cheery engines, the ship's passage indelibly marks the marine environment—as the preceding sentence continues—"an endless spout of water and refuse was splashing from her rusty side into the Yellow Sea [...] the *Oedipus Tyrannus* poured out black smoke, mephitic and black from her one enormous funnel [...] it was the one smudge on all that glad serenity" (22–3). Unlike the scene on deck, the noisy, hot space of the engine room is a source of erotic fascination and fear (Figure 2.3): looking down from above, Dana watches

FIGURE 2.3 Lascar (Indian or Southeast Asian) stokers in the engine room of a P&O steamer shoveling coal to keep the fires burning. © Reinhold Thiele Hulton Archive/Getty Images.

the engines, a maelstrom of noise which crashed on his brain; it was humiliating to watch the nicety with which lever weight and fulcrum worked, opening and closing their hidden mechanisms and functioning with such an incomprehensible exactness! He thought of the whirling clanks holding horribly in their nerveless grip the penetrating shaft that turned the screws, that internal dynamic thing, the life of the ship.

(23)

Even when he is ashore, the sound of the ship's engine returns to him, signifying a mechanical, if only partly reassuring, continuity. Rejected by the cooks and sailors he serves in the messroom, Dana becomes attracted to the firemen serving the engines, who "seemed to get more fun out of life than the seamen, and somehow to be better, in some queer way to be nearer God" (23). The voyage of the *Oedipus Tyrannus* is transitional, and while Lowry's deployment of experimental style and his erotic fascination with the very "incomprehensible exactness" that provoked Conrad's disdain looks to the future, the old ship belongs to the past. *Lord Jim*, in 1900, and *Ultramarine*, in 1933, both share the sense that the cultural value of the practices of the sea that they represent have changed.

GLOBALIZATION, CONSOLIDATION, AND EXPANSION

Before the Second World War, the freighters that opened markets for European trading companies, like much of the industrial world, were fueled by coal. However, a trend from coal to oil for heating and propulsion, coupled with an emerging worldwide automobile market, increased oil consumption sixfold between 1913 and 1937. In the Royal Navy, conversion to oil-fired boilers had begun in 1905 and spread throughout the merchant fleet. To secure fuel for the new oil-burning navy, in 1914 Winston Churchill negotiated a 51 percent share in the Anglo-Persian Oil Company, the forerunner of British Petroleum (Paine 2013: 543). Oil fields developed in locations that were far from European consumer markets, such as Latin America, the Persian Gulf, and Southeast Asia. Transportation of oil was about 5 percent of all sea-borne trade in 1914, quickly rising to 21 percent in 1937 (Miller 2012: 250).

As the transportation of oil by sea became strategically important, and to connect remote production sites with refineries and consumers, oil companies sought to control their transportation infrastructure by building tankships of their own. The "cistern ship" or oil tanker was pioneered by oil producers in Russia in the late nineteenth century because of the high costs of shipping liquids as breakbulk cargo and the difficulty of constructing pipelines to deliver refined products to consumers (Tolf 1976: 52). Previously, oil producers had been shipping their products aboard sailing vessels and breakbulk steamships packed in barrels or metal cans. The *Glückauf*, built for Standard Oil in Great Britain, was the first purpose-built ocean-going steam tanker (although powered by coal), and on her maiden voyage, she carried 910,221 gallons of petroleum in large tanks (78). Nations with easy access to coal, such as Britain, tended to retain their coal-fired ships longer, while others such as the Norwegians, Dutch, Russians, and Japanese, who depended on other nations to power their vessels, moved quickly to oil and diesel power. Powering vessels with relatively clean-burning oil instead of coal had advantages for owners of cleanliness and the reduction in crew size. Oil-burning ships did not require stokers and trimmers to feed the liquid fuel to their boilers. Still, in 1935, coal drove 80 percent of cargo and passenger ships in all the world's trades (Paine 2013: 544).

The Second World War brought an effective end to the small ships and small companies such as the one described in *Ultramarine*. Even though trampers and family-based shipping companies continued into the twentieth century, the war definitively changed the maritime industry. Michael B. Miller (2012: 282) argues that a decisive factor during the war was successfully organizing and applying the knowledge of maritime practitioners: "The vital issue was less getting ships than knowing how to use them," he writes. Shipping and stevedore company managers were experts at preventing port congestion, ship delays, and cargo and labor problems. All the major twentieth-century changes in transporting cargo had their roots in logistical experiments undertaken during the war: RoRo (roll-on roll off) suggested by landing craft; palletization, widely adopted by US supply services; and containerization, suggested by lashing boxes of cargo to the decks of ships to maximize carrying capacity (288). After the Second World War, the knowledge gained during the conflict, added to the quick sales of excess Liberty Ships and T-2 tankers, gave new leaders such as Onassis, Nicharos, and McLean the start they needed to build the massive fleets that changed the global ocean.

In the second half of the twentieth century, expanding tanker fleets accounted for the largest portion of the enormous increase in world shipping tonnage (Miller 2012: 307–8). The rapid growth of petroleum and dedicated dry bulk carriers changed ship design and company organization. European oil imports between mid-century and the 1970s increased tenfold. Single-product liquid and dry bulk vessels—carrying single cargoes from fixed point to fixed point, such as from oil field to refinery—had no need of the versatility of the break bulk freighters and small tankers of previous generations. Building one gigantic ship was cheaper—and cheaper to crew and operate under reduced manning and maintenance rules—than several smaller ones (308). While the typical coal-powered tramp freighter of the 1930s may have displaced 5,000–6,000 tons, tankers built during the Second World War displaced about 21,000 tons. By the 1960s, the size of new ocean-going tankers was

FIGURE 2.4 A Wessex helicopter owned by the Bristow Helicopter Group flies over the Shell supertanker *Melania*. The Group uses its helicopters to fly out crew members, pilots, and engineers, and mail to the supertankers. © Hulton-Deutsch Collection/CORBIS/Getty Images.

approaching 200,000 tons. In 1979, by some measures the largest ship ever built, the tanker *Seawise Giant,* was launched, with a loaded displacement of 646,642 tons (USCG n.d.). Similarly, typical dry cargo ships went from about 15,000 to 200,000 tons between the 1950s and 1970s. One of the largest container ships afloat in 2018, the 399-meter *CMA CGM Benjamin Franklin,* displaces just over 237,000 tons (USCG n.d.) and can carry the equivalent of 18,000 twenty-foot containers. However, the largest ships afloat today are not container ships or tankers but bulk carriers designed to sail on fixed routes between Brazilian iron ore mines and steel mills in China. At 362 meters, the 402,347-ton *Vale Brasil* dwarfs earlier freighters and tankers (Det Norske Veritas n.d.). With the development of these gigantic vessels in the twentieth century, fleet numbers (and crews) shrank. Between 1968 and 1975, in the UK fleet, the number of large ships decreased from 4,020 to 3,662, but overall, the fleet's total cargo carrying capacity *increased* from 21.9 to 33.2 million tons (DeSombre 2006: 80).

CONTAINERIZATION

Anticipating the value of applying the logic of tanker operators to transporting break-bulk freight, in 1956 the American trucking entrepreneur Malcolm McLean converted a small tanker to carry individual consignments of cargo in aluminum containers fastened on deck. His innovative ship, the *Ideal X*, in some ways represented a revolutionary insight, but it was the product of a long period of development.[5] His real innovation, though he did not recognize it at the time, was imagining the myriad small and large consignments of heterogeneous cargo that made up a typical break bulk voyage as a single commodity. Although there are many versions of McLean's fable of success, they all share the trope of a hard-working and frustrated truck driver having to wait for his goods to be unloaded, sorted, and reloaded on pallets to be delivered pier side and put on a ship. Of his inspiration, McLean later wrote that he thought, "Wouldn't it be great if my trailer could simply be lifted up and placed on the ship without its contents being touched?" (Allen 1994: 13).

In the same way that petroleum companies in the late 1800s moved from shipping oil in crates of five-gallon cans to running specialized vessels to dedicated port facilities carrying large volumes of liquid cargo in bulk, containerization transformed the dry freight business. The new model essentially treated individual consignments as bulk cargo in aggregate by specializing the design of the vessel. Instead of using their own gear to load and discharge the thousands of products that cargo vessels had done for centuries, the "container ship" was loaded and discharged using very specialized and expensive equipment in a dedicated central port. The cargoes were simplified into identical metal boxes of standard dimension fitted to special guides and secured using special "twist-lock" pins provided for them.

McLean saw freight as simply "something added to the cost of the product" and throughout his career sought to reduce that added charge by as much as possible (Allen 1994: 15). Even "maritime" came to have an unstable meaning under containerization, as sea and land integrated (Miller 2012: 320). McLean's company name, "Sea-Land," anticipated this effect of the logistics revolution. When he registered his Pan Atlantic Steamship line with regulators in 1955, McLean stated that he was employing ships as "sea tractors" to carry trailers, emphasizing his break with the traditions of marine transportation. Changing the name of his steamship company from Pan Atlantic to the more descriptive "Sea-Land" signaled his second major innovation: "intermodal" freight that was packed once by the shipper and never opened again until received by the customer.

Malcolm McLean's rags-to-riches story has been burnished by magazines and books, but besides revolutionizing ocean transportation, McLean was a pioneer of the leveraged buyout. This disruptive financial tool radically changed corporate finance and the global capitalist economy in the 1980s and 1990s. McLean's Pan American Steamship Corporation bought up the ships, docks, and wharfs of its parent but was only able to do so by borrowing over 80 percent of the purchase price (Klose 2015: 89–90). Similarly, the economics of scale that encouraged increases in ship size—and the exorbitant costs of retooling for the container trade—also increased the amounts of capital needed to build ships. Previously, owners would build or buy a ship with close to 100 percent equity, but by the 1970s banks were lending up to 90 percent of the cost of a new ship. Speculative owners built larger and larger ships as "it was not difficult to pay off mortgages with one years round of voyages and then plow profits back into new ship orders" (Miller 2012: 309). However, with more shipping capacity than cargo demand to fill it, in the 1980s many ships were repossessed from bankrupt owners. With no advantage to sell such recovered vessels for scrap, their new owners—governments or banks, not the savvy maritime operators of the first half of the century—kept them running, adding to a general downward pressure on rates (DeSombre 2006: 80–1). Since bankers usually know little about effective ship operations, they hired third-party managers to operate them profitably. Such ship management firms soon realized that there were vast profits to be earned by operating larger fleets of vessels, and following them, specialized subsidiary firms arose to handle the tasks of hiring crew (human relations), maintenance, and the other aspects of managing fleets of ships. Where once the shipping line office or the captain engaged crew directly, now it is common for seafarers to be hired through independent shipping agencies operating on commission with no connection to either the seafarer's community or the shipping lines that contract with them (81).

Containerized freight substituted "intermodality" and "logistics" for the traditional techniques and cultural ways of moving cargo that had held for generations (Miller 2012: 320). Globalization made ocean transportation a key part of a larger transportation chain in which freight costs were often inconsequential, so ships, with their enormous size and capital expense, became even more important to the global economy. Paradoxically, however, their importance was based on the extent to which their massive size and low operating costs provided the savings that helped sustain the near-costless basis for commodity-driven supply chains. Ultimately, McLean and the others' contribution was "to reduce the oceans to a system of highways—to dry up the seas, in essence" (Klose 2015: 103).

INTERNATIONAL REGULATION: SOLAS TO IMO

Early marine transportation developed in a laissez-faire environment that often accepted the many hazards of the trade as the natural course of things (Boisson 1999: 45). Most early attempts at creating and coordinating regulations came from within private communities that historically tried to remain as free from government influence as possible (Silverstein 1978: 11). Eventually a system developed to encourage trade by protecting both ship and cargo and compensating losses based on the idea that the parties with financial investments in commerce each had to bear their share of liability and, before major environmental disasters became a factor, that they were the only parties with any legitimate interest in losses at sea (Boisson 1999: 48). To manage their own exposure to such dangers, maritime insurers encouraged the development of classification societies.[6] Insurers and classification societies worked together to gather intelligence information on individual ships, produce lists of vessels rated according to age and condition, and assure their members and partners of the level of risk associated with particular vessels. However, few attempts were made to develop standards to harmonize national customs and laws governing each trading nation's own ships. Throughout the nineteenth century the legislation adopted by individual nations was based mainly on reactions to major losses suffered by that country and not a forward-looking study of hazards and conditions "or even an objective assessment of the casualties suffered by the world fleets as a whole" (Cowley 1989: 113).

In the early twentieth century, fires and accidents that had resulted in major loss of life in industry ashore forced governments to exert some control over domestic industries, and similar spectacular disasters at sea finally "compelled governments to forego some degree of national control in exchange for greater reliance upon international solutions" (Silverstein 1978: 13). When 146 garment workers, most recent immigrants, many children, lost their lives in the 1911 Triangle Shirtwaist Factory fire in New York, the public was outraged to learn that fire exits and stairwells were locked to prevent workers from taking unauthorized breaks. A year later, in April 1912, when the RMS *Titanic* sank off Newfoundland with the loss of over 1,500 lives the public was again horrified at reports of insufficient lifeboats for the number of passengers aboard. In the US Senate, Robert Lafollette made the connection explicit:

> No one will claim it is safe to crowd people into a theatre or shirtwaist factory and then to lock the doors. Is it not even more dangerous to jam a steamer full of passengers and then to send it out of harbor without having on board the means whereby they may be taken off quickly and safely in case of need?
>
> (quoted in Fink 2011: 96)

Following the RMS *Titanic* disaster, both maritime safety and labor reform gained inexorable momentum (Fink 2011: 95). In January 1914, the first Convention on Safety of Life at Sea (SOLAS) met in London to address radiotelegraphy, lifesaving equipment including lifeboats, construction of ships, and signaling protocols (SOLAS 1914). Enforcement was left to the nation-states that subscribed to the agreement, and then only in their ports and aboard ships registered under their flag. In the United States, seafarer's union leader Andrew Furuseth objected to the treaty, predicting that capital investment would flow to the lowest-cost, least-regulated flag, taking seaman's jobs and any progress toward safer ships with it. Of the thirteen delegations attending the London conference, only five nations ratified the convention: the UK, the Netherlands, Norway, Spain, and Sweden (Phillips and Sirkar 2012: 27). SOLAS 1914 never went into full effect due to the outbreak of the First World War. Nevertheless, the convention encouraged more extensive national regulations seeking to improve safety at sea in the UK, France, the United States, and Scandinavia (Boisson 1999: 54; Cowley 1989: 114). Later SOLAS agreements, in 1929 and 1948, further extended the 1914 convention as first eighteen and then thirty nations agreed to adopt the international protocol.

FLAGS OF "CONVENIENCE": PANAMA AND LIBERIA

Because international regulations left enforcement responsibility mainly to flag states, conventions such as SOLAS could not compel universal compliance. This helped to promote the race to the bottom predicted by Furuseth, as shipowners and cargo owners sought the lowest-cost, lowest-regulated flags under which to register vessels and transport freight. The hazards of war also helped encourage the practice of "flagging out." During the First World War, oil and gasoline became vital strategic commodities, and tankers became prime targets. The United Kingdom and United States responded by vastly enlarging their fleets with new building programs; once the United States entered the war, to sail under a "neutral" flag many existing ships were reregistered—mostly to Panama with some choosing other Central and South American nations.

At the beginning of the First World War, the entire world's tanker fleet was approximately two million tons. From 1919 to 1921, American yards alone produced 316 new tankers totaling just over three million tons (Devanney 2006: 19). The resulting postwar oversupply created opportunities as oil companies and speculative independent operators quickly became global corporations with large fleets. Panama's close relationship with the United States attracted American shipowners who were prohibited from putting their newly acquired war-surplus ships in direct competition with other US flag vessels (Carlisle 1981: 20–1). In 1925, new Panamanian laws were passed that favored shipowners and Panama's consulates provided convenient remote registry to foreign corporations. In 1935, Standard Oil of New Jersey (ESSO) established a new Panamanian firm called Panama Transport Company to reflag its vessels from Danzig (Gdansk) to Panama (Carlisle 2013). Acquiring ships in the ESSO fleet gave the Panama flag global legitimacy, and consequently Panama's government worked to retain the ESSO ships and attract other corporate shipowners (Carlisle 1981: 58–9).

By 1939, Panama's flag was recognized in shipping circles as a "convenient" registry (70). However, during the 1940s, labor activism and political instability threatened the operation. The European International Transport Federation (ITF) considered boycotts against the Panamanian fleet. Meanwhile, a week of rioting in 1947 followed by a disputed presidential election in 1948 made American shipowners concerned that the Panamanian Flag of Convenience (FOC) system might not be as stable as they had hoped (112).

Following the Second World War, as they had a generation before, tanker owners with foreign policy connections in the United States sought more favorable conditions by starting a new flag in the West African nation of Liberia. During the war, American officials feared that Liberia could provide a "jumping off" point to invade the Americas through Brazil, so the US Navy built a small installation protecting the main port of Monrovia. In 1947, a firm owned by Edward Stettinius, American Secretary of State under Franklin D. Roosevelt, entered a profit-sharing arrangement with the Liberian government, with a subsidiary, the "Liberia Company," conducting business in the country (Carlisle 1981: 116). From 1947 to 1949, Stettinius and his aides were actively writing the Liberian Maritime Code while operating tankers registered in Panama as the American Overseas Tanker Company (AOTC) (120). The document was carefully designed to meet the postwar needs of oil companies and tanker owners and was vetted by executives of ESSO and other shipping and banking interests in the United States before becoming Liberian law in December 1948 (Carlisle 1981).

The flourishing trade in ship registries has spread far beyond Panama and Liberia, although those are still the major "Flags of Convenience" today. There are real benefits for shipowners and nations providing "convenient" flags and many firms have sprung up to serve loosely regulated international commerce. Elizabeth R. DeSombre (2006) writes that in the early twenty-first century fees charged for ship registration in Panama contributed 5 percent of the national budget, while in Liberia revenue from the registry accounted for 10 percent of the national budget before their civil war (1989–2003) and as much as 90 percent during that conflict. More recently, the Liberian registry is reported to account for one-sixth of total annual revenue. The registry in Cyprus is worth $10 million per year. Often nations offering Flags of Convenience engage professional ship registry firms to manage their accounts, many of which operate out of the United States. "International Registries," a firm based in Virginia, runs the day-to-day business of the Marshall Islands flag and, until recently, Liberia. The ship registry firms are profit-making businesses apart from the funds they provide to their flag state; International Registries earns an 18 percent commission on gross revenue. For states that run so-called "open" registries, there are currently few disadvantages (DeSombre 2006: 78–9).

FRANCISCO GOLDMAN: *THE ORDINARY SEAMAN*

In "Duty and Mutiny" Geoff Quilley makes a point that remains as true in the twenty-first century as it was in the eighteenth century: "in his professional capacity as a productive labourer, [the sailor] was of necessity removed from society. In this sense, his cultural identity was located at some level in the imaginary" (2000: 82). While logistics firms advertise aeolian connectivity and frictionless, nearly cost-free transportation services, seafarers are pushed to the margins of representation and society. Now-iconic news images of broken ships aground and others undergoing "recycling" on the toxic beaches of Chittagong, Bangladesh, and Alang, India, have replaced the heroic ship portraits of the eighteenth century. Maritime workers "vaguely remain as visual traces while their material and manual labor undergoes erasure" (Naimou 2015: 49).

The first twenty-first-century sea novel was *The Ordinary Seaman*, by Francisco Goldman, although published in 1997. In this narrative, a crew of Central American men is sent to join a ship moored in Brooklyn, New York. The men are greeted by "the revenant of a ship," a "dead ship, a mass of inert iron provocatively shaped like a ship" (Naimou 2015: 54; Goldman 1997: 38). Their new home is the burned-out Panamanian-flagged coastal freighter *Urus*, bought at auction by two Americans who hoped to see a quick profit under the cover of their front company, the Achuar Corporation. The inexperienced crew arrives with high hopes, willing to see the ship as a good prospect. The central character, Esteban, sees "a perfectly regular-looking ship, sturdy and capable, and he was going to work on it. Who cared that it was berthed in the middle of desolation? What difference would that make in a few days, when they'd be out to sea?" (Goldman 1997: 20).

However, for the Americans, the venture is from the beginning a scam predicated on manipulating the weakness of international regulation and the porosity of flag state control. The Achuar Corporation operates within the labyrinth of open registries, as part of the complex legal infrastructure that supports global capital. Angela Naimou writes:

> The transaction of registering a ship under a flag of convenience is a transaction that takes place within the formal economy but whose value as a transaction comes from the formal cover it provides for a shipowner to operate within the range of informal economic acts, from hiring undocumented workers to withholding wages to using violence as a means to control the labor force.
> (2015: 71–2)

The scheme is described in the text by Elias, the owner and prospective captain, with a breathless optimism reminiscent of young "Jim's" infatuation with his imagined life of adventure at sea. In this echo of Conrad's ambiguous protagonist, the ideological position of the seafaring adventure hero shows its toxicity. The futility of Elias's irredeemable plan does not lessen the deadly consequences for the subject crew. Elias elaborates: "Get one of those cheap flag of convenience registries and incorporations. Import the cheapest possible crew, even have them pay their own airfare. Work night and day, repair the ship fast, in a month to six weeks. Keep expenses to a minimum, pile up debts" (Goldman 1997: 276). As much as their plan borrows elements of classic sea adventure and American "bootstrap" rags-to-riches fables, and obliquely promises a "trickle-down" benefit for all, there is no thought of ever operating the ship in trade. Theirs is a fable of a corporate raider, a character from a specific late twentieth-century social imagination. Once the ship is repaired, Elias and his partner, Mark, always intend to sell and turn a quick profit: "[we] should be able to get a half a million dollars *at least*, for a decent working ship like this. *Then* pay off the crew, the port fees, the equipment rentals and everything else" (276, emphasis in original). The crew are promised that one day, soon, the ship will move, but in the meantime, they are forced to stay onboard in grim and deteriorating conditions, prisoners of their status and their remote and dangerous location in the backwaters of late 1990s Brooklyn.

Cold, without power or water, and subsisting on dwindling supplies of rice and canned sardines, the crew works haphazardly to repair the burned-out electrical panels that keep the engine from turning. Determined but inexperienced, they "didn't know what a true ship, a true capitán was like and acted as if they had no choice but to believe that when the ship was fixed, she'd sail. Look at all the tools onboard! [...] What's is all for, Viejo? Why else are we here?" (Goldman 1997: 58). As Naimou explains, in joining the ship the crew members have become "something like"—adrift between different categories of identity: "they have become something like slaves without literally being enslaved, they have become something like seamen without ever setting sail or receiving the work papers that would declare them as such, and they are something like stateless persons without formally losing their citizenship from their respective Central American states" (2015: 54).

Though a work of fiction, *The Ordinary Seaman* lives up to its title: "ordinary seaman" is the entry level, lowest-skilled position in the deck department aboard ship, and the experiences the men in Goldman's novel face are unfortunately not extraordinary. As one speaker at a 1999 maritime insurance conference reported, "owners who cannot afford (or do not wish) to spend money maintaining their ships tend not to spend money on their crews either" (quoted in International Labour Office [ILO] and Seafarers International Research Centre 2004: 159). An estimated 10 percent of ships regularly trading in European ports continue despite being in "sub-standard" condition. The ILO warns that "the level in many parts of Africa, Latin

America, and the Middle and Far East must be substantially higher" (161). While unscrupulous owners and complicit masters are easy to blame, the ILO points out that the problem is structural: "the shipping industry's historical regulatory structure [...] has been fragmented as a result of flagging out to sovereignties incapable of duplicating the web of negotiated consent of the older maritime states" (163). Francisco Goldman discusses the background of *The Ordinary Seaman* in his acknowledgements. He writes that in 1982, a story in the New York *Daily News* about an abandoned ship's crew caught his eye. In subsequent visits to the ship and the Seaman's Church Institute facility in lower Manhattan he began the research for what would become *The Ordinary Seaman*. He later discovered that, remarkably, the owners of the actual ship had escaped prosecution and although banned by the Liberian Registry from ever again registering under that flag they had not ceased their efforts: "Amazingly, the ship, once seized and auctioned off as scrap to a machinery company in Brooklyn, was repurchased by those hapless owners; sometime again they were caught trying to work the same scam, with the same ship, in Staten Island; and then again in the Caribbean" (1997: 384).

At the end of the novel, in an act of desperate defiance, a smattering of the skeleton crew finally starts the ship's engine and cuts the *Urus* from its moorings: "Tomaso shouted, 'That's why we're stealing this fucking ship! Get that hijo de puta capitán in even more trouble!' [...] 'We're going home' shouts Tomaso Tostado again, laughing, his gold tooth glinting" (376–7). Although the pilotless ship only drifts across its basin and crashes into another decrepit pier and most of the crew disappears into the projects and barrios of Brooklyn, with this act of nihilistic rebellion the novel rejects marginalization or acquiescence, the only narratives the men are presented with on the fringes of twenty-first-century America. *The Ordinary Seaman* is a sea novel that rejects tropes of the sea, the ship, the voyage, and even late capitalist ideas of post-national sovereignty to celebrate the radical and collective autonomy of its liberated crew.

LOGISTICS AS ONTOLOGY

Logistics promises instantaneous and seamless communication of goods, people, and information over a fluid and invisible global network: "Logistics makes markets *live*," as one provider's advertisement boasts (Cowen 2014: 203, emphasis in original). "Logistics space" seeks to make physical space and distance insignificant. Geographer Chris Connery observes that the logistics ontology, which he describes as "annihilationist," is "emblematized by a 1990 Merrill Lynch advertisement, a two-page spread photograph of a scene in the open sea, with the caption, 'for us, this doesn't exist'. For the cyberneticized world of total connectivity, the materiality of the sea—pure distance—is indeed something to be superseded" (2006: 497). Alexander Klose neatly summarizes the "world picture" that obtains when viewed through the lens of logistics:

> In the world picture that the transport network of goods and information jointly create, the physical world is almost disembodied. If the notion of the Internet as an immaterial communications system succeeds in concealing tens of thousands of tons of cables, circuit boards, and housings, then the vision of the container world succeeds in making millions of tons of heavy metal appear weightless and frictionless, moved as if by magic. And it is, above all, this image of a frictionless, well-ordered organization through standardized containers that makes containers so attractive as a structural metaphor. It evokes the image of a neutral medium, a pure movement of units of information, production, and consumption on the circuits of systems.
>
> (2015: 75–6)

As information networks have risen in cultural significance, supply chain management and logistics firms have been quick to adopt the internet metaphors of "clean and durable technology […] that will eventually be extended everywhere at little cost" (Starosielski 2015: 13) to describe international shipping services. Government regulators and corporate managers agree that disruptions in the global logistics system should be eliminated wherever possible: that, like "noise" in an electronic circuit, these disruptions—whether accidents, equipment failure or breakdown, labor disputes, or actions by political and environmental protesters—pose an unequivocal threat to the security of the system. Yet others, such as Alan Sekula, insist that we "counter the fantasy, common among elites, that information is the crucial commodity, and the computer the sole engine of our progress" (2002: 582).

Despite modern efforts to subsume the unpredictability of the ocean into "an integrated national and international architecture of risk-based, layered, and networked security" (Cowen 2014: 89), the sea remains a radically unstable space. Ideally, the public never notices the marine transportation system. However, when it fails, it does so spectacularly. Then, social and environmental catastrophe brings this critical but largely invisible commercial infrastructure into the light (Klose 2015; Virilio 2007). The wrecks of the MV *MSC Napoli* and MV *Rena* (Figure 2.5) showed television audiences devastating scenes of environmental damage that disintegrated the myth of frictionless movement, as shipping containers from the MV *MSC Napoli* washed ashore leaving consumer and personal household goods scattered on the rocky English coastline. Sekula notes that "the key popular economic struggles of the past few years have come from the transport sector" and the maritime world is a world "not only of gargantuan automation but also

FIGURE 2.5 A navigation error led to the grounding of the Liberian flagged MV *Rena* in October 2011, which broke up in January 2012, spilling 350 tons of fuel oil and 100 containers near New Zealand. © Handout Getty Images News/Getty Images.

persistent work, of isolated, anonymous, hidden work, of great loneliness, displacement, and separation from the domestic sphere" (2002: 582).

CONCLUSION: ROBOTS AND MEMORIES

The long history of heterotopic iconography as well as the formal similarity between an actual sea voyage and a romance or adventure plot, has led to seafaring's identification with heroic narratives of individual struggle and national glory. However, in the global age, the ship-as-state metaphor has been shaken. The most recognizable twenty-first-century "cultural imaginaries" of the sea arise in a sentimental mode rich with nostalgia. Seemingly endless repetitions of seafaring fantasies such as *The Pirates of the Caribbean* (2003–17), *Black Sails* (2014–17), and even the extremely popular Aubrey–Maturin series of historical novels (1969–2004) by Patrick O'Brian that inspired the 2003 film *Master and Commander* obscure the realities of contemporary ocean commerce while they reinscribe a heroic fantasy, often celebrating political nationalism accomplished through individualism and masculine action. On the other hand, dissenting contemporary interventions, even those with radical activist intent, can be drawn into "a risky mimesis or replication of the very design and function of the abstract spaces of logistics" (Toscano 2018) and sentimentally render workers as negative idealizations of alienated or victimized labor.[7]

Oceanic discourse is freighted with romance and nostalgia—which effaces the lived experience of seafarers whenever it romanticizes a half-remembered heroism. Nor, when considering the present picture, should critics condemn the many changes that have made seafarer's lives better, safer, more connected to family and communities ashore. "Tradition" justifies the valorization of many elements of this strange, insular, and evanescent community of temporary inhabitation. Self-sufficiency, individual achievement, and the aura of an ancient skilled craft can attract new recruits to a life at sea, but these can also mask the persistence of gender inequality, bullying, sexual abuse, and social alienation that continue to cause lasting harm. The UK's Mission to Seafarers reports that the "rate of suicide for international seafarers is triple that of shore workers, and they are 26 times more likely to be killed at work" (The Mission to Seafarers n.d.). Moreover, the functioning of the quasi-digital infrastructure of globalization that, to cite the title of Rose George's recent popular book on the subject, carries *Ninety Percent of Everything* (2013) still depends on the skill and lonely perseverance of this sparse and decreasing population of men and women. Despite changes to the ideal of autonomy at sea, the day-to-day operation of the ship is still largely the independent

FIGURE 2.6 An employee of a Philippine marine staffing agency for seafarers mans the recruiting booth at a seafarer's park in Manila on October 24, 2008. © Luis Liwanag AFP/Stringer/Getty Images.

responsibility of the shipmaster and crew. In the United States, the United Kingdom, and many Western European nations, these are well-compensated, sought-after positions requiring extensive professional and academic training. In many Eastern European countries, training at a maritime university can lead to a satisfying career earning much more than average incomes at home. Coming from the Philippines and Asia, many enjoy challenging but productive and comparatively lucrative careers in positions that can also earn the respect of families and communities who understand the stresses and deprivations of the job (Figure 2.6).

Even with mechanized propulsion, modernized cargo gear, and progressively more reliable—some would say intrusive—navigation, communication, and management systems, ships continue to sail the same routes in many ways using the same techniques as their predecessors did centuries before. Conrad's *fin de siècle* prediction that seafaring "is an art whose fine form seems already receding from us on its way to the overshadowed Valley of Oblivion" (1988: 30) did not come to pass during the twentieth century, but for many in the industry, the transfer of autonomy from the fully crewed and self-sufficient merchant vessel to a robotic MASS, feels threateningly like "another step forward upon the way of universal conquest" (31). More disturbing is the widening gap between the "first world" ships whose owners can afford to maintain and crew them according to modern international standards and the enduring substandard fleet whose crews often suffer unthinkable conditions while their ships limp from port to port scratching out an income for invisible trading companies. Maritime workers' numbers wane even as cargo tonnage continues to rise; their seclusion from population centers and their own communities renders them more and more imaginary in the contemporary regime of globalized trade. Many wonder what will be left in this world besides robots and memories.[8]

CHAPTER THREE

Networks

The Fluid Culture of Maritime Diplomacy

JOHANNA SACKEL AND ANNA-KATHARINA WÖBSE

The twentieth century witnessed the emergence of global environmental regimes concerning the oceans of the world. This chapter looks at the transition and increasing interconnection of networks that were decisive for developing the discursive, legal, and material frame for such governance. Essential for this development was the understanding that oceans, hitherto understood as infinite spheres, turned into fragile entities, since they were subject of numerous newly evolving usage categories. As an increasingly contested sphere, the oceans were also a projection surface for manifold worldviews and interests, for resource dreams as well as for ecological concepts of wholeness.

There is a metaphorical ambiguity to the term network. On the one hand it signifies the cooperation of interest groups governing the planet's oceans and on the other hand it reminds us of two means for navigating and exploiting the seas: a network is not only a set of interconnected people but also an arrangement of intersecting horizontal and vertical lines—a measure for mapping the seas and avoiding the risk of getting lost in these vast open spaces. There is also the net as such—the instrument most efficient for catching fish. This ambiguity and its somewhat ambivalent connotations offer an appropriate set of references for outlining the constantly changing approaches toward interpreting and governing the planet's oceans. The networks that shaped international debates and discourses had to integrate these often conflicting priorities. We argue that the idea of global maritime commons was a guiding theme in the twentieth century, propagated by maritime diplomatic networks that framed the sea as a connecting sphere and challenged by competing concepts of how to deal with the oceans.

Maritime diplomacy and law was not necessarily the outcome of a closed circle of judicial experts. It evolved from a public discourse that echoed a growing interest in shared spaces and the changing attitude toward a previously rather ignored blue sphere that reached out beyond national boundaries. Thus, it was not only the business of official diplomats but rather a growing field of stakeholders from maritime business as well as environmentalists and scientists participating in maritime negotiations and regime building. Who were these people involved in framing conceptions of the oceans and what were their ways of getting in contact and building coalitions? Who set the agenda for discussing the sea as a common sphere and heritage and whose narratives and imaginaries of the ocean managed to set the tone? Which changes did the culture of maritime networking undergo?

Our interest in networks is grounded in environmental and diplomatic history. By studying the debates in international organizations and the communication of non-governmental organizations (NGOs) we can identify actors, their networks, and their different types of debates. Moreover, we can track down changing narratives and competing concepts over time. We argue that the maritime networks diversified during the twentieth century, since maritime usage categories multiplied and new actors evolved, generating competing concepts that concurred with the construction of the ocean as a common.

The idea of a global common has come a long way (Löhr and Rehling 2014). Originally denoting the fields and spheres local communities shared and used accordingly to a set of rules, it stirred new interest in academic and political discourse in times of accelerating transnational exchange and global connectedness. In 1968 the American biologist Garrett Hardin published an article called "The Tragedy of the Commons" (1968). Clearly inspired by the debates on population growth, dwindling natural resources, and environmental deterioration, the paper suggested that any regime of unrestricted open access would necessarily lead to the ruin of the common due to its diminishing resources and the interest of the individual users in maximizing their own profits. Hardin's reading was a pessimistic one. Various actors in international, intergovernmental and Non Governmental Organisations, however, promoted the global commons rather as a common heritage and focused on finding and establishing reliable rules for using the shared natural assets. Moreover, the concepts of the global commons and common heritage offered a virtual bracket embracing humanity as an actor and the planet as a shared sphere. This planetary approach and the idea of a universal humanity related to moral-economy regimes evolving around the global commons debates in the late 1960s. Such normative systems called for universal regulation and emphasized values such as "reciprocity, cooperation, transparency, mutual aid, and equitable sharing of resources, risks, and responsibilities" (Disco and Kranakis 2013: 42). Over the twentieth century the oceans would be a testing ground for negotiating and administering rules, values, and procedures of exploitation evolving around the open maritime space.

This chapter emphasizes the environmental and material aspect of the debate as well. On the one side maritime mammals, fish, and mineral resources played an essential role for framing the sea as borderless and supranational realm that actually gave impetus to very concrete jurisdiction. Environmental debates related to contemporaneous visions of a supposed global community, united and connected by the vast oceans. On the other side they were subject to conflicts between different interest-based networks, revealing competing concepts that propagated other visions of how to deal with the oceans, for instance the nationalization of fishing resources.

In a first step we take a look at the growing criticism of unregulated exploitation strategies of the oceans from the turn of the century onwards. Scientists, popular writers, and nature lovers suggested new approaches toward governing the seven seas. They framed the oceans as an interdependent system tied together not only by humans traveling and communicating across the oceans but by ecological relations. Especially whales turned into icons of global creatures threatened by extinction calling for concerted action. International networks of conservationists and ornithologists identified oil pollution as the first global environmental problem. Such voices would find an echo in the League of Nations. The organization saw various attempts to come to terms with this transnational sphere by suggesting international jurisdiction. These initiatives paved the way for the League's successor, the United Nations, to continue the debates and negotiations on maritime law.

Due to accelerating globalization and technological progress, the second half of the twentieth century saw an institutionalization and then the diversification of networks. They were established around new ocean issues or extended and condensed along reform processes in maritime law. While the internationalist Elisabeth Mann Borgese purposefully rallied an informal network round her, based on personal relationships, and tried to use this network for urging reformatory visions for the oceans, Greenpeace was a growing community of nonconformists, grounded in counter culture that networked with civil societies and celebrities at different places of the globe. Other maritime networks were even formed on the occasion of concrete conflicts, for example, an alliance of South Pacific island communities opposing deep sea mining—which in turn was a result of intensifying industrial networking.

This chapter sheds light on the many different approaches toward a global— and even glocal—framing of the oceans as commons suggested or questioned by multiple actors and stakeholders working in fluid networks.

PEACE FOR THE SEA: EARLY CONCEPTS OF SHARED HERITAGE

Today, the concepts of the global commons and the common heritage of humankind present important and yet constantly challenged principles of law, which are negotiated and governed by international institutions and protected by international conventions. The idea of framing such supranational domains and establishing a network for negotiating individual and universal interests has come a long way (Löhr and Rehling 2014). First, we would like to explore how these concepts came about in regard to the oceans and who brought them up *avant la lettre*. The late nineteenth and early twentieth century saw an intensification and acceleration of such concepts anticipating a global regime for governing the oceans. In 1861, the popular and widely read historian of the French Revolution Jules Michelet published another bestseller: *La Mer* (The Sea), an outstanding analysis of human interaction with the sea. He set out to integrate the maritime sphere into a far-reaching historiography that took into account aspects of exploitation and preservation of the riches of the sea, the rise of technology in industrial societies, and theories on health and leisure. Michelet not only explored the multidimensional relationship between humans and the oceans but also paid tribute to the fact that planet Earth was actually covered and dominated by water. Yet, the historian challenged the idea of oceanic boundlessness that prevailed at that time. He read the signs of the times: in his lifetime, the use of fossil fuels accelerated the exploitation of marine life significantly. Steamships and railways carried fresh fish to inland markets. The modern British trawling fleets served as a role model for the expansion of industrial fishing and whaling (Roberts 2007: 136–7). Watching the fundamental change in exploiting the oceans, Michelet pleaded for an international jurisdiction of the sea to end the unsustainable use and to pay respect to the "gentle" and "benevolent" sea. To him the oceans not only seemed a marvelous source of inspiration and recreation but also a supplier of resources. However, according to Michelet, humanity exploited those riches without considering its finite generosity. To illustrate his argument he drew attention to maritime mammals—peaceful and yet vulnerable creatures traveling the seven seas. Whaling and sealing played a decisive role in many national economies and had turned into a vital source for fat and oil (Tønnessen and Johnson 1982). To Michelet marine mammals as well as fish represented the victims of modern societies' greed and unbridledness. Resulting from his diagnosis of the ongoing depletion of cetaceans and seals he proclaimed:

> Peace! I say again; peace for the Whale, the Sea-Cow, the Sea-Elephant; peace for all those precious species which man's inhumanity has so nearly crushed out of existence. A long, a sacred peace should be granted to them

[...]. For all, whether Fish or Amphibii there is needed a season of perfect rest, like the *Truce of God*, which in the olden day prevented the chivalry of Europe from butchering each other.

(Michelet 1861: 324)

Nations had to find ways to warrant such periods and spaces for the marine creatures' peace and establish closed seasons and reserves—even out on the high seas. Michelet's postulations echoed a fundamental shift in looking at the moral, cultural, and political obligations nation-states had in regard to governing the oceans. The framing of the maritime sphere was just about to change fundamentally—maritime science started to investigate systematically the diversity and interconnectedness of the marine habitats. Field stations along the coasts taught the public about new lifeforms, the beauty of jellyfish, or the miracle of migrating species (De Bont 2015; Egerton 2014). Michelet's sweeping concept of shared duties and binding regulations signaled that the spatial and cultural interpretation of the maritime sphere was being linked to political behavior. Neither a single author nor a book make a network, but Michelet's arguments and metaphors anticipated the need for coordinated governance. The tangible experience of depleting stocks of whales, seals, and fish led to some local and multilateral regulation and more systematic research (Figure 3.1). Marine science increasingly promoted international cooperation. Especially Northern European countries, whose economies depended heavily on fishing, sought pragmatic solutions to prevent the depletion of plaice, cod, and herring. The establishment of the International Council for the Exploration of the Sea in 1902 indicated a rather pragmatic way to deal with the fact that fish and whales ignored national borders (Kurlansky 1999; Rozwadoswki 2002). Its approach focused on the setting of quotas on landings of fish and managing marine stocks for national economies.

In 1910, the Swiss gentleman scientist, Paul Sarasin, tabled the issue of deteriorating populations of whales and seals due to overexploitation at an international conference of biologists in Austria. His appeal to his colleagues, intended not only to voice concern about the future of wildlife in general but also to build networks and get involved in political debates on resource issues, resulted in an international conference in Berne in 1913 to set up a global convention on nature preservation (Wöbse 2012).

The First World War brought a halt to most transnational cooperation. Michelet's ideas, however, were to reemerge on an international agenda. One of the results of the Paris Peace Conference was the founding of the League of Nations. Its principles represented a fundamental shift in diplomatic history. It was the first international organization whose mission was to maintain peace by ensuring collective security and applying negotiation, arbitration, and collaboration instead of aggression and confrontation. However, nobody

FIGURE 3.1 Onlookers visit the carcass of a slaughtered baleen whale, England, 1900. © Universal History Archive/Universal Images Group/Getty Image.

seemed to think about governing the oceans as a shared natural sphere of the international community. When the League was established in 1920, it had no intention to put spatial and cultural issues such as a global maritime commons on its agenda. Nevertheless, soon it became clear, that the debates arising from legal issues concerning the high seas had to be dealt with. The use of marine resources and struggles over fishing rights had already caused diplomatic negotiation and posed a potential problem that corresponded to the League's obligation to contain conflicts and promote international peace (Juda 1996). There were two central questions triggering such debates: the riches of the sea and oil pollution. In 1924, the League's council established a committee of experts to "prepare a provisional list of the subjects of international law." One of the committee's members, the eminent Argentine professor of law José León Suárez, insisted to include the question of the exploitation of maritime resources (Wöbse 2012: 174–202). The committee appointed him to report on the issue in 1926. Suárez's report is a remarkable and outstanding analysis of the status of the evolving debate on the use of the global commons. He combined moral with economic and ecological issues and framed the oceans and its aquatic life as a heritage of humanity: "The wealth constituted by the creatures of the deep is not fixed in the sense of being confined to one region or latitude but varies from year to year according to the biological, physical and chemical circumstances affecting the plankton among which they live" (Suárez 1928: 4).

Only little was known about the complex migration patterns of the maritime fauna (Morais and Daverat 2016). It was sufficient, however, for Suárez to assume that it had to be taken into account when drafting any future jurisdictional maritime law: "the biologico-geographical solidarity" of migrating species "should find its counterpart in a legal solidarity in the sphere of international law in which we are working" (Suárez 1928: 2). He did not only suggest a new approach toward the international governance of the shared heritage—"which, being today the uncontrolled property of all, belongs to nobody"—but also presented a management plan for securing the sustainable use *and* protection of whales as such. Suárez's visions were clearly inspired by an evolving internationalism and anticipated the challenge of paying tribute to the limits of oceanic flora and fauna and governing the oceans accordingly by a supranational regime.

While one of the most prominent members of the committee, the eminent German expert of international law Walther Schücking, applauded so broad an approach, the other legal experts hesitated to support Suárez's ambitions (Schrijver 2010: 25–6) (Figure 3.2). The imaginative power of how to deal with such a sprawling vision had been overburdened. Nevertheless, the committee agreed on the "urgent need of action" and as it was lacking

FIGURE 3.2 Diplomatic networks discussing the future of international waters: Walther Schücking (*first row on the left*) and José Suárez (*first row on the very right*) in the League of Nations' committee on the codification of international law. © United Nations Archives at Geneva.

any expertise it sent out a questionnaire to get advice from the League's member states. While the majority agreed on the fact that the issues had to be discussed internationally, the nations made sure that their spheres of interest were not to be effected. In the long run, Suárez's master plan was reduced to a rather meagre draft for the regulation of whale hunting as it was a highly profitable industry. It was plain to see that this economic branch was extremely vulnerable to the ongoing overexploitation of the stocks and had the potential for causing international and economical conflicts. Thus, the initial plan for a coherent global maritime management scheme was abandoned (Cioc 2009: 127–9; Dorsey 2014; Juda 1996).

This had long-lasting effects: as there was no integrative body established for managing the maritime domain the questions of whaling and whaling regulation was dealt with by the Economic Section of the League. In 1934 the British government approached the League of Nations' secretariat to settle the fast-growing environmental problem of oil pollution—mainly caused by the shift from coal- to oil-driven vessels, which washed their tanks along the coast and pumped oily sludge over board. The British called for a transnational solution. The secretariat did not link the issue to the question of regulating fisheries and whaling but instead transferred it to the section responsible for transit and communication. Again, the committees of the League soon agreed that oil pollution was an issue of high relevance.

Over the years, various British NGOs for bird and animal protection had watched and commented on the growing numbers of victims threatened by the pollution: sea birds. The activists initiated campaigns to raise public awareness and had forced their government to take the issue to Geneva. Soon, such campaigns, emphasizing the transnational nature of migrating birds, were supported by their corresponding organizations in Europe and the United States. The secretariat of the League set out to collect data, expertise, and advice. Already in 1935, the committee of experts presented a draft convention—a rather weak compromise that prohibited oil dumping in coastal areas, encouraged the shipping industry to install separators, and to introduce "oil diaries." The NGOs had asked for much more radical measures: simply no oil should ever reach any waters or, as they had put it, "the nations cannot, so to speak, sweep the oil into the middle of the oceans and leave it there" (Royal Society for the Protection of Birds 1922: 18). The transnational character of floating oil had surely fostered their perception that the high seas apparently were a shared sphere under threat and that the creatures of this sphere—such as sea birds and maritime fauna—were to be protected (Wöbse 2008: 527). In the end, not even the compromise entered into force. The League was increasingly paralyzed by growing aggressions in world politics.

However, the League of Nations surely played an important role in identifying conflicts caused by the use or misuse of the resources the oceans provided. Both initiatives of the League set out to cope with maritime problems and started to frame the idea of a natural heritage of humanity. For the first time ever, it offered at least a political forum to discuss the issue of what would later be framed as the global commons. The League of Nations opened a forum for discussing new approaches for thinking transnationally. This embraced many new ideas about "humanity" and its heritage. Historians, archeologists, and literary studies had promoted the idea of thinking in terms of a cultural heritage of humanity. Preservationists set out to file nature under such heritage—especially landscapes of outstanding beauty and threatened species (Rehling 2017: 263–6). Moreover, as Schrijver observes, this period marked "the beginning of an era of treaty making during which international organizations played a role in facilitating the drafting and conclusion of multilateral conventions, and [...] acted as registrars of treaties" (2010: 27). It provided a visible, accessible, and reliable space for open diplomacy—or at least that was what it intended. Thus, it was essential for discussing norms and values—but it failed to translate them into transnational political action. In fact, it turned into a stage dominated by self-interested political strategies of national governments. One reason for the League's failure to initiate or realize any fundamental maritime environmental jurisdiction was not only the dominance of national interests but also the lack of a central agency promoting such issues. Rather, the League—due to its administrative deficiencies and the lack of own expertise—fostered the fragmentation of the field. The problem of whaling was discussed in the economic section, oil pollution in the transit and communication section, and the question concerning nature reserves and natural heritage was dealt with by the section of intellectual cooperation.

The conflicts between the various stakeholders that characterized the debate in the League of Nations would reemerge after the Second World War. The ideal of a shared responsibility for the maritime sphere clashed with national and individual interests in exploiting the riches of the sea. So did the emerging networks, which were organized along the lines of the conflicting ideals and interests.

THE "RESOURCE TURN" IN THE POSTWAR OCEANS

The Second World War brought a halt to many diplomatic initiatives of maritime interests. Large parts of the seas turned into battlefields. Some stocks, under severe pressure before, recovered. Some parts of the most fished waters along the northwestern coasts of Europe were completely closed to fisheries. The Second World War, however, helped to improve technologies for maritime exploitation and political responses to immediate postwar market problems. The experience of resource scarcity and hunger would foster the growing interest not only of the nation-states but also of international organizations in framing the oceans as a field for harvesting proteins, oil, and minerals and set the stage for the Great Acceleration after 1945 (Holm 2012). When the successor of the League, the United Nations, took over after the end of the Second World War, it soon faced the unsolved questions of the prewar era. Among the fundamental questions concerning the peaceful future of humanity, many had in one way or another an environmental dimension. Oil pollution had not ceased. While whales had enjoyed a kind of a ceasefire during the war, the hungry population of Europe was waiting to be fed with cheap fat. The environmental shadow of the war was huge as reconstruction and reorganization led to a growing demand for resources of all kinds.

The global dimension of environmental problems and resource issues became a topic addressed at international forums such as the United Nations Educational, Scientific and Cultural Organization (UNESCO), the Food and Agriculture Organization of the United Nations (FAO), and the World Health Organization (WHO) (Sluga 2010; Speth and Haas 2006; Staples 2006). The composition of networks would change over the next decades. International organizations such as the UN turned into important hubs for voicing concern about the management of resources and spheres. In the run of the 1950s and 1960s the UN institutions, especially UNESCO, involved protagonists from a growing civil society to discuss the state of the natural world and the conflicts caused by its human use (Wöbse 2011). The fabric of the networks discussing oceanic matters became multilayered. The growing input of NGOs at least counterbalanced national and economic interests in the oceans.

The struggle on the prerogative of the use and interpretation of the oceans loomed ahead almost immediately after the war. The minutes of two parallel UN conferences in the summer of 1949, for instance, the United Nations Scientific Conference on the Conservation and Utilization of Resources (UNSCCUR), convened by the Economic and Social Council of the UN, and the International Technical Conference on the Protection of Nature, convened by UNESCO and the International Union for the Protection of Nature (IUPN; later IUCN) marked a decisive point on the diplomatic way toward an integrated and sustainable governance scheme of the oceans (McCormick 1991: 136–8). While both received their impulse from the notion that resources had been generally overexploited due to the war effort, the conferences offered conflicting interpretations on how to respond to this problem (UN 1950; UNESCO and IUPN 1950). The experts of the UNSCCUR showed a strong tendency toward large-scale planning, offering universal instructions on agricultural management and advocating the exploitation of "underfished" seas or the "vast" tropical rainforests. The preservationists and ecologists of the small conservation networks in the IUCN and UNESCO still struggled to frame the complex and yet unknown interaction of humans and the biosphere. While the former pressed for the acceleration of the current course of action, the latter insisted on the deceleration of certain technical interventions. The prevalent development paradigms generally banked on the forced use of chemicals, large-scale planning projects and the introduction of exotic and protein rich species. The ecologists, in contrast, pleaded for conducting fundamental research before applying such strategies to the so-called underdeveloped world. In retrospect, the two conferences exemplify the antagonism inherent in the UN and its promise of modernity (Linnér 2003; Mahrane et al. 2012; Wöbse 2012).

As far as the maritime regime was concerned the FAO, for instance, fostered the expansion and industrialization of fishing fleets all over the world and featured—in cooperation with UNESCO—programs to map the deep sea as a yet underexploited reservoir for protein. At the same time, the United Nations' specialized organizations featured networks that would not only voice environmental concern but also provided the empirical evidence and scientific knowledge to back it up and put it on the agenda (Schrijver 2010: 121–2).

The conception of the oceans as a resource reservoir was supported by developments in the international system. With decolonization, newly emerging states entered the stage and claimed their right to nationalize the land-based resources to gain independence not only at the political but also the economic level. "Resource sovereignty" became a prominent term and was transferred to the ocean. In this sense, nationalization meant to ban the "fishing imperialism" of the Global North in the waters of the Global South. Thus, marine resources became part of a moral economy that was debated in UN forums as "new international economic order" (Gilman 2015).

Whereas pioneers of global environmentalism such as Michelet and Suárez had chosen whales for framing the problem of governing a shared sphere, the charismatic animals now seemed to be boiled down to mere resources. The system of managing rather than preserving the maritime resources of the high seas prevailed. Whaling soon turned into a bloody and profitable business again. Accordingly, the International Whaling Commission, founded in 1946, turned into an institution *for* rather than *against* whaling and made sure that any nation interested in exploiting the blue whales and humpbacks would get its share (Epstein 2008).

As far as oil pollution was concerned, the environmental activists and their organizations were much faster to get onto their feet again: in 1952, the British Section of the International Committee for Bird Preservation set up an independent advisory committee on oil pollution and secured the cooperation of other NGOs. In 1953, the network convened an international conference in London with twenty-eight countries to discuss the problem of fouling the high seas with fossil fuels. This surely helped to animate the British Government to organize an international conference of forty-two nations. After some years of negotiation, the International Convention for the Prevention of Pollution of the Seas by Oil (OILPOL) came into force in 1958: the first international environmental agreement dealing with the sea. In 1958 the United Nations International Maritime Organizations took charge of handling OILPOL (Campe 2009: 145), while the International Whaling Commission dealt with whaling issues, and the FAO set out to frame a global fishery regime. Idealism seemed to have squandered its credibility. Instead of considering the big picture of governing the global commons and preserving the heritage of humankind that oiled birds and whales had epitomized in early debates, international organizations and economic networks seemed to focus on administering maritime assets.

The role of the international organizations, however, was ambivalent: they definitely provided a central stage for framing the ocean as a global space and managed to find at least partial solutions to some pressing questions concerning the utilization of the riches of the sea. It might seem as though the early advocates of a global oceanic regime in the international organizations and from civil society had forestalled the future maritime agenda and anticipated many of the potential detrimental effects the globalized economy and exploitation would have. The extend of such effects and the fundamental changes in maritime discourse and practices, however, proved to be more dramatic than they had envisioned.

DIVERSIFICATION OF OCEAN ISSUES

During the second half of the twentieth century the oceans became the venue of an accelerated technical change. Industrial fishing expanded all over the globe, since the opportunity to freeze fish immediately at sea allowed fishing fleets to reach distant regions and to develop new kinds of resources, for example krill in Antarctic waters (Heidbrink 2011; Kehrt 2014). This was not only true for living resources. Moreover, innovations in marine technology and oceanography gave rise to new opportunities to exploit the riches of the sea on the ocean floor. The evolving possibilities of offshore drilling heated up profit expectations on the sector of the oil industry and even prompted US president Harry S. Truman to proclaim the continental shelf as national territory. The "third dimension" of the oceans came into the focus of scientists and the industry. This development was boosted, when John L. Mero published his book on the economic potential of deep seabed minerals (1965). Resource dreams were transferred to a three-dimensional ocean space and launched the establishment of "ocean engineering," which seemed to be a promising field of activity for the industries mainly of the Global North. Furthermore, the engagement for a prospective exploitation of minerals from the seafloor implicated hopes for resource independence within the industrialized states, which seemed to become necessary in the context of an emerging "North–South conflict" and apprehensions concerning political instability in the young states of the Global South (Sparenberg 2015b: 154).

This run on seabed resources had two side effects. Firstly, it caused a decades-long reforming process in the law of the sea, beginning with two United Nations Conferences on the Law of the Sea (UNCLOS I and II) in 1958 and 1960. The "tragedy of the commons" became evident under the "freedom of the seas": this concept, which had shaped seafaring for centuries and consequentially ensured unrestricted access to marine resources, seemed to be outdated in the light of the new utilization opportunities, whose promises induced states to take unilateral actions such as the expansion of territorial waters (Wolf 1981: 48).

Since UNCLOS I and II had failed to provide legal certainty, the seabed issue was captured by the Maltese ambassador to the United Nations, Arvid Pardo. In 1967 he pleaded before the General Assembly to declare the ocean floor and its resources as common heritage of mankind. In his view, the common heritage was a principle for the management of resources that should replace the traditional concept of property with trusteeship. It implicated intergenerational as well as intragenerational resource equity, since the resources of the seabed should be governed *by* mankind *for* mankind including the coming generations and by taking into account the special needs of developing countries (Pardo 1975). Thus the concept of common heritage of mankind contained the idea of global commons and seemed to be an alternative draft to the principle of the freedom of the seas as well as to the concept of national or private property. While the former predominantly benefited the Global North with its technological supremacy, the latter was bound to resource exclusion based on territorial claims. The commons idea Pardo captured with the common heritage principle provided an alternative approach to both. Pardo's speech turned out to be an initial spark for convening the third United Nations Conference on the Law of the Sea (UNCLOS III), which took place from 1973 to 1982 and ended up with the Convention on the Law of the Sea (coming into force in 1994). In many aspects, Pardo's ideas echoed Suárez's visions. Both pleaded for supranational monitoring and management of the oceans. Nevertheless, both of them narrowed their proposals to specific ocean issues—Suárez to marine species and Pardo to the ocean floor. In either instance this was a reaction to undermining interests that challenged the idea of the commons and to make it acceptable to the highest possible number of maritime actors. This fundamental problem was also reflected in the Convention on the Law of the Sea that eventually acknowledged "that the problems of ocean space are closely interrelated and need to be considered as a whole" and furthermore recognized "the desirability of establishing [...] a legal order for the seas and oceans which will facilitate international communication, and will promote the peaceful uses of the seas and oceans, the equitable and efficient utilization of their resources, the conservation of their living resources, and the study, protection and preservation of the marine environment" (UN 1982). While this sounded like a triumph of the commons it was rather a lip service, since the common heritage principle was only juridified for the ocean floor and its resources. Although the marine environment was recognized as a global common—which was a result of the growth of environmental awareness during the 1970s (Macekura 2015)—hard issues such as protein supply, navigation, and maritime industrialization prevented its installation as a guiding principle in international law and practice.

DIVERSIFICATION OF NETWORKS

The second side effect, going along with these developments, was the transition of maritime networks. Since the negotiations at UNCLOS III implicated nearly all ocean-related issues—from fisheries and deep-sea mining to environmental protection and marine science—these multiple ocean uses were mirrored in the diversification of actors involved in maritime diplomatic networks. This found notable expression during the so-called Pacem in Maribus convocations that served as some kind of parallel forum to UNCLOS III. The aim was not only to weave a web of maritime diplomats and experts but also to promote the idea of the oceans as a common heritage.

The ocean of Elisabeth Mann Borgese

Pacem in Maribus was initiated by Elisabeth Mann Borgese. She was the youngest daughter of the German novelist Thomas Mann and seized with the question of a new world order. Shaped by the disturbing events of the Second World War and by her time in exile, she had worked on a "Draft of a World Constitution" during the 1940s at the University of Chicago, together with her husband Guiseppe Antonio Borgese and other academics. She was electrified by Pardo's speech, since it reflected the idea of the Chicago group to declare the human resources earth, water, air, and energy as "common property of mankind" (Committee to Frame a World Constitution 1948; Holzer 2003).

For Elisabeth Mann Borgese the ocean was a big laboratory for a new world order: considering the ocean as a whole and establishing a new "ocean regime," which would involve all stakeholders at all levels from the local to the global, could have been the first step to launch a global change. Furthermore, it was a global laboratory with regard to a fair allocation of resources as well as to a new international economic order (Borgese and Pardo 1975). In this sense, the ocean was not only a nature space worth protecting but also it provided huge potential for resource development which it was necessary to mobilize to meet the growing needs of world population for protein and energy:

> Yet, no one can seriously propose that industrializations of the oceans be haltet. A "zero-growth economy" for the seas is the most atopian of all utopias – and, worse still, it is a rich man's dream that would become a nightmare

for the majority of peoples whose survival requires full development of the world's resources. Luddism did not work on land. It will not work under water.

(Borgese 1970)

Thus, for Elisabeth Mann Borgese the ocean offered the means to solve global inequalities, at least when the exploitation was rational. Hence, it had to be subject to an integrated and functional management, taking into account all the stakeholders involved in ocean matters. Accordingly, the actors in her "drama of the oceans" were seafarers, fishers, oil entrepreneurs, miners, engineers, and scientists (Borgese 1976).

The Pacem in Maribus convocations reflected this diversity of actors: there were fisheries experts, representatives of mining and oil companies, intellectuals, and delegates who at the same time participated in the negotiations at UNCLOS III. The aim of Pacem in Maribus was to "think three years ahead of official thinking" and provide an informal frame to think about ocean issues in a more interdisciplinary manner (Figure 3.3). The convocations became a well-frequented forum for exchange among the different kinds of maritime diplomats. Some regular guests became crossers between the sector of state diplomacy and the field of informal diplomacy, such as Ambassador Hamilton S. Amerasinghe, president of UNCLOS III and at the same time chairmen of the board of trustees of the International Ocean Institute (Figure 3.4). The institute was initiated by Elisabeth Mann Borgese as well and served as planning council for Pacem in Maribus. It obtained observer status as NGOs at UNCLOS III (Borgese 1993).

Though this network of ocean diplomats around Elisabeth Mann Borgese was an amalgamation of the public and the diplomatic spheres it was mainly an elitist network (Heine 2013), based on personal connections, and more or less dissociated from social movement networks or citizen networks. While the latter either tried to influence the negotiations from outside of the framework with moral appeals or by providing information for the delegates (Levering and Levering 1999), Elisabeth Mann Borgese tried to use her network to mobilize involved persons to support her vision of an ocean regime. Furthermore, starting in 1978 with the aid of the International Ocean Institute, she established training programs for experts from developing countries to secure not only their participation in the global commons but also in the administrative machinery. Accordingly, "training" for prospective deep-sea mining, fisheries management, and marine research was also a kind of mobilization for implementing the common heritage of mankind in the sense of sharing in knowledge concerning marine resources, marine technology, and in ocean management (Chircop 2012). To make these knowledges—which were concentrated in the Global North—accessible to experts from developing countries, the International Ocean Institute cooperated with actors from highly industrialized countries, for instance with the German

FIGURE 3.3 Participants of Pacem in Maribus in Malta. Photograph from Pacem in Marbibus II, 1971. Elisabeth Mann Borgese fond, MS-2-744, Box 169, Folder 28. © Dalhousie University Archives Halifax/Nova Scotia.

FIGURE 3.4 Presentation to Ambassador Hamilton S. Amerasinghe, the president of the third United Nations Conference on the Law of the Sea at Pacem in Maribus (*in the foreground on the right*); Elisabeth Mann Borgese is sitting at his side, 1973. Elisabeth Mann Borgese fond, MS-2-744, Box 178, Folder 31. © Dalhousie University Archives Halifax/Nova Scotia.

mining company PREUSSAG and research institutions such as the technical university RWTH Aachen who provided technological facts (Draft Minutes of the 15th Session of the Planning Council 1978). In this sense, not only were marine resources constructed as commons but also knowledge about technical solutions to exploit these resources. In Elisabeth Mann Borgese's view, the concept of common heritage of mankind provided the opportunity to communize the oceans as a whole for the profit of all mankind and by involving all concerned stakeholders. In this respect, such partnerships between industry, science, and civil society mirror the interrelations between the different maritime sectors and at the same time reveal the diversification of maritime networks in response to the interconnectedness of ocean issues as Elisabeth Mann Borgese had diagnosed it.

Although the Borgesian multi-stakeholder networks integrated the different sectors of science, economy, state diplomacy, and cosmopolitans, and therefore retrospectively seem like a forecast on today's efforts for integrated ocean governance, it would be a mistake to generalize these constellations for the second half of the twentieth century. Often different maritime networks turned out to be opponents in gaining the prerogative of interpretation concerning the ocean and its resources and remained self-contained. Due to different "social constructions" of the ocean (Steinberg 2001), maritime networks evolved within various operational and ideological frames that were scarcely to harmonize.

This will be demonstrated through two more case examples with regard to their formation conditions, aims, and network structures, revealing the miscellaneous scenery of maritime networks.

The miner's ocean

Mining provides an appropriate example to examine inter-industrial relations. When the deep seabed became a projection surface for resource dreams in the late 1960s, the "golden era for manganese nodule research" began (Glasby 2002: 162). Manganese nodules contained nickel, copper, and cobalt and therefore provided the opportunity for the industrialized states to become independent from decolonized states as primary producers. This seemed to become much more important during the boycott policy of the OPEC states in 1973, which demonstrated the alleged resource power of the Global South (Dietrich 2017). It was also a reaction to assumptions of resource depletion and concerns about the "Limits to Growth," which Dennis Meadows and colleagues had alerted in their famous study for the Club of Rome (Hays 1998; Meadows et al. 1972). Mineral resources seemed to provide an alternative to the shrinking resources on land. Since most of the manganese nodules were located in areas beyond national jurisdiction, moreover, mining the deep seabed could have been currency-free. Because the ocean was seen as a promising resource reservoir, mining companies gained financial support from their governments to explore mining sites and technologies as was the case in Germany. To spread the risk and to profit from competencies of other companies the mining corporations allied in consortia—at first on a national scale and then, when they realized it was very big business, they chose an international cooperation. In 1975 the Ocean Management Incorporation (OMI) was established, one of six mostly multinational deep-sea mining consortia incorporated between 1974 and 1982. Partners in the OMI were a German syndicate of mining companies, a Japanese corporation, a Canadian nickel producer, and a US-offshore drilling company (Sparenberg 2015a: 132). With high-tech research vessels and refitted drilling ships they explored the ocean floor in the Pacific Clarion-Clipperton Zone and conducted pilot mining tests. In 1978 they demonstrated that seabed mining was principally possible and thereby reinforced the conflict potential at UNCLOS III, where diplomats were negotiating if and under what terms companies should have access to the "common heritage of mankind." Nevertheless, these joint ventures and consortia decelerated their efforts at the start of the 1980s, due to a disproportionate expenditure, a lack of legal and political securing, and sinking prices for nickel and copper in the global market (Sparenberg 2015a: 138–40).

This example of economic networking within the frame of inter-industrial relations reveals some generalizable characteristics of maritime economic networks. Firstly, such networks were built around profits. Where the rise of marine treasures was complicated because of a hostile environment and therefore carried risks for single companies, a network of several associates worked like a safety net. It reduced the costs and risks and helped to open up new markets. Secondly, the maritime economic networks were subject to conjunctures. When the companies became aware there was no profitable mining in the near future, they loosened the network nods. Their networks were fluid since they had to adapt to new circumstances, whether in the form of new marine resource potentials or according to developments in the law of the sea.

When the Canadian corporation Nautilus Minerals Inc. got a license for mining the seabed in the waters off Papua-New Guinea, this prompted an opposition of civic activists, organized in the "Bismarck and Solomon Seas Indigenous Peoples' Council" in 2008. These people felt overlooked in the process of selling parts of a common heritage to states and declared: "Our livelihood and culture is based around these oceans, and it is an inseparable part of our culture identity and way of life. Our lives are interconnected with the cycles of the sea, it is our calendar and we are dependent on it for our survival" (Schertow 2008). This statement suggests that the network of subaltern groups had built their subject-based network on the basis of a common conception of the ocean. For them, the ocean was not only a resource reservoir or an emblem of ecological wholeness but also the basis for their existence.

This concurred with the agenda of networks such as the OMI consortium that was bound to a concept of the ocean as a resource reservoir and sphere of economic value. Therefore it was something like a counterpart to conceptions of ecological wholeness that implicated the need for protection. It also concurred with the idea of trusteeship, inherent in the concept of common heritage of mankind as Elisabeth Mann Borgese considered it.

Due to the emerging awareness of environmental degradation, resource depletion, and population growth the 1970s saw a turn to an unprecedented environmental awareness. In international politics this was perceptible by the 1972 Stockholm Conference on the Human Environment, which was also attended by more than a thousand NGOs. Most notably in the Global North, growing parts of democratizing and liberalizing societies not only called for peace but also for a change in dealing with nature and its treasures (Kupper 2003).

Greenpeace's ocean

Along with the ascent of new social movements during the 1970s, different maritime networks emerged from the grassroots level and conceptualized the ocean as integral part of the human environment, both strange and simultaneously familiar since it represented the "womb of life" and hosted animals connatural to humans. When a small group of hippies and Quakers called themselves "Greenpeace" and moved out to the North Pacific to fight against nuclear tests, they implemented both the peace movement and the environmental movement. They used new forms of action that one of their founders, Bob Hunter, called the "mind-bomb." The small group, getting through to a growing group of like-minded supporters, stage-managed their actions by mass media, assuming that a "global village" received their message through catchy pictures, which would launch a mind shift. This was really different to "traditional" lobbying at parliaments and international organizations, which Hunter, especially, found to be debilitating and little promising (Zelko 2014: 38–9). They professionalized this method of public action during their campaign against whale hunting. While "traditional" conservationists such as the Sierra Club aimed for the preservation of whales as well but found it legitimate to use them as resources as long as species did not become extinct, the members of Greenpeace mythologized whales as a symbol for ecological wholeness and the "wisdom of nature." Whale hunting was not only ecological destructive in their view, it was also a morally reprehensible expression of human hybris and cruelty against nature (7–8).

This approach to the ocean and its mammals also became evident during their campaign for seals in the Arctic, where they staged their fight against the bloody slaughter of seal pups with good publicity, involving celebrities such as Brigitte Bardot to gain attention. During these early years of Greenpeace their network was structured by a core of activists around the founders in Vancouver but with connections to famous individuals and with loose ties to other grassroots movements in different parts of the world acting in the name of Greenpeace. Unified by the conception of the oceans as fragile ecosystems worth protecting, this trans-local network kept growing and the Greenpeace subsidiaries institutionalized. These processes of professionalization and spreading came along with the requirement for consolidation. The loose ends of network threats had to be bundled with the aim to retain the brand Greenpeace (manifested in their iconic ships, see Figure 3.5). Consequently, Greenpeace transformed from a network of trans-local grassroots movements into an international organization with a central structure and a headquarter in Amsterdam (Zelko 2014: 269). This "NGOization" (Kaldor 2003: 92) provided new opportunities for Greenpeace and they mixed their methods of direct action and "mind-bombing" with traditional lobby work. They became an important voice of global civil society and the structure of the Greenpeace network changed to a system of national subsidiary organizations that were subdivided again into regional and local organizations and individual associates, all of them under the umbrella of a centralized council (Zelko 2014: 272–4).

The "world wide web" of Greenpeace became evident during the Brent Spar campaign in 1995. When the Shell concern decided to dump their offshore

FIGURE 3.5 Greenpeace's *Arctic Sunrise* in the harbor of Halifax/Nova Scotia.
© Johanna Sackel, 2016.

installation Brent Spar in a Norwegian fjord, Greenpeace argued with the risk of chemical residues that would affect the marine environment in the North Sea. To draw attention to that danger they started a campaign based on effective pictures and public information that led to political interventions in Scandinavia and Germany. The latter even saw a consumer boycott of Shell (Owen and Rice 1999). The Brent Spar campaign foregrounded the pollution of the commons, caused by profit interests of multinationals. At the same time they established a direct connection between the consumer and the sea. Who tanked up at Shell was co-responsible for marine pollution and the destruction of a common good. The concept of the global commons shines out in that campaign, but Greenpeace rather saw nature as a stakeholder on its own. For them it was an entity with its own interests—and humans had to be its attorney.

Although the media-effective direct actions are still the brand essence of Greenpeace, their professionalization and bureaucratization makes evident that a powerful network is needed as backing for lobby work and offering expert knowledge in international organizations and national parliaments. Furthermore, it helps to gain credibility, which is needed for the production of norms on an international level and for influencing the global civil society.

Though Greenpeace is not a prototype of a maritime non-governmental network (the wide range of different organizations forbids generalizations), its history combines in some measure two sorts of maritime networks. On the one hand it may represent the diverse field of (international) NGOs acting within a multilevel system. On the other hand the organization structure of their early years especially stands for trans-local networks developing on a subject-related basis.

A WEB OF MARITIME REGIMES

We can identify five different types of maritime networks: diplomatic networks, expert networks, grassroots networks, NGO networks, and profit-oriented economic networks. All of them are interest-based networks, though their interests depend on different conceptions of the ocean, ranging from the ocean as global commons and common heritage of mankind, as resource reservoir, and as ecological sphere to the ocean as livelihood.

Since the coming into force of the Convention on the Law of the Sea in 1994 the ocean is the subject of enhanced efforts for an integrated ocean use management. This functional differentiation, similar to the vision of Elisabeth Mann Borgese's ocean regime, takes place within the framework of the convention but exceeds the legal dimension. Thus, the ocean floor beyond national jurisdiction is governed by the International Seabed Authority and exclusive economic zones up to two hundred nautical miles (370 kilometers) by the coastal state, grounding on territorial principles. Furthermore there are functional regimes for the management of living resources, such as regional fishery bodies and management organizations, for the prevention of pollution, and also for the regulation of marine research (Mondré and Kuhn 2017). This web of maritime regimes illustrates the interconnectedness of ocean issues and moreover implicates an increasing exchange between actors belonging to different networks on levels from the local to the national, the regional, and the global. But a multi-stakeholder system like the ocean entails also lots of target conflicts as has become evident, for instance, in the case of Greenpeace against whalers and oil pollution. Due to their different conceptions of the ocean, entanglements between the different maritime networks take place on a case-by-case basis. Points of intersection merely develop along similar interests since networks are bound to shared values and norms (Schulz 2007). According to this, meetings between participants in different networks take place if it serves their particular interests as it is the case in cooperations between private economy and NGOs or between different NGOs with relating aims. Despite these interfaces, their networks keep their coherence.

Indeed, real fluid maritime networks often were networks of official diplomats. As border crossers they watched the scenery from above, since they had no vital or concrete interests in the ocean or its resources itself. For most of them the conception of the ocean as global commons emerged from their own cosmopolitan lifestyle and a "rational thinking" that implicates the insight that the ocean could only be governed under equal and just circumstances if it was managed by all concerned stakeholders.

CONCLUSION

The concept of the global commons turned into a historical leitmotif in international maritime debates, occurring in various formulas, reaching from "biologico-geographical solidarity" (Suárez) to "heritage of mankind." Such concepts never went uncontested and therefore were never able to pacify the very different charges various stakeholders attributed to the oceans.

Due to the accelerating use of ocean resources starting at the end of the nineteenth century, there was a growing demand for negotiating the various interests evolving along the utilization of the aquatic life and riches. With the application of new techniques—reaching from pelagic trawling to seabed mining—the number of stakeholders grew steadily. So did concerns about the vulnerability of marine ecosystems. Apart from environmental issues the debates on a fair and just share of marine riches became an issue on a global agenda. Neither the economic nor the moral aspects could be dealt with only by bi- or multilateral consultations. The biological complexity of oceans called for new ways of negotiating how humanity as such should find a way for sustaining the ocean as livelihood and resource reservoir.

Just as the number of stakeholders grew over time so did their networks. These networks sought ways to transfer their issues into global politics. Early commons advocates set the stage for debating such concepts but did not manage to establish influential networks. It was only after the Second World War that these diplomatic networks conglomerated and made clever use of the institutionalization of international maritime organizations. With the concept of a common heritage of mankind the global commons gained a prominent position within maritime law and politics but were contested by economic desires and spiritual perceptions at the same time.

At the end of the twentieth century we find a massive fragmentation of interests and maritime regimes coming along with a multitude of networks involved in negotiating ocean governance. This became evident during the Ocean Conference in 2017, when participants from all types of maritime networks gathered in Stockholm to negotiate the protection of the ocean environment. While subaltern Fidjian citizens opened the conference with a traditional ceremony and praised the ocean as a giver of life, nongovernmental groups and economic actors held side events concerning deep seabed mining, "blue economy," and the future of ocean governance (UN 2017a). Hence, the international organizations and their diplomats might provide open forums for the separated networks. The culture of maritime networking, however, is characterized by diversity and ongoing debates on what the commons actually defines.

CHAPTER FOUR

Conflicts

Underneath the Quiet Waves

SIMONE M. MÜLLER

INTRODUCTION

The water's surface was at its calmest as it slowly swallowed the massive steel construction of the SS *LeBaron Russell Briggs*. Gently, the ocean's waves touched and embraced the ship's outer wall. A splash here and there, but hardly a white crest was visible and the sun sparkled and mirrored vis-à-vis itself as if to exist a thousandfold on the ocean's surface. Meanwhile, unseen by the human observers encircling the site, ocean water gushed greedily into the ship's body and through the cracks that human will had deliberately created. The explosion had been quick but massive. With brute force, it had ripped open the ship's hull to allow the water to enter. Slowly but steadily the cold saltwater filled the *Russell Briggs*' compartments and pulled the old liberty ship and its hazardous cargo ever deeper into both their ocean graves (US Naval Photographic Center 1970).

Many hundred miles out on the Atlantic, the calm marine scenery belied the great excitement that the United States Pentagon's mission CHASE had triggered on land. Cut holes and sink 'em: CHASE was an acronym for a secret military operation through which the United States rid itself of outdated chemical weapons from its stockpile, a practice common among militaries around the world. Onboard the SS *Le Baron Russell Briggs* were 418 steel jacketed, concrete vaults that encased 12,500 M55 rockets containing Sarin nerve gas and one container of VX gas. On August 18, 1970, the US Army towed her out 282 miles east of Cape Kennedy, Florida, and scuttled the ship in 16,600 feet (4,900 meters) of water (Sherman 1972). Sunk on the ocean bottom, they hoped, ship and cargo would be out of sight, out of mind, and, ideally, also out of harm's way. Widespread concern about marine ecosystems, however, sparked an international debate on the dumping of hazardous materials that pathed the way to the passage of the London Dumping Convention in 1972. The Convention was the first UN governance format on global marine protection and CHASE 13 the last mission of its kind.

Over the course of the twentieth century, myriad conflicts have erupted on as well as over ocean space. During the century's different military conflicts, maritime space has always represented an important stage for military engagements (Lehman 2018; Morison [1963] 2007; Roy 1995; Symonds 2018). Similarly, nations, businesses, or individuals competed for the oceans' vast resources, ranging from fish to oil and minerals (Holm, Smith, and Starkey 2017; Heffernan 1981; Hook 2012; Jónsson 1982; Steinsson 2016). In the face of the voluminous global naval histories of the two world wars, the dramatic Cod Wars between Great Britain and Iceland, the Tuna Wars between the United States and Mexico, or the ongoing territorial struggle between China, Brunei, Taiwan, Malaysia, Indonesia, the Philippines, and Vietnam in the South China Sea, we easily forget about a much quieter and slower environmental conflict that is yet so pervasive to the maritime history of the twentieth century: the battle over the use of ocean space as dumping ground. The controversy whether the world ocean is pristine nature in need of human protection or an enormous dumping ground with seemingly endless assimilative capacity is integral to the rise of modern environmentalism, the growth and expansion of ocean science, as well as the disenchanting of older, mythical imaginations of the deep sea. It strongly links to questions of the costs of modern means of production and consumption-and who is bearing them-and testifies to societies' practice to externalize their waste (Lessenich 2016). Finally, the slow and yet violent environmental conflict over the use of ocean space as dumping ground is emblematic for how humans have understood what they call nature, how they define their relationship to it, and whether they see themselves as part of it.[1]

Industrial nations in particular have competed with other nations, with nonhuman actors, and with future generations over the use of the world ocean as habitat and resource on the one hand or as dumping ground on the other hand. The ocean has provided humans not only with food and mineral resources, but also with an apparently limitless capacity to assimilate an ever-growing amount of waste. In the twentieth century, various actors from militaries, municipalities, or industries purposefully turned to the world's maritime space on their search for the "ultimate sink" (Tarr 1996). Via pipelines or barges, they transported unwanted objects, such as sewage sludge, chemicals, low- and high-level nuclear material, dredge spoils or outdated chemical weapons, out to sea to designated dumping areas. Often also simply where currents and wind would take them.

The practice of open-water dumping relied on the ocean's ability to put unwanted objects out of sight and out of reach while mitigating potential conflicts about waste dumping on land. The waters' flowing quality, its opaque nature, its depth, but particularly the ocean's vast container made it look like the perfect final receptacle. Ocean dumping seemed a natural human activity.[2] Often, a lack of data made it difficult to prove otherwise. Additionally, century-old cultural tropes about the ocean as "a sea that can wash away all evils," allowed people to consider ocean dumping as environmentally sound and harmless (Patton 2007). Questioned about CHASE, Acting-Assistant Secretary of the US Army, Charles L. Poor, explained how the military had always looked on the ocean floor "as a kind of 'Davy Jones Locker' remote and inaccessible where 'things could be put and forgotten'" (quoted in Selin and VanDeveer 2013: 499).

As of the late 1960s, people from all strata of society and all regions of the world increasingly wondered about the limits of the ocean's assimilative capacity. Due to the growth and expansion of ocean science as well as the rise in cinematic access to deep ocean life, marine space had become less of a terra incognita. Despite its primarily terrestrial focus, modern environmentalism, too, recognized a need to protect the oceans. Water's fluidity, together with the ability of other chemicals to diffuse through water, made open waters problematic disposal sites. Unwanted materials might stay hidden, but they were unlikely to stay put (Müller and Stradling 2019). In smaller waters, the practice of open-water dumping had already led to a series of dramatic and visual pollution incidences, such as the proclaimed deaths of Lake Erie, the Rhine River, and the New York Bight (Cioc 2002; Egan 2017; Langston 2017; Stradling and Stradling 2015). Soon, the ocean too might become a dead zone, so some scientists. Concern over marine ecosystems led to a series of regional and international marine protection treaties such as the London Dumping Convention (1975), the Oslo Convention (1972), the Kuwait Convention (1979), or the Abidjan Convention (1984). As of the 1990s, these transnational environmental protection governance systems covered almost all maritime regions. Yet, neither the practice of ocean dumping nor the controversies about it have truly stopped.

This chapter foregrounds the rather quiet environmental conflicts connected to ocean dumping and the slow violence inherent to it (Nixon 2011). The chapter opens with an oversight of ocean dumping practices before it discusses how century-old cultural tropes of the ocean have informed the practice of sea-dumping rendering it a seemingly environmentally harmless practice. It then introduces the different international regulations intended to protect ocean space from dumping, such as the London Dumping Convention or the Oslo

Convention. In its final section, the chapter discusses the continuous return of both drowned materials as well as the issue of dumping itself.

DAVY JONES'S LOCKER

In 1946, the US military launched a secret mission called *Operation Davy Jones Locker*. With this name, the military invoked the gruesome history of nautical superstition. From at least the eighteenth century on, Davy Jones's Locker was the idiomatic expression for the bottom of the sea. The term characterized a remote place, the reign of Davy Jones—the sailors' devil—where drowned sailors and shipwrecks were irretrievably bound never to return to the surface (Bane 2014). In 1946, the term became a euphemism for drowning hazardous waste as the US military planned to dump outdated, defect, or captured war munitions from the Second World War. Calling the operation Davy Jones's Locker signified how the military, but also a full host of groups ranging from industry, science, or local and national governance, felt about the deep-sea and marine space. Many people assumed an entitlement to use the ocean as the ultimate sink. Ultimately, so Wilson Talley of the United States Environmental Protection Agency (EPA) in 1975, the ocean was "the sink for the waste that [was] created on the land, and it was a natural choice to use it as a dumping ground" (Talley quoted in Subcommittee on the Environment and the Atmosphere 1975: 196).

Open-water dumping has its origins with earliest human settlements by water. The practice increased dramatically in the late nineteenth century with a steep rise in both quantity and toxic quality of the material following the synthetic-chemical revolution and the Second World War. The remnants of industrial production and synthetically produced consumer products, marine trade infrastructure, and urban growth found their ways into the world's seas. Municipalities dumped sewage, the corps of engineers dredge spoil, industries their chemical wastes, and the militaries outdated chemical weapons to name a few. Some of the actors dumped in coastal waters and within the national territories of the continental shelf, others beyond it in international waters. Some marked where they dumped material, many did not.

The world's militaries are probably the most clandestine actors to link the forceful conflicts of the twentieth century with what was going on more quietly underneath the oceans' waves. They accumulated millions of tons of chemical weapons ranging from artillery shells to Agent Orange. Some of these chemical warfare agents were old and abandoned, others newly manufactured and stocked over the course of an escalating retaliation and containment strategy of the Cold War (Hart 2008: 55; Müller 2016: 264, 275; Souchen 2018). The problem of all of these chemical warfare agents was that they were not made to last or to store indefinitely. Over time, many chemicals became less stable and their containers more susceptible to leaking (Christianson 2010: 132). Eventually, the militaries needed to dispose of their stockpiles so that they were equally out of harm's way and out of the enemy's reach.

Military officials turned to the sea as the ultimate disposal ground, particularly the North Atlantic, the Baltic, and the North Sea, since these waters were easily accessible from the major battlefields. Already in the 1920s, Belgian authorities systematically collected war materials from the First World War and dumped or scuttled them on ships. Much of this dumping occurred in shallow water in an area called Horse Market (*Paardenmarkt*) in the North Sea (Hart 2008: 55). Meanwhile, the Allied Forces dropped stockpiles of captured German blister chemicals into the Mediterranean, the Irish Sea, and the Atlantic (Mitchell 2013; Peterkin 2005). With the end of the Second World War and the ordered demilitarization of Germany and Japan, ocean dumping turned into large-scale

FIGURE 4.1 Members of the Royal Army Ordnance Corps place shells on gravity rollers that take the ammunition over the side of the ship and into the sea. © Imperial War Museum (IWM), H 42208.

FIGURE 4.2 Barge on its way to the ammunition dumping ground Beaufort's Dyke off Cairnryan, Scotland. © Imperial War Museum (IWM), H 42204.

operations (Arison 2014: 20). Indistinctly, British, American, French, and Russian forces dumped much of the war's remains in open water. Between 1945 and 1949, the British disposed of some 120,000 tons from their occupation zone in the Skagerrak, an area between Norway, Sweden, and Denmark that connected the North and the Baltic Seas, and sank several barges near Ireland (Figures 4.1 and 4.2). US forces, too, used the Skagerrak (Plunkett 2003a: 7). One of the greatest post-Second World War dumps occurred off the coast of South Carolina in the North Atlantic between 1946 and 1948 (Christianson 2010: 132–4). Following the Second World War, also the Pacific became a site of ocean dumpings as material was dumped off the coasts of Japan and Australia (Mitchell 2013; Plunkett 2003a: 8–12).

Many more ocean dumps happened during the Cold War. After the Korean War, the US military ordered the mass destruction of obsolete lewisite gas weapons from their stockpiles and created dumpsites about 185 kilometers off the tourist beaches of Chincoteague, Virginia, and Assateague, Maryland (Christianson 2010: 134). In the mid-1960s, the US Army launched Operation CHASE to get rid of newly aggregated stockpiles of chemical weapons in the North Atlantic (Müller 2016: 274). With the Cold War in full force, there seemed to be no end of aging and corroding weapons that eventually had to be disposed of.

Militaries were far from the only ones that looked to the sea as the ultimate dumping ground. The oldest practice of ocean dumping is probably that of sewage dumping. First with pipes leading into open water and eventually with barges, sludge dumpers usually unloaded the material at explicitly marked dumpsites. With the advent and then continued improvement of sewage treatment facilities over the course of the twentieth century, sewage contained increasing amounts of toxic substances such as cadmium, PCBs, or mercury. This in turn induced municipalities around the globe to move their sewage dumping sites further out at sea. New York City, for instance, moved from a 22-kilometer dumping site to a 196-kilometer dumping site in the mid-1980s (Subcommittee on Environmental Pollution 1985: 11). Throughout the first half of the twentieth century, municipalities, industries, and federal agencies all around the world expanded open-water dumping, for instance, in the New York Bight, the Gulf of Mexico, or the Santa Monica Submarine Canyon. By 1972, almost 250 official dumpsites existed off US coasts (122 Atlantic, 56 Gulf of Mexico, 68 Pacific) for all sorts of materials (Council on Environmental Quality 1970: 1).

Alongside sewage and other municipal wastes, a wealth of industrial wastes, such as organochlorinated compounds, PCBs, or tailings found their ways into ocean water. As of 1938, for instance, Chañaral Bay in the Pacific became the site of massive waste dumping from two Andean mines located in the North of Chile. From 1938 to 1962 alone, about 125,000,000 metric tons of tailings were dumped there. Over time, the dumping created an artificial beach ten kilometers long and covering an area larger than four square kilometers. Dumping only ceased in 1989 due to a judicial order, long after the Organisation for Economic Co-operation and Development (OECD) had classified the practice as a serious incidence of marine pollution in the Pacific Ocean (Cortés et al. 2016: 19; Paskoff and Petiot 1990). Over the course of the twentieth century, Norway became one of the largest dumpers of tailings into the ocean with seven official tailing dumping sites along its Atlantic coastline and some more in its inland fjords (Friends of the Earth Norway 2015: 2).

Dredge spoils represented the largest group of material dumped into the ocean. Dredge spoils originated from the practice of underwater removal of debris or sediments of harbors or waterways and referred to "unconsolidated, randomly mixed sediments composed of rock, soil, or shell materials" (European Marine Observation and Data Network 2018). With the vast expansion of the shipping industry, the advent of the containership, harbors attempted to accommodate ever more and bigger ships that made dredging a regular and necessary activity. According to a US study, by the 1960s, dredge spoils accounted for about 80 percent by weight of the material dumped in open water—in the Atlantic Ocean, Pacific, and Great Lakes—rising to almost 90 percent by weight by the mid-1970s. The issue with the dredge spoils was that they contained contaminated sediments originating from older environmental abuses and agricultural, industrial, or municipal discharges into marine water. About 34 percent of the dredge spoils was polluted (Committee on Merchant Marine and Fisheries 1980: 3, 48; Council on Environmental Quality 1970: 3).

Finally, radioactive waste, too, ended up in the ocean. It came from nuclear energy, nuclear-powered vessels, industries, hospitals, scientific research centers, or nuclear weapons facilities. Prominent nuclear sites were Sellafield in the UK, LaHague in France, or Dounreay in Scotland from where the pipes with effluents usually ran directly into the sea (Hamblin 2008). Between 1946 and 1993, fourteen countries, starting with the United States, the Soviet Union, and Great Britain, and as of the 1950s also France, Switzerland, the Netherlands, Japan, New Zealand, South Korea, Italy, and Sweden (amongst others), used more than eighty sites in the Atlantic, the Pacific, and the Arctic to dispose of radioactive waste (International Atomic Energy Agency 1999: 12; Vartanov and Hollister 1997: 7). Material comprised liquid and solid wastes as well as nuclear reactor vessels, with and without fuel (International Atomic Energy Agency 1999: 6). Originally, such nuclear dumping took place solely under national authority. From 1968 onwards, the European countries moved to joint dumping operations that took place annually at the same site and were organized within the OECD's European Nuclear Energy Agency (Calmet and Bewers 1991: 417–18; Hamblin 2008: 8).

In contrast to most other hazardous material dumped into the seas and oceans, and with the exception of the Soviet Union, radioactive material was not dumped indiscriminately or without political debate (Aust and Herrmann 2013: 2). Throughout the 1950s and 1960s, the Soviet Union used the issue "as a vehicle for waging a propaganda war against the West," especially the United States and Great Britain. Ironically, while the Soviet Union raised the loudest voice of disapproval accusing the Western countries of poisoning the shared resource of the ocean, they secretly did the same. Only in the early 1990s, President Boris Yeltsin disclosed that in addition to effluent and packaged waste, the Soviet Union had dumped sixteen nuclear reactors from submarines and icebreakers, some still with nuclear fuel, most of them in water less than one hundred meters deep (Hamblin 2008: 2–3).

THE SEA CAN WASH AWAY ALL EVILS

Water covers more than 70 percent of the earth's surface. More than 90 percent of this is ocean water. Scientists customarily divide the world's ocean into several principal oceans, such as the Pacific, Atlantic, Indian, Southern (Antarctic), and Artic Oceans, as well as smaller seas, such as the Mediterranean, Baltic, or North Sea. The average marine water's depth is nearly 3,700 meters whereby mean depth can vary greatly from sea to ocean. There are bodies of water, such as the Pacific that reach a mean depth of 4,000 meters and is home to the Mariana Trench—the world's deepest point—with 10,911 meters. Then, there is the Baltic Sea that has a mean depth of only 52 meters and is much shallower than, for instance, Lake Ontario with an average depth of 86 meters (Charette and Smith 2010; Czub 2018: 1485). The world ocean, to use a term that covers all marine space, is the habitat of 230,000 known species, but because much of it is unexplored, the number of species that exist in the ocean is much larger, possibly over two million (Drogin 2009).

Although ocean science has rapidly advanced throughout the twentieth century, we still know relatively little about this vast aquatic space and the effects of human presence and interference with it (Haward and Vince 2008: 9). In the context of ocean dumping, knowledge in the form of both facts and presumptions, hard data and mythical imaginations played a key role. People have dumped all sorts of material into the seas and oceans not necessarily based on what they knew about the marine environment or potential hazards effected from dumping. Rather, they did so based on what they presumed to know about the qualities of ocean water and the assimilative capacity of sea spaces.[3] Hard data was difficult to get for both sides of the argument and many a scientific controversy was born from the conflict over the effects and abuses of ocean dumping throughout the twentieth century.

The imagination of ocean space and its vast assimilative capacities intricately linked to ancient visions of marine space as well as a cultural turn in nineteenth-century marine art and literature. Painters J.M.W. Turner and Winslow Homer, most explicitly, turned their artistic gaze away from older depictions of harbors or ships representing marine space. Instead, they pioneered with depictions of light and movement on canvas (Gillis 2013: 11). In their paintings, Turner and Homer directed their viewers' gaze to encompass the gigantic premises of the ocean, which in the literatures, too, increasingly gained attention as a space upon which to imagine modernity (Cohen 2010) (Figure 4.3). Both forms of art gave expression to a general newly awakened recognition and passion for the ocean that led to a vast expansion of humanistic and scientific knowledge of the sea "as a three-dimensional living thing with a history, geography, and a life of its own" over the course of the nineteenth and twentieth centuries (Gillis 2013: 12). At the same time, they also gave expression to a fascination with the ocean's breadth that a century later were at the core of the attraction for open water dumping.

FIGURE 4.3 J.M.W. Turner, *Seascape*, 1828. © Tate.

When it came to ocean dumping, people saw the vast expanses of the ocean in relation to limited space for disposal on land. Particularly decision makers "located in crowded or geologically unstable countries with active population groups that resist land dumping," such as Japan or Great Britain found ocean-dumping attractive (Hamblin 2008: 28; VanDyke 1988: 82). For instance, when in the mid-1970s, Japan began to plan for the ocean disposal of its low-level radioactive waste, Takehiko Ishihara, director of Japan's Radioactive Waste Management Program, argued that it was "quite natural" for Japan to opt for sea disposal given the vast premises of the Pacific in contrast to Japan's limited territorial space (quoted in VanDyke 1988: 87). Similarly, New York City argued that due to the lack of adequate land for disposal within city premises it must dump its sludge into New York Bay. Sewage sludge from New York contained heavy metals that ruled out any land that could be used for agricultural usage as a potential dumping ground. Instead, the land you put it on had to be forever designated to nonagricultural use that was difficult to find in New York City (Subcommittee on Natural Resources, Agriculture Research and Environment 1981: 4). Ultimately, marine space appeared as "a logical dump site" to many decision makers, simply because there was "more ocean" (VanDyke 1988: 82; Subcommittee on Environmental Pollution 1985: 6).

In addition to the oceans' vast premises, it was the water's flowing quality that played a crucial role in the attraction of ocean dumping. Through much of human history, flowing water was the most desirable disposal site, since water flushed away wastes. As far back as the ancient Greeks, people followed Euripides' statement that "the sea can wash away all evils." According to Kimberly Patton, throughout history, a "wide range of cultures have sacralized the sea, trusting in its power to wash away what is dangerous, dirty, and morally contaminating." They believed that the sea made "life on land possible by keeping it 'pure'" (Patton 2007: jacket). Marine pollution practices of the twentieth century were partially inherited from these beliefs.

Generally, many people followed the premise that the "solution to pollution is dilution" and the idea that large water bodies thinned down whatever was put in them through the sheer quantity of water available (Subcommittee on the Environment and the Atmosphere 1975: 101). Marine space represented an "unlimited [...] reservoir for waste assimilation," so a widespread belief up until the 1970s and 1980s (Subcommittee on Fisheries and Wildlife Conservation and Subcommittee on Oceanography 1971: 138). Scientists assumed for instance that at the dumpsite off the coast of New York City, the city's sewage sludge would, ideally, dilute by a "factor of 5,000 or more within a few minutes of dumping and by 100,000 or 1 million within 1 or 2 days." Then, the material would be "flushed out of the dumpsite in less than a week" (Subcommittee on Natural Resources, Agriculture Research and Environment 1981: 23). Industries had a similar apprehension of the ocean. The ocean had "tremendous assimilative capacity" and was a "natural and ultimate repository for waterborne residues from man and nature," so William Galloway, director of Environmental Affairs at DuPont (Subcommittee on the Environment and the Atmosphere 1975: 77). When interrogated about operation CHASE in 1971, Under Secretary of the US Army, Thaddeaus Beal, argued that "immersing" outdated chemical weapons in sea water would "dilute and detoxify the chemical agent when it escape[d] from the vaults." While the military could not guarantee that there would be "absolutely no effect on the environment at the disposal site," they believed it would be "inconsequential" (Subcommittee on Oceanography 1970). Similarly, the British Ministry of Supply justified its dumping of atomic waste in 1949 stating that its amount was "much too small to have any harmful effect on fish or human life" (British Ministry of Supply 1949, quoted in Hamblin 2008: 27). Despite a rudimentary state of knowledge, ocean dumping often appeared even to scientists, such as oceanographer Richard Fleming, as the safest, most economical, and environmentally soundest disposal method for a number of hazardous wastes, including radioactive (Bearden 2007: 8; Hamblin 2008: 29, 34).

For communities, industries, and government agencies alike, finally, the various attractions of dumping in water were "in its relative ease, its obvious convenience, and its economic efficiency" (Weinstein-Bacal 1987: 887). Historically, many cities have been located on coastlines as such a position brought with it transport, food, and ecological benefits. Products and money would flow into these cities through their ports and so nourish their growth.

Today, eight of the top ten largest cities in the world are located by the coast, among them Tokyo, Mumbai, São Paulo, New York City, Shanghai, and Lagos (United Nations 2006–16). When over the course of the first half of the twentieth century, these ocean communities were facing "decreasing capacity of existing disposal facilities, lack of nearby land sites, higher costs and political problems in acquiring new sites," it was convenient to simply drop the material beneath nearby waters. As a participant at the 1966 international conference on ocean dumping pointed out, the "great economy" of discharging urban sewage, industrial wastes, or dredge spoils into near-shore waters was "inherent." If these waters could be reached "within the bounds of economy, the grim specter of an expensive treatment plant grew dimmer and dimmer, [...] to the great satisfaction to those [...] who have to pay the bill." In the end, "good old ocean [did] the job for free" (quoted in Subcommittee on Fisheries and Wildlife Conservation, Subcommittee on Oceanography 1971: 138).

TERRA INCOGNITA

Up until the 1960s and beyond, people all around the world—scientists included—presumed that open water dumping would cause no or little environmental harm to the oceans. At the same time, people harbored such presumptions often without the appropriate scientific knowledge base. Although ocean science and marine biology vastly expanded over the course of the twentieth century, both could still contribute little to a public and governance debate on the short- or long-term environmental effects of ocean dumping. What should be the discharge limits for certain materials? How should material be discharged of in the first place, at which depth and at what rate? How was the decay different for material dumped in shallow water or the deep sea? How could scientists trace contaminants such as PCBs or mercury? And how should one surveil the dumpers and monitor the dumpsites? In 1975, environmental activist Kenneth Kamlet of the US National Wildlife Federation warned that the ocean would become "a vast wasteland long before [humanity] could answer all [the] questions about natural processes and the fate and effect of pollutants in the marine environment" (quoted in Subcommittee on Fisheries and Wildlife Conservation, Subcommittee on Oceanography 1971: 26).

This lack of knowledge was often based on missing basic research related to decades of negligence, to secrecy, and to particular characteristics of the ocean itself. Up until the late 1960s, both military and civilian sources kept few records of how much they dumped or where exactly they dumped materials. To this day, the precise coordinates of many of the early dumping grounds are completely unknown. Equally, dumpers did not necessarily determine whether the material was problematic for human health or the marine environment, whether it dissolved in open water or would most likely stay put (Bearden 2007: 11). In a time prior to satellite supported navigation, finally, many dumpers were unsure if they had released the material at the designated dumping site, since marine space was not a highway where you could easily navigate to an exact spot ("Appeal on Seabed Dumping" 1970).

Aspects of secrecy played a particularly important role in military dumping operations. Hardly ever did military agents release information on their dumpings and many records were only declassified in the new millennium (Christianson 2010: 134). A rare moment of transparency happened in 1970, when the British military admitted that a poison gas leak from their dumpings probably caused the death of more than 17,000 seabirds on the shores of the Irish Sea the year before. Another when the US military had to report about its CHASE missions before US Congress that same year (Anable 1970; Furphy, Hamilton, and Merne 1971: 34–40). Only in 2001, however, the public learned that US disposal of chemical weapons in the ocean until 1970 had been more common and widespread geographically than acknowledged. The Pentagon also reported that some of the weapons dumped had been damaged or leaking at the time of disposal (US Army Research, Development and Engineering Command, Historical Research and Response Team 2001). In 1997, a public outcry ran through Great Britain when people learned that—contrary to past statements—also Beaufort's Dyke in the Irish Sea had been used as a dumpsite for the country's radioactive waste ("Radioactive Waste was Dumped in Irish Sea" 1997).

Matters looked equally bleak on the civilian side, if for different reasons. When in 1971, the United States started considering marine protection as one of the first nations around the globe, none of their experts knew "the volume [...] of wastes that [had] been dumped in the oceans in the past years" (Subcommittee on Fisheries and Wildlife Conservation and Subcommittee on Oceanography of the Committee on Merchant Marine and Fisheries 1971: 1). The Council on Environmental Quality could only go back as far as 1968—two years—by estimating that the United States had dumped about 48 million tons at sea that year alone (1970: 1, 10) (Figure 4.4). One of the problems was that questions on the effects of ocean dumping had "scarcely" been asked "and then only by an obscure group of scientists, known as ecologists" (Subcommittee on Fisheries and Wildlife Conservation and Subcommittee on Oceanography of the Committee on Merchant Marine and Fisheries 1971: 1). When in 1972, the United States passed the Marine Protection, Research and Sanctuaries Act, also known as the Ocean Dumping Act, it did so "recognizing that little was known of the assimilative capacity" and demanded to both "strictly limit or prohibit" ocean dumping and to expand oceanic research (Lee [1981] 1983: 1).

Knowledge gaps continued to exist after first national and then international marine dumping regulations were in place and research programs established. Assessing the situation in 1975, ocean activist Kenneth Kamlet concluded that

FIGURE 4.4 Barge loaded with ashes on its way to ocean dump 05/1973. © US National Archives College Park, photo no. 412-DA-5412.

serious information deficits were still as valid as prior to the London Dumping Convention (1972; ratified in 1975). Scientists struggled to separate the effects of ocean dumping from the broader issue of marine pollution (Subcommittee on the Environment and the Atmosphere 1975: 50). Meanwhile the amount of sewage sludge or dredge spoils dumped into the ocean steadily increased. In 1973, the United States had dumped 4.3 million tons of sewage sludge; in 1982, 7.3 million tons. By 1982, ten years after the country's Ocean Dumping Act, "almost a decade of research" had not offered policy makers "cohesive data upon which to evaluate current and proposed ocean dumping policies" (Lee [1981] 1983: 1). Researchers urged governments to fund more basic science while admitting that such kinds of research tended to be painfully slow (Subcommittee on the Environment and the Atmosphere 1975: 170).

The dumping of radioactive waste was the first kind of sea disposal that triggered calls for emission standards and thresholds. In the early 1950s, the US Atomic Energy Commission and the US National Bureau of Standards both pressured oceanographer Richard Fleming to define thresholds of safety for the ocean dumping of radioactive waste. Initially, the oceanographer struggled with the task. There was "so little known about the effects and he was uncomfortable with the idea that radioactive waste would safely disappear into the oceans without significant consequences." Despite lacking data, Fleming settled in the end for a document recommending that "surely, some radioactive waste could be put into the sea" (Hamblin 2008: 11). Considering the precise amount of this ominous *some*, scientists at the time followed the critical pathways approach presuming that if levels were safe for humans they were safe for marine organisms. Consequently, discharges should be limited by the pathways by which levels of radioactivity could reach humans in a specific environment. Marine space was not worthy of protection in itself, only in so far as it concerned humans (219).

Following up on Flemming, the Commission of the European Communities inaugurated Project Marina to assess the radiation exposure to Europeans in the seas around Northern Europe in 1985 (Hamblin 2008: 252). Yet, despite the beginning of some more meticulous monitoring, many questions concerning the effects of, for instance, radioactive waste dumping, remained unanswered. In the late 1980s, scientists were puzzled that sea anemones from one of the main Atlantic dumpsite in the outer Bay of Biscay sampled in 1979 had strontium-90 and cesium-137 concentrations at least ten times higher than those found in samples taken in 1966, although the use of the site had been discontinued in the meantime. One possible explanation was that adverse effect simply might have taken years before they appeared. Yet, studies done at that particular dumpsite were "far too sketchy to give definite answers" and prior inaccuracy about the amount and location of dumped material haunted later scientists. At the time, they also could not conclude on the question of what had happened to the waste. In the end, they warned that because of the legacy of the pre-1970s era and their still "limited knowledge about [marine ecosystems], disturbances [were] not likely to be noticed unless they [were] 'enormous'" (VanDyke 1988: 91). Instead of filling their existing knowledge gaps, however, the opposite happened. In 1993, the members of the London Dumping Convention voted on a total ban on radioactive waste disposal at sea, to be reevaluated every twenty-five years. With this decision, they also terminated accompanying research programs monitoring existing dumpsites (Aust and Herrman 2013: 9).

PROTECTING THE OCEAN

The danger of dumping material at sea became apparent when in the 1960s and 1970s the reappearance of dumped material intersected with the rise of modern environmentalism, a series of marine environmental catastrophes, and an older legacy of underwater imagery that made it possible for the average person to peak beneath the oceans' waves. All four factors allowed the terrestrial human beings to *feel* connected to the vast habitat that covered much of the planet (Alaimo 2014: 188).

The golden age of underwater moving images started in the 1930s with a host of technological and scientific innovations that allowed divers and photographers to capture the vast richness of underwater life. After the war, it penetrated society. In 1956 Jacques-Yves Cousteau's film *The Silent World* reached audiences all around the globe with its vivid colors of a highly diverse underwater world (Cohen 2018: 81). Almost at the same time, marine biologist and writer Rachel Carson published her book *The Sea Around Us*. In 1953, its film adaptation won the Oscar for best documentary (Carson [1952] 1961). These works not only illustrated the richness of the vast ocean, but also stressed the importance of preserving it and although modern environmentalism of the 1960s and 1970s primarily focused on terrestrial issues, Cousteau and Carson had laid the seeds to an awareness that the marine environment, too, was in need of protection. A series of high-profile maritime accidents and events drew attention to the need to govern marine protection internationally. In 1967, the wreck of the oil tanker *Torrey-Canyon* off of the British coast illustrated the vulnerability of wetlands. The 1969 Santa Barbara oil spill only underlined the message (Simcock 2010: 29).

Ocean dumping came under first scrutiny when drowned objects reappeared. Not all of the dumped munitions, for instance, remained truly out of reach. Generally, chemical weapons agents are denser than sea water and so tend to remain on the ocean floor rather than float to shallower waters (Bearden 2007: 9). Repeatedly, however, they washed ashore or were accidentally retrieved as in the shallow waters of the Skagerrak and the Baltic Sea. Over the course of 1968 to 1970, several reports were filed in the Scandinavian countries from swimmers and fishermen receiving burns, apparently from mustard gas leaking out from seabed dumps. West German fishermen were temporarily blinded after they had hauled up an odd canister and five children playing with seaweed near Lübeck had received skin burns (Anable 1970).

Chemical warfare agents were not the only objects to resurface. In 1975, US Senator Lautenberg related to Congress his experience of flying over the New York Bight and witnessing the residues of sewage sludge that remained even after a long time in the ocean as well as the "mutated marine life" (Subcommittee on Environmental Pollution 1985: 7). Another issue with sewage sludge was the slime that formed from a mixture of natural mud bottom, human hair, fibers from sanitary napkins, and varieties of treated sewage. Fishermen reported how it entwined with their nets or occasionally would even tear their nets apart. At points, they had found the slime as far as 130 kilometers from the coast (27). With these reports about reappearing materials, it dawned upon people that objects—while drowned—were unlikely to stay put. In its 1977 film *Empire of Ants*, Hollywood took up a simmering fear about the potential effects of such reappearances from their ocean graves, centering their storyline on a washed-up canister of radioactive waste producing a colony of enormous ants in the Florida Everglades (Hamblin 2008: 3).

The reappearance of dumped material triggered a full host of responses from marine nations all over the world in order to mitigate the dawning conflict between those favoring and opposing ocean dumping. In the 1960s West Germany, for instance, launched an operation to locate and detoxify poison gas from the Second World War that had been dumped in the Baltic Sea. They fished some of them from the bottom to move them to deeper dumping grounds in the Atlantic (Anable 1970; "Gas Wells Moved" 1960: March 9; Helcom 2018). In 1968, with the launch of the German vessel *Matthias I*, West Germany and other European nations turned to ocean incineration as an alternative method to ocean dumping. Ocean incinerated materials were largely organochlorine wastes that were difficult and costly to dispose of on land. By 1973, the quantity of wastes annually incinerated were over 80,000 metric tons. By 1981, the number had increased to 117,000 metric tons. All incinerator ships operated in the North Sea (Suman 1991: 562–3). The turn toward ocean incineration was the first step away from understanding the deep sea as *empty space* where all sorts of material could be dumped indiscriminately.

Australia, in contrast, responded more rigorously and much earlier than any other nation across the globe to the reappearance of ocean dumpings. As early as the 1920s, pollution was washing up on beaches around Sydney as well as around Melbourne and Adelaide. Ships routinely discharged loads of garbage just off the coast. In Sydney this waste included offal, organic refuse, waste collected by municipal councils, and ashes. In addition to being a pollution nuisance, such sea-disposal also caused net-snagging problems with Australia's recently established deep-sea trawling industry and possible obstruction of the increasingly busy navigation routes. To combat pollution, Australia's federal government introduced the Beaches, Fishing Grounds, and Sea Routes Protection Act of 1932 to control the dumping of boats and to prohibit the dumping of "any garbage, rubbish, or organic refuse" in designated exclusion zones. The Australian legislation was enacted some forty years before there were any international moves to control sea dumping (Bearden 2007: 9; Plunkett 2003a: 7).

Internationally, environmentalists and governments alike started considering that also the vast ocean needed protection irrespective of human presence or dependence in the late 1960s when news broke of Operation CHASE. "More than just a few startled squid [had] been stirred" about the Pentagon's plan to dump 22,000 tons of poison gas munitions into the North Atlantic (Anable 1970; Müller 2016). The British government officially informed the United States of "mounting concern" acting on behalf of the governments in the Bahama Islands and Bermuda ("Britain Voices Concern on Nerve Gas" 1970). Iceland, which by way of the Gulf Stream had a direct connection with the dumpsite off the coast of Florida, complained to Washington that nerve gas would "harm her fisheries." Additionally, Iceland used the United Nations Committee on the Peaceful Uses of the Sea-Bed to push for an international conference to draw up a treaty preventing pollution of the marine environment. Led by Iceland, the committee appealed to all governments to "refrain from using the seabed and the ocean floor as a dumping ground for toxic, radioactive and other noxious materials" ("Iceland Calls for a Parley To Bar Pollution of Seabed" 1970). It was the first step toward the London Dumping Convention of 1972.

While nations around the world were resenting the American ocean dumping mission, operation CHASE stirred anxieties that were already close to the surface. In Europe, people had become astutely aware that not only the North Atlantic but also their own waters were far more polluted with dangerous chemicals than experts at the time had realized. Otto Kinne, head of Helgoland's Marine Biology Research Station, called the North Sea "the industrial cesspool of Europe." He documented that some 1,200 tons of sulfuric acid a day were dumped within twenty-two kilometers of his station. Journalists further uncovered the story of a cannery that disposed 18,000 tons a formalin a year off the coast of Norway. Similarly, oceanographers stated that similar pollution was behind the fact that the Baltic's bottom waters are what they called "dead" (Anable 1970). On the other side of the world, in Japan, public concern mounted regarding dangerous discharges from factories, including cadmium and mercury, into Tokyo Bay and other waterways (Müller 2017).

Over the course of a year, a worldwide consensus had developed that ocean dumping was an issue of great concern for the entire community of nations. When in September 1971, the *Stella Maris* attempted to dump 650 tons of toxic chemicals in the North Sea, opposition from Norway, Iceland, Ireland, and the United Kingdom forced the Dutch freighter to return to its homeport (Simcock 2010: 29; Suman 1991: 562). That same year, Norway invited a group of European nations to attend the Oslo Conference to draft the first international dumping convention. On the other side of the Atlantic, the United States prepared its Marine Protection, Research, and Sanctuaries Act, better known as the Ocean Dumping Act, which it passed in October 1972 (Weinstein-Bacal 1987: 898). After a series of conferences in London, Ottawa, Reykjavik, and Stockholm, eighty nations adopted the Convention on the Prevention of Marine Pollution by Dumping of Wastes and Other Matter, generally called the London Dumping Convention, in December 1972 within the UN framework. On August 30, 1975, it entered into force (Chasek 2010: 58–9; Hassan 2006: 80).

In the early 1970s, these different dumping conventions established a regime of marine protection from ocean dumping while recognizing that the ocean could also assimilate certain material. They neither prohibited ocean dumping nor banned all material. The London Dumping Convention (LC), for instance, works with a regulatory structure based on black and gray lists. On the black list—prohibited—you find materials such as high-level radioactive wastes, and chemical and biological warfare agents, concentrated heavy metals, and synthetic chemicals. Dumping of substances on the gray list, such as sewage sludge or dredge spoils, in turn, is possible after the dumper has obtained a special permit (Suman 1991: 568; Zeppetello 1985: 620). In 1996, members of the London Convention adopted the 1996 Protocol (LP), which updated and improved the LC and should eventually supersede it. On March 24, 2006, ten years after its adoption, the LP entered into force (Hong and Lee 2015).

One important aspect to the London Convention is the encouragement of member states to develop regional agreements to prevent ocean dumping. The first of such regional agreements was the Oslo Convention that was negotiated in February 1972, even prior to the London Convention. In 1992, the Oslo Convention was updated through the OSPAR convention (Du Pontavice 1973: 126; Suman 1991: 564; UN 2017b: 380). In 1974, those nations bordering the Baltic Sea adopted the Helsinki Convention. Similarly, the deteriorating ecological state of the Mediterranean Sea brought fifteen countries bordering this body of water to sign the Convention for the Protection of the Mediterranean Sea Against Pollution (Barcelona Convention) in 1976. It entered into force two years later (Suman 1991: 569–71). As Table 4.1 below illustrates, several more regional conventions on the protection of marine environments from pollution and ocean dumping entered into force in the 1980s or updated existing conventions in the 1990s. Today, most nations are part to one or several of these conventions that relate to sea dumping. Among the exceptions are some of the largest twenty economies of the world as well as some of the Pacific Island nations that while suffering the most from the effects of radioactive waste dumping argue that the different conventions were not strong enough (UN 2017b: 382; VanDyke 1988: 86).

TIDAL RETURNS

At the end of the twentieth and the beginning of the twenty-first century, we witness yet another turn in the long history of ocean dumping, a chapter that is characterized both by continuities as well as changes. To this day, ocean dumping is still a legal and common practice. To this day, it also remains difficult to assess the amount or the effects of it based on a lack of data on the dumpsites, knowledge about the deep sea and its marine environment, as well as a reluctance of the international community to face these two issues. The London Dumping Convention and the London Protocol, for instance, both ask their member states to submit annual reports on their ocean dumping activity. Most member states are not responsive. From the reports submitted, we learn that the largest amount of material ocean dumped are still dredge spoils, while the amount of sewage sludge has declined as nations recognized

Table 4.1 Existing International and Regional Ocean Dumping Conventions.

Name of Convention	Area of Concern	Date of Adoption	Date of Entry into Force
Oslo Convention	North Sea and Northeastern Atlantic Ocean	February 15, 1972	April 7, 1974
London Convention	Worldwide	December 19, 1972	August 30, 1975
Helsinki Convention	Baltic Sea	March 22, 1974	1974
Barcelona Convention	Mediterranean Sea	February 16, 1976	February 12, 1978
Kuwait Convention	Persian Gulf, Gulf of Aman, and North Arabian Sea	1978	1979
Abidjan Convention	Marine environment of the Atlantic coast of the West and Central and South African Region	1981	1984
Lima Convention	Southeast Pacific	1981	1986
Jeddah Convention	Red Sea and Gulf of Aden	1982	1985
Cartagena Convention	Marine environment of the wider Caribbean environment	1983	1986
Bucharest Convention	Black Sea	April 1992	1994
OSPAR	North East Atlantic	1992	1998
London Protocol	Worldwide	1996	2006
Antigua Convention	Marine and coastal environment of the Northeast Pacific	November 14, 2003	August 27, 2010

that this material was a potential contributor to eutrophication problems (UN 2017: 383). Similarly, while new technologies are available many ocean dumpsites, such as those harboring radioactive waste from OECD countries, have not been monitored regularly and over a long period of time (Aust and Herrmann 2013: 9).

At the same time that there exists this reluctance to face the ocean, in particular over the last decade of the twentieth century, several nations have started to physically revisit their ocean dumpsites with new equipment and technology, taking an interested peak underneath the water's surface. When it came to chemical weapons in particular as of the 2000s, actors all around the world started attempts to map existing dumpsites and catalog what and how much the different militaries around the world had dumped where. One of these location projects is carried out by the Baltic Marine Environment Protection Commission (HELCOM), another by OSPAR (UN 2017: 384). Often, it is the militaries themselves that want to know more about what rests underneath the ocean's surface (Plunkett 2003b). Information is compiled with an eye toward proper monitoring and—if possible—remediation, yet little has been concluded so far. The question of who should be responsible for the cleanup of disposal sites and how liability could be enforced is complicated by several factors, such as the passage of time, the commonality of the practice, the connection of dumping activity to the conduct of war, or safety and engineering issues (Baine 2004: 2).

Similarly, also the question of radioactive waste dumping has vehemently returned to the surface twice since the 1990s. First, when after the end of the Cold War in 1992, the Soviet Union disclosed that it had dumped large amounts of high-level radioactive waste into shallow waters of the Arctic Ocean since the 1960s. Concerns mounted particularly among those countries with an Arctic shoreline. A Norwegian-Russian committee was formed to investigate radioactive contamination at the dumpsites and a team of scientist undertook several excursions to the respective sites, taking samples from the ocean bottom and sea water (UN 2017: 384). Second, when in 2011 the accident at the Fukushima nuclear power station again raised public awareness of contamination of the ocean through radioactivity. It put the monitoring of dumpsites back on the agenda of the different marine protection conventions (Aust and Herrmann 2013: 9). Pressure to reinvestigate the issue mounted further when public protests opposed the dumping of the radioactive material from the fall-out. The general debate on ocean dumping remained static after Fukushima if compared to earlier discussions and controversies over the course of the twentieth century (O'Connor 2017).

Over time, people have found many arguments for and against the practice of dumping waste in the ocean. Essentially, they circle around what marine scholars W. Jackson Davis and John VanDyke had made out already in 1982 to be the major controversies: (1) the oceans are a living, interconnected environment that can return wastes to humans via the ocean food chain; (2) the ocean is a formidable environment, destructive of human structures such as radioactive waste containers; (3) despite recent rapid strides in the oceanographic sciences, the ocean is still largely an unknown environment; (4) the ocean represents a global resource, the birthright of all people and all generations; and (5) damage of this global commons by a minority of people is contrary to principles of international law (1982). To this day, we have found no profound answer to any of these five controversies that render the issue of ocean dumping into a Flying Dutchmen bound to continually return to the table of political debate and social and environmental controversy. It remains a conflict yet to be resolved.

CHAPTER FIVE

Islands and Shores

War in the Pacific

REBECCA HOFMANN

ISLANDS IN THE GLOBAL AGE

The Global Age marks the beginning of an accelerating yet conflictive development: the move toward the world's shores. Already, over 600 million people or about 10 percent of the globe's population live in coastal areas that are less than ten meters above sea level (Ocean Conference 2017); projections see this rising to a billion by 2060 (Berger 2015). In the words of environmental historian John Gillis: "We are used to oceans crashing against the shore, but now for the first time it is a human wave that is rolling seaward" (2012: 187). In the twenty-first century, however, the human urge toward the shore conflicts with accumulating environmental challenges such as rising sea levels, increased wave and storm activity. Discourses around climate change classify islands as particularly vulnerable due to their high land–coastline proportion, limited resources and restricted alternatives, and many island societies have become poster children as first climate change victims.

The destinies of islands and their inhabitants have always been intriguing to people living on continents. In current as well as in historical narratives, especially smaller islands are caught between ambivalent presentations as either places of longing or doomed places. Often, they have and continue to serve as perfect little laboratories, in which biophysical but also social dynamics can be easily studied (Hofmann and Lübken 2018). The island topos was transferred even to our planet by the globalization of environmental issues in the 1970s that depicted "Spaceship Earth" as our small island in the width of the universe (Höhler 2008: 69). In the end, however, imaginaries of islands as small, isolated, and distanced still predominate and neglect the role islands have played in world politics of the past century. Embedded in narratives of colonialism, decolonization, and liberation, in nation formation and the quest for their own identity, islanders around the world thus struggle against the marginalized position outsiders ascribe to their lifeworlds and to them as islanders. A new way of telling the story of islands and shores and thus also of the cultural history of the sea is inspired by late Pacific scholar Teresia Teaiwa who suggested to make island a verb. The verb "islanding," she argues, cracks characterizations such as isolated or vulnerable because the projection object vanishes. In contrast to continental formations, islanding additionally mediates and emphasizes the agency and potency of islanders. This chapter challenges the imaginary of the Pacific Islands—also called Oceania—as an isolated utopia by sketching out the cultural history of the islands and shores along bellicose encounters and conflictive proceedings that variously have centered them right in the middle of world politics and global dynamics.

MARTIAL OCEANIA

The Pacific Ocean is two times bigger than the Atlantic and contains twice the volume of water. It includes the Bali Sea, the Bering Sea, the Gulf of Alaska, the Gulf of Tonkin, the Coral Sea, the East China Sea, the Philippine Sea, the Sea of Japan, the South China Sea, and the Tasman Sea. Its tropical waters between Australia, the Philippines, and America contain some 7,500 islands, reefs, and atolls with a land area of about 1.3 million square kilometers, dispersed over about 70 million square kilometers. Oceanic islands have a transient existence, determined by tectonic and volcanic activity, by long- and short-term climatic conditions, and not least by anthropogenic engagement. About 2,100 of the islands accommodate some 17 million people (Mückler 2009a: 15), clustered by European explorers into rough cultural areas known as Polynesia, Melanesia, and Micronesia (Figure 5.1). UN projections reach up to 31.5 million in 2050 (Ortmayr 2009: 190, 220). The possible prospect of losing their islands and thus becoming citizens of a landless nation much sooner due to climate change is certainly an existential threat, yet not the first battle Pacific Islanders confront. Islanders were caught in belligerent disputes amongst themselves, and of course, with European and American colonizers, missionaries, and tradesmen long before they staged dramatic scenes during the Second World War and subsequent Cold War. All together, the waters of the *Mare Pacifico*—as Portuguese explorer Ferdinand Magellan named the largest ocean in the world in 1520—have been little peaceful.

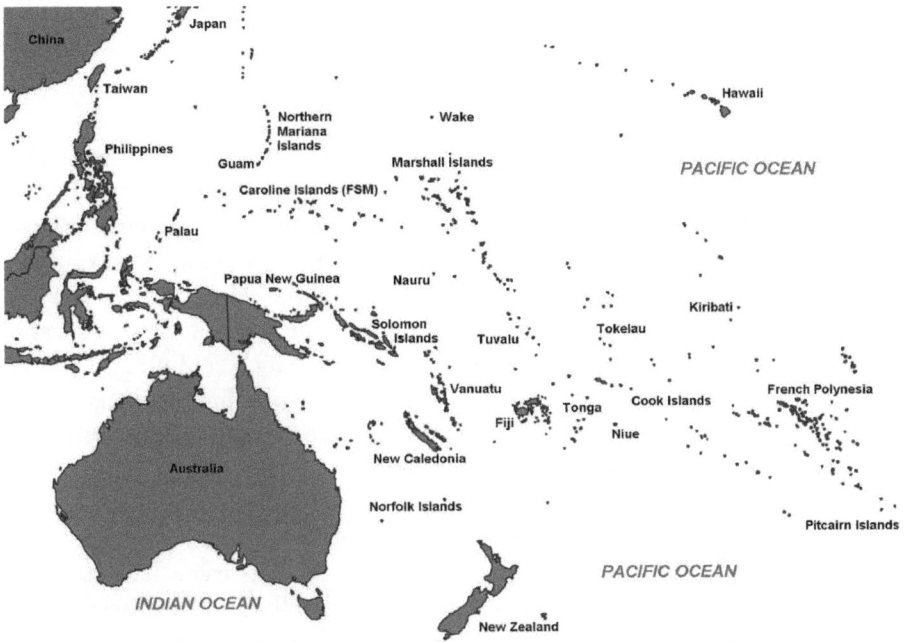

FIGURE 5.1 Islands of Oceania. Draft by Florian Gaschick, 2016. © Wikimedia Commons (public domain).

Oceania was the last part of the world to be settled. Most Pacific Islands became fit for human population some two thousand years ago as sea levels reached their current level. Although early theories attributed the settlement of the islands to a series of storm- and sea current-driven coincidences, it is widely acknowledged that settlers acted purposely, loading their canoes with livestock and plants to take up residence on new lands in which they rooted their sense of belonging. Surrounded by the sea, they also developed a maritime culture with exceedingly sophisticated navigational and seafaring skills. Oceania's lifeworld, thus, is one of mobility and place attachment, which islanders understand to be complementary and formative to their identity. Thus the islands' shores from the start have been places of arrival and departure and therefore have seen both happy and sad scenes. They hosted joy as people took claim to land after weeks on the open sea, or as family members followed. Until today, the landing spots and the chronology of the arriving groups have special significance to the people as the foundation of their land rights, their political claims, and their family history. Yet, the shores also dried up tears of farewell as people took off—be it out of curiosity, to alleviate overcrowding, or as expellees. They soaked up blood in battles between settlers and newcomers. On shores, trading partners or clan mates from various islands gathered and reinforced reciprocal allegiances, exchanging goods that were scarce on their own islands, ensuring survival in the Oceanic island-scape. According to Mückler (2009b: 138), trade events were the only peaceful encounters of clans who otherwise were in permanent war conditions with each other.

In the maritime island-scape, the central reason for war was land. The history of Oceania can also be read as a war story around the emergence and decline of partly extensive kingdoms or chiefly dominions that characterize the region up until today. The martial island culture, in Kiribati, for example, included suits of armor made of coconut fiber or animal skins that covered the whole body, finished by a helmet made of dried stingray or blowfish skin and armed with spears and swords full of shark teeth (Mückler 2009b: 266–7). Moreover, successful and brave war acts were one way of achieving social status for men all over Oceania; for instance, Melanesian headhunters were really hunting prestige. Long before the severe repercussions of anthropogenic global warming, climatic and environmental conditions were already influencing the sociocultural development and conditioned competition amongst settler groups. "Times of plenty" and "times of less," marine archaeologists argue, have induced transformations of settlement structure and diet as well as social cohesion and political organization with increased fortification due to environmental stress and food shortages especially during the little ice age (1350–1800 CE) (Carson 2014; Nunn 2007; Nunn and Britton 2001).

From the sixteenth century on, European missionaries, beachcombers, traders, and soldiers arrived along with firearms and new ideas of power, giving island war new motives and a new quality. The first colonial encounters, however, might have taken place with curiosity and awe on both sides and romanticizing descriptions from contemporary European witnesses initially shaped and transported the islands' imaginary as utopian places where Rousseau's "noble wild" show alternatives to life on the old continent at the time, as this appraisal of Tahitian society testifies:

> Yet I can tell you that it is the only place on earth in which the people live without vice, without prejudice, without needs and without discord. Born under the most beautiful sky, nourishing on fruits from soil that is fertile without human work, governed by family fathers rather than kings, Tahiti's inhabitants know no other god but love.
> (Tahiti ou la Nouvelle-Cythère; zit. N. Hérubel, M. ed., *Voyage autour du monde par la frégate "La Boudeuse,"* quoted in Bitterli 1980: 250, translation by R.H.)

Others, however, saw the "small" and "isolated" islands as the epitome of a nearly impossible life, harsh and full of deprivation—thus as feasible only at the price of internal barbarism or outside dependency. European impressions of Melanesian societies have been especially appalling. An early description states:

"Hundreds of years ago the country which is called New Guinea was shaded black on the map and called the Islands of the Bad People" (Beaver 1920: 40, quoted in Knauft 1990: 251). Melanesians became the prototype for uncivilized societies where barbarism, cruel war acts, headhunting, and cannibalism ruled—a motive that reverberates in William Golding's dystopian novel *Lord of the Flies* (1954). Certainly, the increasing number of European and American people establishing themselves and their businesses in the islands, along with new diseases and shady trading practices or outright exploitation, nourished notions of revenge and retaliation in islanders.

Throughout the twentieth century, a dialectic of trade and violence between islanders and foreigners accompanies Oceania's history. Along the course of colonialism, European powers have turned the islands into well-established commercial outposts with productive copra (dried coconut meat) plantations that substituted the declining resource of train oil around the globe. At the same time, the new economic and political system fueled competition for leadership positions, rearranging loyalties and allegiances within and between groups that continue to play out in today's civil disturbances as shown further down. Trade and colonialism, hence, connected the islands in the far Pacific to the rest of the world. In the end, however, war was what really placed them into global history.

In Micronesia, for example, the Japanese seized the islands from German colonial rule with the beginning of the First World War in 1914, when they also invaded US-governed Guam. At the end of the war, the forerunner of today's United Nations—the League of Nations—formalized Japan's claims under their mandate in the Treaty of Versailles. The goal was to establish a settler colony as part of Japan's southern expansion doctrine. They aimed at acculturating the islands to Japan and keenly went to the task of developing the economy, bringing wage labor opportunities, Japanese literacy and customs, yet also isolation to prepare for mass immigration of Japanese who soon outnumbered Pacific Islanders. While it had immense sociocultural effects, they were only a taste of the lasting impacts and meanings of the Second World War in which the islands, their shores, but also the waters between and the air above them staged the Pacific theater. While the military history of the Pacific War is meticulously documented, descriptions of the islanders' situation and perspectives are captured mostly in the islanders' oral history, which preserves the little-known but often cruel experiences of islanders through intergenerational storytelling. The following account thus delineates how the formerly imagined paradises have become prey to war parties that came from far beyond their shores. Geographically placed in the crosslines between the United States and Japan, the islands hosted some of the fiercest battles of the Second World War. In Micronesia, military campaigns took place that were decisive not only for the Pacific War theater but that determined the war as such.

THE PACIFIC ISLANDS BETWEEN HOSTILE WORLDS: THE SECOND WORLD WAR

Starting from the early 1920s, Japan's policy for the islands shifted from settler imperialism to the militarization of the islands. In 1933, Japan made its intention official by withdrawing from the League of Nations. As it sealed the end of civil administration in the islands, the Japanese started to extend their dominion and established major military outposts all over Oceania (Mückler 2012: 216–21). The heavy Japanese fortification led to major changes in the island-scape. In Chuuk Lagoon (today part of the Federated States of Micronesia), for example, people were forced to level down half an island for the construction of an airfield. Oil tanks, coal storages, roads, and channels further modified the island-scape and islanders still remember the sight of the deforested island hills, from where rockets and missiles were launched. Although the trees have grown back by now, caves, tunnels, and rusting weaponry are still visible reminders (Figure 5.2). In addition, whole stretches of the surrounding coral reef were blasted for the passage of large battle ships. Chuuk was no longer a Garden of Eden, but became the "fortress of the Pacific" (Poyer 2008: 226) that hosted a major part of the Japanese Navy with severe consequences for the local island population.

FIGURE 5.2 Japanese Second World War Gun in Chuuk Lagoon. © Rebecca Hofmann 2012.

Some islands thus served as agricultural stations to supply the military or to grow cash crops and were turned almost completely into fields and plantations. For the islanders, this meant forced labor, confiscation of land and houses, the draining of taro swamps, and the chopping of breadfruit and other fruit trees, which accounted for a significant part of their diet and thus led to severe food shortages, which have become a significant part of local war legacy.

Chuuk Lagoon became eternally inscribed into the war's history after Japanese bombers attacked the US military base of Pearl Harbor in Hawai'i on December 7, 1941, which destroyed the American Pacific flotilla and cemented Japan's dominion in the Pacific. In consequence, the US formally entered the Second World War and thus Oceania ultimately became embroiled. For the Pacific, it marked the beginning of a new military epoch with aircraft carriers and submarines populating its waters, while the islands turned into chess pieces in outsiders' war strategies. In retaliation for Pearl Harbor, the US Air Force started with neutralization air raids on Japan's marine in Chuuk in 1944, beginning almost two years of continual bombing. In the end, hardly any coconut trees were left standing, much of the reef was damaged, and famine and incredible suffering ruled (Poyer 2004). That same year, US military also started to drop bombs on Guam and the Northern Marianas followed by an amphibious assault to recapture the islands. Impressive is the sheer number of troops and material that flooded the islands. During the campaign, 535 US military ships carrying 127,570 military personnel approached the islands of Saipan and Tinian. Some 180,000 shells sprinkled the islands, accompanied by heavy naval and aerial bombing for two days to prepare the shores and islands for the amphibious landings. Walking them today, one still finds artillery shells and caves with blackened rock from flamethrowers used to drive out hidden soldiers.

For the Sixtieth Commemoration of the battles for Saipan and Tinian (Commonwealth of the Northern Mariana Islands) in 2004, students from kindergarten and schools listened to their elders accounting their own experiences during war or as they were told by their parents and kin. In these memories, the contemporary witnesses who were children at the time, report how they have seen their fathers, pregnant mothers, siblings, and kin injured or shot dead by crossfire, how they became prey to the bombings, etc. None of the witnesses has survived the assault without scars on their bodies or their souls as the Japanese drove the local Chamorro population into the hills where they had to endure severe hunger, thirst, and fear in caves and dugouts (Tuten-Puckett and Pacific STAR Center for Young Writers 2004).

In the end, 3,426 American soldiers died, 13,099 were wounded. On the Japanese side, 24,000 had been killed, 1,780 captured. Some 8,000 Japanese escaped imprisonment by jumping off the cliffs on the northern end of Saipan after they had pushed their family members to death. Nearly one thousand islanders did not survive the liberation. When the islanders could finally leave the camps to which they had been allocated after the assault, they found their islands devastated, with houses and trees flattened. For the Pacific War as much as for the Second World War, the battles of Saipan and Tinian were decisive as on August 6, 1945, the US airplane Enola Gay took off from Tinian to drop the first atomic bomb on Hiroshima (Tuten-Puckett and Pacific STAR Center for Young Writers 2004: vi–vii).

The Second World War turned the Pacific waters and islands into a mass grave for American and Japanese soldiers. As such, Oceania is inextricably bound to the respective national histories, and American and Japanese veterans and descendants of dead soldiers visit the islands in remembrance. As indicated above, also the islanders keep the war actively alive as part of their collective cultural memory—all the more as time perception and historicity in Oceania differ from Western concepts of lineal temporal progress: "I have memories of a war that took place before I was born" (Diaz 2001: 155). With this sentence, Micronesian historian Vicente Diaz speaks to the way(s) even younger generations still feel the war's impact on the islands as memories of the war are saved, preserved, and passed on in local stories and songs. "These stories inhabit my mind and body," Diaz continues, and at the same time, he is "becoming increasingly aware of the political costs of such memories and the narratives they spin as they bolster American hegemony on this island" (155). The war's legacies are thus manifold and prominent in today's island life all over Oceania.

WAR LEGACIES

On the island of Guam, every July 21, the landing of American military forces and the successful recapture of the island from the Japanese in 1944 is commemorated and celebrated with colorful parades, a fair, and other events. "Liberation Day," however, leaves local historian Vicente Diaz pondering upon the motive for the American military operation, which was for strategic reasons rather than to free the Chamorros. To him, the festivities thus touch questions of decolonization and Chamorro identity. "How to unpack that one day?" (2001: 157), he wonders, which means different things to different people: to some, it is a sign of continuous loyalty to the United States. Others use it to demonstrate their resistance to the ongoing American military presence on the island, renaming the day "Reoccupation Day" (169). Diaz explains this ambivalence as a process of postcolonialism: while the local norm of reciprocity admonishes the Chamorro to pay back liberation and the material goods and food the Americans brought after the military intervention with loyalty, love, and land, they more and more become disillusioned, as reciprocity seems to be never ending and is never returned. Instead, ongoing US strategic interests have led to struggles over land for military usage and keep pushing the islands into other nations' war games (162, 169), as for example in 2017, when North Korea threatened to launch nuclear missiles against US military facilities on Guam as a reaction to US President Trump's provocations.[1]

The most peculiar display of Indigenous appropriations of material and behavioral aspects that came from beyond the island shores, especially during the Pacific War, are probably the so-called cargo cults of Melanesia where the sheer existence and amount, but also the seemingly wasteful usage of material goods—cargo—the colonialists and soldiers brought to the isolated villages awed the locals. During the war, allied troops brought masses of military and other technical equipment, fridges, radios, canned foods, and other goods. Flown to and dropped at isolated places attached to parachutes, they deeply impressed upon the islanders. In lack of any other explanation, it was clear to the islanders that the ancestors were the only might that could accomplish such a task, and the foreigners therefore must have a special relationship to them. When the delivery of new cargo stopped after the war, the locals—under the leadership of charismatic individuals—tried to lure the ancestors into more cargo by taking up behavior and practices they had observed from the soldiers. They built wooden airplanes and antennae, made new airstrips, remodeled uniforms, lit beacons, and waited. In some cases, their conviction of the return of cargo was so strong that they forwent gardening and other customary practices, resulting in far-reaching sociocultural change (Diaz 2001: 116).

Thus, for the Pacific Islanders, the war represents a caesura that brought novelty and disruption, evoking, challenging, and finally transforming former structures in the islands. After the war, however, the islanders found themselves reapportioned to previous colonial domains and the exploitation of their lands for mining, their waters for fishing, and whole islands for military installations continued colonial economic and political logic. As islanders became increasingly dissatisfied with their political dependency and economic exploitation, they started independence movements and protested the foreigners' operations at their shores and on their islands. Although the gradual political liberation has been celebrated as the dawning of a new Pacific Way, formal decolonization has also brought stormy waters. Secessionist movements and civil unrest from the late 1950s on demonstrate how difficult the process of nation building can be when different interests have to be integrated.

This is especially true for Melanesia, which is the most populous as well as ethnically, culturally, and linguistically most diverse area of Oceania. Be it the civil war between the State of Papua New Guinea and the islanders of Bougainville between 1988 and 1999 (Mückler 2000: 13) or the military putsches in Fiji, what seem to be mostly ethnic conflicts are just as much a struggle for power, jobs, and resources and as such is the outcome of various postcolonial developments. In the Solomon Islands, for example, islanders from Guadalcanal revolted against Malaita Islanders who hold most economic key positions while people from Guadalcanal take little or no part at all in economic activities. This dates back to the recapture of Guadalcanal by US troops from the Japanese and the subsequent set-up of a large military basis that later turned into the capital Honiara. Islanders from neighboring Malaita were massively employed during the construction and kept moving to Guadalcanal ever since. Yet, while the imbalance between the capital and the other islands in the periphery, together with disputes over land rights on Guadalcanal, feed the conflict, also this is only seemingly a rivalry between island groups and has in fact a long history, interlinked with colonial complexities and postwar developments. In his detailed analysis, Mückler points to the heterogeneous and small-scale societal set-up of the many dispersed islands that knew little cooperation or were outright antagonist before they were pooled to become the nation of the Solomon Islands in 1978.

For some islands in Oceania, the war paradoxically also accounts for today's only worthwhile tourist attractions in the form of diving. At Espiritu Santo, Vanuatu, the diving spot "million dollar point" marks the location at which hundreds of vehicles and tons of other material were drowned after the war as it was cheaper than return the transport (Mückler 2009b: 115–16). In Micronesian Chuuk, where the US drowned the Japanese Navy in "Operation Hailstone" in 1944, the wrecks of ships and planes have been conquered once again over the years—this time by corals and other marine life and thus offer some of the world's finest diving (Figure 5.3). Currently, however, the dive treasures

FIGURE 5.3 Bow gun on the *San Francisco Maru*. © Brandi Mueller/Getty Images.

represent a turning tide as the wrecks grow into ticking time bombs and the corrugating material starts to set free the machineries' heavy oil and other pollutants.

These war legacies illustrate how political and sociocultural proceedings indeed link the Pacific Islands to world history. Yet, especially the world's postwar division into east and west, respectively the Cold War between the United States and the Soviet Union poignantly steered Oceania's history and linked it eternally to the rest of the world. With the end of the Second World War, the Micronesian Islands, for example, came under a unique "strategic" trusteeship of the United Nations under the administration of the US Department of the Navy. The Trust Territory of the Pacific Islands (TTPI) was not to answer to the General Assembly as other trust territories but to the Security Council in which the United States exercised veto power. While the United States considered former enemy Japan as an ally, the Micronesian Islands now played the central military strategic role as a bulwark between United States and Soviet ideology, which greatly influenced the region's development. The day after the Japanese attacked Pearl Harbor in 1941, the US Navy commissioned anthropologists and other scientists from prestigious universities including Yale to collect whatever information was available on the islands and to compile military handbooks on the region (Kiste and Falgout 1999: 11, 17). The region, however, was not only of military strategic interest but also has become a promising market for the United States, and in 1946, the United States Commercial Company carried out an economic survey with additional data on labor, agriculture, forestry, marine resources, mineral exploitation, transportation, and the like (Hanlon 1998: 88). By 1980, the United States conducted more trade across the Pacific than across the Atlantic (MacIntosh 1987: 1). Thus, as in colonial times, traders and soldiers again acted hand in hand and the United States saw the Pacific as an "American Lake" at their disposal. The islanders, however, once more gained only little from it, because while the United States hermetically closed its dominion to outsiders, inside development was restricted to military policy and the Trust Territory soon resembled rather a "Rust Territory." Thus, apart from their function as a military bulwark between the United States and the Soviet Union, the islands seem to have moved to the edge of the world again. This did not change once the reign had shifted to civil administrations as contemporary writer Willard Price sums up:

> They are administered by the Department of the Interior, yet they are as far exterior as any land could be. Are they inside of outside? Domestic agencies of the national government won't touch them because they are outside. They don't qualify for foreign aid because they are inside.
>
> (1966: 217)

The gamble of the islands' place in the world characterized also the debates about political independence that commenced in the 1960s. As representatives from the six island districts could not agree on a common Micronesian solution for independence, they engaged in individual negotiations with the United States in which both sides knew about the other's importance for themselves. While the Micronesians have become dependent on outside money to finance their government and state services, the United States was keen to keep transit and porting rights as well as land use rights for their military bases and testing grounds. Eventually, they entered into Compacts of Free Association, which, however, manifest and perpetuate neocolonialism where the United States obtains full international defense and security authority in return for funding the government.[2]

With the bombings of Nagasaki and Hiroshima in 1945, the Second World War came to an almost sudden end—at least officially and regarding direct war action. The Pacific Islanders, however, found themselves once more between competing and conflicting nations, who continued to ignore or blatantly disregard the islanders' lives and island environment. Only three months later, the United States decided on its atomic bomb program Operation Crossroads. The first bomb exploded on July 1, 1946, at the Bikini atoll, Republic of the Marshall Islands. The UK and France also had nuclear programs in Oceania. Hence, the end of the Second World War did not mean the end of civil unrest or militarization in the Pacific. In fact, it heralded a new dimension of conflict and military history, the darkest chapter of which might be the years of nuclear testing in which the Pacific Islanders "have become pawns in East-West rivalry" (McIntosh 1987: 7).

THE NUCLEAR PACIFIC

My island is contaminated. I have three tumours [sic] in me, and I'm frightened. I don't know whether I should have children or not, because I don't know if I will have a child that is like a jellyfish baby. All I know is that I must travel the world and share our story of the bombs, so that we can stop them—before they get to you.

(Darlene Keju, Marshallese activist and educator 1951–96, quoted in Maclellan 2014)

In 2014, people of Oceania commemorated the sixtieth anniversary of the explosion of "Bravo"—a nuclear device one thousand times as powerful as the bomb of Hiroshima and thus the largest and most powerful atomic bomb ignited by the United States in history. The explosion took place on March 1, 1954, at Bikini atoll in the Marshall Islands, which are part of Micronesia (Figure 5.4). The 150 Bikini Islanders were given one month's notice to vacate the atoll with the argument that their land was needed for testing "for the good of mankind

FIGURE 5.4 Nuclear Weapon Test at Bikini Atoll, Micronesia, July 25, 1946. © John Parrot/Stocktrek Images/Getty Images.

and to end all wars" as Commodore Ben Wyatt, the military governor of the Marshall Islands, explained to them (Niedenthal 2002).

Moreover, the detonation of "Bravo" at Bikini atoll demonstrates the hubris of the United States regarding the exploitation of people's health and well-being. Contrary to US announcement, the wind carried tons of contaminated fallout material to the south instead of to the north of the by-then emptied Bikini atoll and adjoining waters. Five centimeters of radioactive dust settled on the inhabited atoll of Rongelap. Its inhabitants, however, were evacuated only days after. The deathly dust also reached other atolls, affected US service personnel, and led to the death of a Japanese fisher in the area (McIntosh 1987: 125). Years later, in 1982, the Defense Nuclear Agency admitted to have known about the shifted winds some six hours prior but did not stop the test. The contaminated islanders reportedly were kept unclear about their destiny, playing in the fallout dust. Eventually, they were moved to Kwajalein and tested by US doctors that were flown in for the cause, while the radiated American service personnel were flown home and dispersed (128). The laboratory that was commissioned by the US Department of Energy to conduct studies on the effect of radiation on the islanders concluded that the 239 irradiated Marshallese provide the only knowledge about the effects of radioactive fallout on human beings, for example, about the "chromosome damage that knows no temporal or genealogical limit" (DeLoughrey 2013: 171). It results, for example, in high levels of thyroid cancer and leukemia, or in the deformation of newborn babies as this woman testifies: "Some of the women gave birth to creatures like cats, rats and the insides of turtles. Most women had miscarriages, including myself who gave birth to something unlike a human. Some women gave birth to things resembling grapes and some women even stopped having children, including me" (Alcalay 2002: 28). In spite of its disastrous consequences, until 1958, twenty-two more bombs were dropped on Bikini. The United States nevertheless declared the atoll safe for resettling in 1970, but corrected its conclusion only eight years later. Bikinians had to return to their nuclear exile along with people from Rongelap of which one women comments: "For almost 60 years, we have been displaced from our homeland, like a coconut floating in the sea with no place to call home" (Maclellan 2014: 7). Difficulties to adjust to unfamiliar ecological settings on other islands additionally aggravated the loss of their homeland.

Answering to public outrage and a plea to court by Bikini and other atoll islanders, the US military assented to a return to some of the islands after a basic clean up. Contaminated soil was transferred to the island Runit in the Enewetak atoll and dumped in a crater left by a previous nuclear explosion. The crater is filled with 101,498 cubic meters of radiating material and capped with a concrete dome—the Runit Dome. The dome measures a diameter of 120 meters, cost about $239 million and is supposed to seal off the dangerous material forever. The island itself, however, has been declared unsafe for at least 240,000 years. In 1980, the first people started to return to their cleaned islands. Yet, due to the removal of the soil, the sandy atoll islands no longer sustain horticulture and people henceforth rely on US compensation payments (Pazifik aktuell 2018a). How costly the future of the Pacific's nuclear past is shows also in the one hundred million euros France put into a modernized nuclear monitoring system at uninhabited Moruroa atoll in 2018, where the Centre d'Expérimentation du Pacifique bunkers radioactive waste in 140 mineshafts. Atolls, however, are made of porous coral stone through which radioactive material may seep into the ocean. The surveillance thus aims at the coral basis and its potential collapse, for example through storm waves. Although only a few Polynesian workers were hired in the center during the French nuclear testing phase (1966–1996), the compensation payments were a major income for the territory (Pazifik aktuell 2018b).

The tests evaporated whole islands or made them uninhabitable, partly for several thousand years. The damage inflicted upon people and environment will accompany generations to come while they continue their struggle for reconnaissance and compensation. Whole island populations were dispelled from their land and keep waiting for the day they are able to return. Land, it is important to emphasize, does not simply mean property to the islanders but guarantees a continued link to their ancestors and associated sociopolitical claims as well as a to their family's history—ultimately it fosters and secures their identity and sense of belonging. It is a connection with emotional as well as physical aspects as people of Oceania not only feel related to their kin but also to their land. Vandalism or destruction of their land due to radiation and the detonation of bombs or people's displacement from their land equal injury or loss of a family member. Thus, even though the tests have finally stopped, the people cannot find peace as they continue to battle for justice.

Albeit to people of Oceania expropriation and dislocation mean ongoing psychological stress and anxiety as well as concern for subsequent generations, islanders were expelled from their shores and islands whenever foreign nations needed them for their purposes. In continuation of their military program in the islands, from 1959 on, the United States has heavily securitized the United States Army-Kwajalein Atoll (USAKA) and locals are under constant observation, allowed only in certain sections with certain passes. Again, the islands in the middle of the Pacific play a key role to people and their proceedings far beyond the island shores. At Kwajalein Missile Range, intercontinental ballistic missiles fired from Vandenburgh Air Force Base in California are monitored and hosted. The missiles take only some thirty minutes at 16,000 kilometers per hour for the 7,700-kilometer journey and crash into the testing base at the lagoon at 8,000 kilometers per hour, or are the target of anti-satellite weapons fired from Kwajalein. Several hundred flights per month reach the islands to bring American goods that keep US scientists happy there, while Kwajalein people were relocated to neighboring Ebeye, which has become heavily overpopulated and hosts the first slum of Oceania with "apartheid"-like conditions. Although it is unlikely, people still hope to be able to return one day. Their attempt to reoccupy their land in 1982, named "Operation Homecoming," however, led to retaliation by the United States through the withholding of their rent payment to the islanders, worth $1 million (McIntosh 1987: 131, 134). In this action, it becomes clear that Americans continue to see land as saleable real estate, whereas to the islanders, land is central to their identity and feeling of belonging.

In the end, over 230 nuclear and hydrogen explosions between 1945 and 1996 turned the Pacific Ocean into a "nuclear cesspool" (Schmidt 1986: 25). Further pollution was impending when several Pacific Rim nations discussed the underwater seascape as a possible disposal site for their nuclear waste or contaminated test residue. Japan's plan of dumping its nuclear waste into the Marianas Trench was stopped just in time by Mariana Islanders who by chance learned about the proceedings from the newspapers and with the help of a biologist who studied the dumping of thousands of barrels with nuclear waste between 1946 and 1968 off the Californian coast. He argued that there is no guarantee that no radioactive particles escape within years and eventually accumulate in the human food chain. In addition, too little is known about maritime processes and in 1977, of the 50,000 barrels, only 140 could still be localized. The news from the Marianas soon traveled around Oceania and thus added a new dimension to the fight for a nuclear-free Pacific (Vinke 1984: 95–7).

Albeit Western imaginary fixated the islands of Oceania as small and isolated, where the little land and few people are legitimate victim to world safety, their inhabitants reached global recognition and support in their fight against the military exploitation and radiation of their homes. Although at least in the beginning, the development of the Pacific nuclear programs were enticing to island leaders for the prospect of money, infrastructural development and jobs, local and global civil society, churches, women's groups, and others stood up in union for peace and justice, and the Nuclear Free Pacific movement became the world's biggest antinuclear movement. Over decades, Pacific Islands jointly lobbied to establish a regional nuclear-free zone. A major role in its negotiation played the South Pacific Forum (now Pacific Islands Forum), the regional organization of independent South Pacific island states, Australia, and New Zealand, which started its protest in 1971.[3] In 1973, the resistance intensified and was carried across the Pacific by international antinuclear groups, such as Greenpeace. Its vessel "Rainbow Warrior" became a tragic celebrity, when French intelligence agents, killing one of its crew, sank it in Auckland Harbor on July 10, 1985, on its way to Muroroa atoll. Only a few months later, the Nuclear Free Zone Treaty, also known as the Treaty of Rarotonga, was signed in August 1985, on the day forty years after the bombing of Hiroshima and Nagasaki. The treaty zone, however, excludes most atolls and islands with a great concentration of deployed weapons or testing grounds, for example Kwajalein. Ten years prior, the Nuclear Free and Independent Pacific Movement (NFIPM) was established at a conference in Suva, Fiji, and generated a series of other undertakings and declarations, linking the nuclear question to Indigenous campaigns for self-determination and political independence. As a delegate from New Hebrides stated: "The main objective of this conference is to end nuclear tests in the Pacific, but the more we discuss it, it becomes obvious that the main cause is colonialism" (quoted in Maclellan 2014: 10). NFIPM thus campaigned not only against nuclear testing but also against the dumping of nuclear wastes in the Pacific Ocean, the transport of nuclear materials through Pacific island fishing grounds, and the mining of uranium on Indigenous land.

How deeply intertwined the protest against nuclear destruction of the islands and the struggle for their political self-determination were, and what role the United States played, shows the contest over Palau's political future that went on until 1994. Along with most other Micronesian Islands, Palau was part of the US Trust Territory of the Pacific Islands. As Palau negotiated her options of association with the United States along with political independence, the nuclear and military question delayed any agreement, and Palau became the first nation to adopt a nuclear-free constitution in 1979. While the United States were keen on developing military options in the Palauan Islands, which are perfectly located between Japan, the Philippines, and Guam, the islanders vehemently rejected any military prospect in light of the tragedy of their Marshallese neighbors, and in the shadow of the bloody Second World War battles, arguing: "After soldiers come, war comes" (MacIntosh 1987: 135–7). Neither economic pressure nor intensive "voter education" by Americans, arguing that they will keep the Soviets off the islands were successful—the Palauans' had heard the same promise regarding the United States from the Japanese prior to the war. The controversy could not be solved in six rounds of negotiation until 1994. The nuclear consequences and battles over compensation continue also in the Marshall Islands, which encumber the relationship with the United States. With the Compact of Free Association in 1986, the Marshallese received $150 million for nuclear damage compensation but only if people of Bikini atoll and Kwajalein dropped their legal action against the United States with the Nuclear Claims Tribunal (*Newsweek*, August 11, 1986, quoted in McIntosh 1987: 133).

Whereas the idea of enclosed and isolated islands have long nourished their imaginary as perfect laboratories, the nuclear era is certainly the perverted climax of the scientific "use" of islands, their flora, fauna, and human societies. In her intriguing essay on "The myth of isolates" literary scholar Elizabeth DeLoughrey (2013) demonstrates how especially the island metaphor of isolation served the US Atomic Energy Commission to morally legitimate their tests. Pictures and aerial videos emphasized the isolation while the promotion of the tests as "radiation ecology" linked them to ecosystem studies, which are modeled on the idea of a closed system. After the explosion of the fifteen-megaton thermonuclear weapon "Bravo," the contaminated atoll islanders thus became the perfect scientific test group as they are relatively isolated and of the same genetic group. The United States effectively constructed the sandy atolls of the Marshall Islands as isolates and turned them "into the contained spaces of laboratory, which is to say a suppression of island history and Indigenous presence" (172). This way, they created a closed-off space used for scientific experimentation, swiftly legitimizing the relocation of island societies and the long-term destruction of whole islands to be minor sacrifices in return for global security. The story of the nuclear nomads from Bikini and other atolls, however, demonstrate that coral island environments are not simply interchangeable but singularities with varying livelihood options, while the sense of belonging to a certain piece of land is not easily overcome by the people.

To sum up, the legacy of the nuclear fallout settled on the islands, on the shores, on coral surfaces—everywhere—as an unforgiving memory that will last ten thousand years (Fujitani, White, and Yoneyama 2001: 12). In some cases, it even turned the island-scape upside down. "Bravo" left a crater two thousand meters wide and seventy-six meters deep—creating an "anti-island" (DeLoughrey 2013: 171). Furthermore, radiation did not stay on the island but instead traveled around the world. Baldacchino and Clark (2013) cynically resume that through the dispersal of radiation that can be found all around the globe in matter, the world population has ecologically become islanders.

In their resistance, inhabitants of the Nuclear Pacific stirred global consciousness about an increasingly militarized planet (DeLoughrey 2012: 171). Marshallese former foreign minister Tony de Brum, who in his youth had eyewitnessed the destructive impact of "Bravo," received the "Distinguished Peace Leader" prize of the Nuclear Age Peace Foundation in 2012 and the Nuclear Free Future Award in 2015 for his unremitting dedication to a nuclear-free Pacific and to the compensation of harmed fellow islanders. A year prior to his death, he was awarded the 2016 Arms Control of the Year prize together with the Marshallese government and was nominated for the Nobel Peace Prize. He used his experiences in local, regional, and international politics also in fighting for climate change mitigation and justice. Along with de Brum, islanders of Oceania have become role models in global climate change politics. Portrayed as one of the first victims to sea-level rise and other impacts of the changing climate, island nations and activists adopted various strategies to gain attention as well as to gain money and find possible alternatives to deteriorating living conditions in their homes.

CLIMATE WARRIORS

At the turn of the twentieth century, people living in Oceania have to adapt to rising seas and other impacts of climate change, both physically and mentally. Islanders who are used to environmental calamities, have become disconcerted as high tides and storm surges have become more potent while droughts became more intense and tropical cyclones more frequent. In the main lagoon of Chuuk in the Federated States of Micronesia, for example, people used to eagerly wait for the so-called *kúún ennefen*—seasonal high waters—for they brought certain deep-water fish into the lagoon that the islanders cherish. Today, however, the waters ingress further inland, flooding coastal houses, turning paths into slippery mudslides, hampering the kids' way to school, spoiling taro swamps, making life more complicated. When it happened again in 2011, a villager claimed: "This we would not call *kúún ennefen*. This tide is even higher, so we are scared, we don't know why it happens. Now it's coming over the road, into our houses. The high tides come more often now" (Hofmann 2016) (Figure 5.5). While repairing the damage is costly for the villagers, even more disconcerting is how these floods exceed previous experiences and can no longer be linked to established knowledge and response behavior, leaving behind notions of uncertainty and fear.

Inundating and eroding shores and islands, however, also stir the thoughts of people living safely off any coast, and Oceania has become a media-effective

FIGURE 5.5 Flood event at Chukiyénú, Toon, Chuuk, November and December 2011. © Rebecca Hofmann 2011.

projection site for our fears and hopes about the future environmental state of the earth. As a microcosm, or new laboratory for the impacts of climate change, Australian geographer Carol Farbotko suggests that the islands get rid of their imaginary only once they have disappeared and thus represent the "absolute truth of the urgency of climate change" (2010: 47). Elsewhere, Farbotko analyzed the constructions of climate change displacement in an Australian newspaper and illustrates how the marginalizing discourses of vulnerability silences alternative constructions of island identity, which would allow a constitution of them as resilient and resourceful (Farbotko 2005: 279). For though skillful mobility was the prerequisite for the conquest and successful habitation of Oceania, in current discussion about climate-change-related human movement, mobility as a positive expression of successful survival is curiously absent, to give but one example (Farbotko 2012). Instead, a great number of scientific, political, and especially media discourses feed into brute generalizations of "the islands" and "the climate refugee," positioning them in a *pars pro toto* equation that reinforces old imaginative geographies of vulnerable islands and weak islanders in opposition to durable and powerful continents.

Narratives of smallness and isolation thus victimize the islanders without taking into account their adaptive capabilities, which have ensured their survival for thousands of years—forming a new eco-colonial discourse in which islanders position themselves in various ways. After the initial uncertainty, Pacific Islanders recollected their history as warriors and started to substitute their insecurity by fighting spirit. People of Tuvalu reject being pushed into the role of victims by the global discourse (Farbotko and Lazrus 2012), Carteret Islanders named their organization that supervises any relocation "sailing the waves of our own" (Tulele Peisa), and Kiribati lobbies for its "Migrate with Dignity" policy. The island states, thus, approach the issue of climate change with different strategies but unite in their effort of pushing it into global consciousness. To gain moral authority, island leaders effectively appropriate the Western discourse on islands being small and vulnerable, eliciting attention in international meetings and committees. "Smallness," in fact, "is one of the Pacific Islanders' key resources in their political battles with the international community," observes Wolfgang Kempf (2009: 201). For Tuvalu, Michael Goldsmith (2015) delineates this "big smallness" along the massive influx of aid and people (scientists, development workers, journalists, and what could be called voyeurism tourists). Their effort paid off in 2014, when the United Nations announced the International Year of the Small Island Developing States through which the islands received global attention and assistance and even more so in 2017, when Fiji chaired the 23rd Climate Change Conference in Bonn, Germany. Pacific Islands are given and take on the role as exemplary forerunners of sustainable development and green economies. As with previous issues, climate change is not only an ultimate physical threat the islanders themselves did not bring about but also a foreign concept entangled with specific epistemologies and political complexities enmeshed in present North–South relations. In their fight against the life-threatening consequences of climate change, islanders thus simultaneously call for the final decolonization not only of political systems but also of discourses and epistemologies. Former Prime Minister Anote Tong (2012) of Kiribati recapitulated:

> Over the years we have convinced ourselves that there is very little we can do as small island states to influence global events though they will affect our lives so profoundly. Perhaps in our typical trusting Pacific Way, we have always believed that our bigger brothers will look after our interests in this highly competitive global community. And whilst that may be true to some extent, experience has shown us that each have their own priorities [...]. The challenge of Climate Change has been the severest test of the international community's genuine desire and ability to redress imbalances wherever they occur; [...] that the rights of all citizens of this planet to a good life is guaranteed.

Islanders seek the "ownership" of the climate change discourse concerning their world, because, as Barnett and Adger (2003) admonished, the real climate danger might be the dooming discourse and giving-up reactions rather than physical implications. Against this victimizing discourse, Pacific civil society and activists prominently started to rebel. Marshallese poet Kathy Jetnil-Kijiner opened the United Nations Climate Summit in New York on September 23, 2014, with a poem to her baby daughter, promising her that she will not give up their islands without a fight, calling to action the world leaders assembled there. Most media-effective are also the "Climate Warriors" of the Pacific who form part of the global NGO 350°. The homepage clearly states their mission:

> For 20 years we've asked world leaders to take action to stop polluting the atmosphere. We couldn't wait any longer. Now, warriors of the Pacific are rising peacefully to protect the Pacific Islands from climate change. Our message: **We are not drowning. We are fighting.**
> ("Pacific Climate Warriors" n.d., emphasis in the original)

CONCLUSION

The Pacific islands and shores, this chapter has illustrated, play a central role in the world's conflicts of the global age. War has always been part of the sociocultural island life and its impressions and memories are frozen and passed on in myths, stories, songs, sociocultural structure, or land rights. Bellicose campaigns from different groups on the same or between islands have accompanied the very beginning of human settlement in Oceania, yet reached a new blood and death toll with the arrival of colonists and their weaponry. Based in political contentions of foreign nations, the islands were more than once shaken and lastingly affected by acts of war although not a single bullet was discharged on them. Guam in the Marianas, for example, had nothing to do with the causes or the conduct of the Spanish–American War, yet the American victory in 1898 has taken Guam to a crucial turning point in her history as it transformed the island into a major military base, drawing it into the modern global war theater. Since the Second World War, which demarcates a lasting incision in the life of the islanders, triggering cultural adaptions and new social movements, Pacific Islanders had to sail along choppy waters to independence and navigate through challenges arising from civilian conflicts and transformations in the sociocultural system in many of the newly formed countries. Moreover, the Pacific waters continue to bear the scars of nuclear tests, while struggling with the neocolonial exploitation of their natural resources or the current issue of the Great Garbage Patch that marks the transition from the Nuclear into a Plastic Ocean. Nevertheless, the islands of the tropical Pacific continue to be an imaginary rather than a place where European clichés of the islands as paradisiacal gardens still prevail. Doomsday scenarios of sinking islands thus touch also the heart of non-islanders and move their island homes once more into the center of the globe's destiny. Pacific Islanders themselves struggle with how to face a threat that could be the final conflictual encounter and have decided to not to surrender without a fight. For them, land and sea are the source of their livelihood, their history and identity, connected to the surrounding island-scape through family lore and dispersed kin relations. Oceania's history in the *Mare Pacifico*—thus named for its supposedly peaceful waters—has been one of conflict and struggle. Today's Climate Warriors are maybe also an answer to these martial legacies, linked by the islanders' opposition against continental notions such as "smallness" and "isolation." Because to them, their home represents a "sea of islands" rather than "islands in a vast sea" (Hau'ofa 1994). In the unforgotten words of Epeli Hau'ofa from Tonga:

> Oceania is vast, Oceania is expanding. Oceania is hospitable and generous. Oceania is humanity rising from the depths of brine and regions of fire deeper still, Oceania is us. We are the sea, we are the Ocean, we must wake up to this ancient truth and together use it to overturn all hegemonic views that aim ultimately to confine us again, physically and psychologically, in the tiny spaces which we have resisted accepting as our sole appointed place, and from which we have recently liberated ourselves.
>
> (1994: 160)

CHAPTER SIX

Travelers

Vertical and Horizontal Voyaging On and In the Nonhuman Ocean

HELEN M. ROZWADOWSKI

For a cultural history of the ocean the category of "travelers" might appear more terrestrial than oceanic, given that travelers move from place to place, or go to distant lands. "Place" and "land" seem to neglect the sea, even if, perhaps, travelers move over the sea to their destinations. If travelers can refer to nomadic persons, who move around rather than living in a fixed spot, that presents a challenge for an environment like the ocean that people cannot (yet) inhabit permanently. Intriguingly, travelers are also nautical mechanisms that move: usually on iron rings that slide along a rope or rod on a ship, to enable a line to slide freely along a fixed course. This prevents lines from getting fouled, and sometimes permits sails to be untended during a tack or a jibe. The movement of mechanical travelers fits notions of human travel, including the expectation that most travelers journey outward and then return to more or less the same place (in contrast to people who migrate to live in a new place). The analogy of the mechanical traveler is less apt in the strict limits it imposes on wandering sideways. Human travel conjures distance, geography, novelty, and the possibility of deflection rather than a fixed track.

"Voyagers" might seem a more appropriate term for a cultural history of the sea, because most human sea travelers embark on ships. The word "voyage" can refer to "a course or period of traveling other than by land routes" (Merriam-Webster 2019). Voyagers are typically associated with ships as well as exploring ventures to far away or dangerous places. In recent times voyagers can travel into space as well as on oceans and, with submersibles, also move underneath the surface of the ocean. Travelers, by contrast, would seem by tradition limited to the horizontal dimension of the sea's surface, which might prove a difference between land and sea travel. As for the atmosphere with the possibility of flight, it became possible for travelers to traverse the ocean vertically with the advent in the twentieth century of submersible and scuba technology. When that happened, the ancient Greek term Argonaut, originally meaning literally a sailor on Jason's vessel *Argo*, proffered the twin neologisms of astronaut and aquanaut.

Oceans differ from lands in ways that make writing their history challenging, particularly given the terrestrial leaning of most historical scholarship. Is someone a traveler who departs from and returns to the same place on land, if most of the experience is on—or in—the sea? Is it travel if most of the distance covered is vertical rather than horizontal, such as into the ocean's depths rather than across its surface? Are circumnavigations merely one of many forms of travel or are they special in some way? In terms of experience of the ocean, what are the differences between travelers and non-travelers? Are fishers, merchant sailors, or submariners travelers? Or, are people who work every day on or in the ocean perhaps outside the category? In that case, scientists, writers, activists, students, recreational divers, yachtsmen and yachtswomen, cruise ship passengers, archaeologists, filmmakers, migrants, and others would seem to qualify, if their excursions are periodic rather than virtually daily. Perhaps travelers are necessarily landlubbers who go to sea?

Considered historically, travelers by ship in the nineteenth century and before—that is, those who embarked not as part of their permanent careers but for a singular journey or series of voyages—often recorded their experiences and later communicated them to others. Traveling, then, might integrally involve a process of reflection and the use of media and practices to collect, record, and convey information, experience, reactions, and insights. There is a robust linkage between voyaging and writing long recognized as part of a literary tradition, which scientists embraced in the nineteenth century when the ocean became an object of their scrutiny (Rozwadowski 2016). That this tradition extended widely to include women ocean travelers, and even families, is evident through the writings of Lady Annie Brassey who, with her husband and children, lived aboard their luxury yacht *Sunbeam* from 1876 to 1877 on an eleven-month circumnavigation (Brassey 1878). The famous late nineteenth-century circumnavigation by Joshua Slocum, the first single-handed, globe-circling voyage, aboard his eleven-meter sloop *Spray*, profoundly shaped twentieth-century ocean travel. Slocum's example, and especially his 1900 account, *Sailing Around the World Alone,* fueled the pursuit of solitary and record-setting circumnavigations, a trajectory that overlooked Slocum's lifetime of sailing with his first and second wives and their children (Slocum 1901). Voyaging and writing clearly left a stronger impression than mere voyaging.

This examination of the cultural history of travelers on and in the ocean recognizes several binaries that characterize ocean travelers in the twentieth century, including work versus play as the occasion for experiencing the ocean; technology versus imagination as an important mediator for human engagement with the ocean; and extraction versus addition as the primary vectors of flow of material resources, knowledge, and imaginative constructions. Play joined—and in many cases superseded—work as a significant activity on and in the ocean. For example, physical oceanographers on Pacific expeditions in the 1950s dove to explore reefs and local shipwrecks, unrepentantly mixing fun with their scientific work (Rozwadowski 2010b: 170–1).[1] As modern ocean science emerged, however, starting in the nineteenth century and extending into the twentieth century, the sea did not cease to be perceived as the realm of wonder and mystery that it had been to early modern thinkers (Adamowsky 2015). Imagination remained central to twentieth-century travel even as modern technologies revolutionized the access of human bodies to the ocean. Whereas pre-twentieth-century ocean histories emphasize resource extraction—and to be sure massive extraction continued unabated—new imaginative constructions reshaped cultural interactions with the ocean. For example, the cruise industry actively employed marketing to formulate and propagate the addition of new meanings for ocean travel, such as the invention of round-the-world pleasure cruises in the 1920s as a novel personal goal for leisure travel. At the same time these cruises represented the height of conspicuous consumption recognized by critics in the present as associated with profligate use of resources (Chaplin 2013).

To explore cultural engagement with the ocean in the twentieth century, this chapter examines three representative groups. First, and reflecting the importance of considering all of the ocean and not just its surface, the chapter considers travelers who explored the ocean's third dimension—from the relatively shallow waters visited by spear-fishing skin divers to the vast depths reachable with submersibles. Second, it explores the lingering use of sail for long-distance commercial trade routes into the twentieth century, which created a nursery for the development of modern sail training, an activity that extended the experience of voyaging under sail into the era of air travel. "Tall ships," or, more accurately, traditionally-rigged vessels, drew travelers to sea in pursuit of nostalgia, maritime skill, and personal challenge, extending traditional maritime culture in a highly curated way to the present day. Finally, the chapter grapples with the question of whether the cultural history of ocean travelers is limited to humans. Or are marine animals travelers if they move—or are moved—from one part of the ocean to another, either as part of a seasonal migration or as a result of human activity? The environmental turn suggests consideration of nonhuman ocean history and culture alongside the human.

VERTICAL OCEAN TRAVEL

The underwater realm has hosted human visitors as far back in time as coastal people in Africa, Asia, the Caribbean, and other places dove to gather marine resources such as shellfish, engage in acts of warfare, retrieve valuable canon from wrecked ships, and otherwise conduct activities that required access beneath the sea's surface (Dawson 2006). Hard-hat diving enabled construction and other underwater work in the nineteenth century, but twentieth-century technologies freed human bodies to accomplish an astonishingly wide range of work and play in the ocean, allowing travel to and in the depths. The two world wars extended into the sea through submarine warfare, and the Second World War involved the exploits of so-called "frogmen" engaging in underwater reconnaissance and demolition (Waldron and Gleeson 1950). Technologies to enable humans to dive into ocean waters and travel far beneath the surface inaugurated the novel vertical extension of ocean travel.

While diving began as a subsistence activity pursued by specialists within a society, its spread depended on recreation, not work. In the 1930s, the former First World War pilot Guy Gilpatric adapted aviator's googles to make them waterproof and began diving in the warm, clear Mediterranean waters, chronicling his exploits and promoting the new sport in his guidebook, *The Compleat Goggler* (1934). "One day," Gilpatric explained, "I shoved off from shore on an innocent sight-seeing trip [...] to study the submarine scenery" (1957: 2). Observing the fishes' lack of fear of him, he devised a spear and went after them, impressing beachgoers when he returned from the sea with spectacular catches. Goggling drew people, initially men, underwater for recreation, a decisive shift away from the activities of previous subsistence divers. By 1957, when Gilpatric's book was reprinted for distribution to subscribers of *Skin Diver* magazine, men, women, and even children donned googles and fins and either snorkels or Aqualungs, the brand name of Jacques Cousteau's self-contained breathing apparatus (Figure 6.1).

Cousteau's invention derived from his wartime experience in the French Navy combined with the skin diving he began to do in his spare time to find food during the lean wartime and postwar years (Dugan 1965; Marx [1978] 1990). Underwater action was critical during the Second World War, both the well-known submarine war but also the daring activities of military frogmen who engaged in underwater construction, reconnaissance, demolition, and salvage (Waldron and Gleeson 1950). Some early enthusiasts of diving technology expected that its use would be limited to extremely physically fit experts doing military or commercial work and, indeed, from the perspective

FIGURE 6.1 *Popular Science* cover from July 1953. © Public domain.

of the 1950s, prospects seemed bright for the application of human divers in aquaculture, offshore oil drilling, and potentially other industrial activities anticipated for the continental shelves (Carrier and Carrier 1955; Liebers 1962). The economic promise of the undersea "frontier," as its boosters styled it, continued to animate diving throughout the 1960s, particularly the efforts to develop saturation diving to allow underwater workers to extend productive bottom time relative to the time spent in decompression (Rozwadowski 2018: 175). Starting with the commercial availability of Cousteau's Aqualung in 1949, though, the composition of the community of divers took a surprising turn.

The ranks of frogmen, spearfishers, and underwater workers were soon swelled by the addition of civilians, nonexperts, and beginners, including women as well as men and even coming to include children. Their expanded underwater activities extended to include sight-seeing, photography, treasure-hunting, amateur science, volunteer search and rescue, and far more. The first underwater statue, "Christ of the Depths," installed on the seafloor off the northwest coast of Italy in 1954 to mark a fifteenth-century naval battle site, attracted curious camera-toting divers ("Christ of the Depth" 1954). The San Diego Bottom Scratchers club, formed by spear-fishing breath-holding divers in 1933, exemplifies the expansion of underwater activities as its members who adopted scuba in the 1950s recovered ancient Native American bowls and artifacts from La Jolla Canyon, experimented with gear for underwater filming, and assisted staff from the Scripps Institute of Oceanography with scientific research on kelp beds, seafloor geology, and seabed communities (Rozwadowski 2010b). Diving became so important at Scripps that the institution had to develop a system of diving instruction and protocols that became the basis for the first civilian diving course offered in the United States (Hanauer 1994). Whereas in 1956 there were fewer than two hundred dive clubs, mostly in California and some each in New York and Florida, by 1965, six hundred had formed in every part of the United States (Dalla Valle et al. 1963) (Figure 6.2). An international diving organization was founded in Brussels in 1958, a year before an American umbrella group for scuba clubs appeared (Rozwadowski 2013). Thus, while diving began in France, and California beaches acted, according to pioneer diver and diving historian Eric Hanauer, as an "incubator," this new mode for experiencing the ocean spread rapidly in Europe, North America, and other spots around the globe (Hanauer 1994: 11).

The broad appeal and fast growth of diving drew strength from the proliferation of representations of it in books, films, advertisements, and other media, so that ocean travelers were encouraged to explore the undersea based on things they were reading and viewing. This pattern drew upon the strong historical connection between writing and voyaging, whereby explorers' narratives inspired other travelers, coached them about what to expect and do, and in so doing shaped their perceptions of the places they visited and the meaning of their travels (Foulke 1997; Rozwadowski 2016). Popular cultural representations of diving in the 1950s and 1960s functioned similarly (Rozwadowski 2010b). Movies from the late 1950s included undersea scenes, such as the 1955 monster movie, *It Came From Beneath the Sea,* Irwin Allen's 1961 film *Voyage to the Bottom of the Sea*, and the 1965 James Bond thriller *Thunderball*. The popular television series *Sea Hunt* starring Lloyd Bridges, which ran from 1958 to 1961, included final segments where Bridges directly addressed divers among the audience. One occasional actress who also worked as a stunt double for the program, Zale Parry, drew public attention to the depths not only for her work in Hollywood but also because in 1954 she became the first woman to dive below two hundred feet (60.96 meters), a feat that put her on the front cover of *Sports Illustrated* ("Front Cover" 1955).

Scientists who wrote books for general audiences contributed significantly in the mid-twentieth century to reframing the undersea as an inviting and safe place of wonder, a departure from perceptions of the depths as full of monsters and danger. The naturalist William Beebe's spectacular bathysphere dives to depths noted in his 1934 book title, *Half-Mile Down*, helped associate the ocean's remote recesses with the sublime. In the mid-1950s, the marine ichthyologist Eugenie Clark also attracted public notice for her underwater forays. Her 1953 book, *Lady with a Spear*, provided readers

FIGURE 6.2 Scuba diving training at a pool in Madison, Wisconsin, 1961, with instructor Paul Geisler teaching the buddy breathing method to student Stephanie Morgan. © Wisconsin Historical Society.

with an adventurous account of her pioneering underwater research on fish, invertebrates, and, later, sharks, while her example of diving and teaching her husband and children to dive helped domesticate the ocean, rendering it as an environment accessible to ordinary people. Both Clark and the marine botanist Sylvia Earle wrote about diving while pregnant, a practice that seemed quite natural to their doctors and other experts at the time. Clark shared a literary agent with another writer who significantly reshaped popular understanding of the ocean, Rachel Carson, whose 1951 bestseller, *The Sea Around Us*, invited ordinary people to view the ocean as a place of awe, power, and mystery (Kroll 2008; Rozwadowski 2010b, 2013).

Diving appeared not only inviting and accessible, but also its enthusiasts viewed it as transformative to travelers of the ocean's third dimension. According to a diver in the 1950s, access to the undersea conveyed "privilege [...] to enter an ocean full of strange alien beings," relative to the "millions [...] who went about their daily lives totally unaware of this fascinating world just beyond the shore" (Powell 2001: 8). Other diver-writers in the same decade articulated the "intense psychological effect" produced by "this new degree of freedom and mobility in a strange, beautiful and largely unexplored world" (Carrier and Carrier 1955: 14; see also Dalla Valle et al. 1963: 22). In

1960, at the height of his ocean boosterism, futurist Arthur C. Clarke made the striking claim that, "Everyone who goes underwater becomes a scientist" (1960: 164), conveying both the meaning that divers became explorers and also that undersea travelers experienced heightened powers of observation (Rozwadowski 2010b: 182–3).

Commentators further naturalized the transformative power ascribed to the undersea environment by couching diving as an evolutionary *return* to the sea. Early diver-writers remarked on the ease with which people encountered the undersea and attributed "our quick adaptation to the fluid world" to the fact that divers "are returning to the atmosphere in which life began millions of years ago" (Bridges and Barada 1960: 5; Sweeney 1955: 53). Others noted that "man" has been drawn to the sea, "in which he had his beginnings and whose mineral content is still reflected in the composition of his blood" (Carrier and Carrier 1955: 17). Well-known figures such as Hans Hass, Arthur C. Clarke, and Jacques Cousteau drew similar connections (Hass [1957] 1958; Rozwadowski 2012). Clarke and the rocket scientist Wehner von Braun asserted that human exploration of space extended the evolutionary journey that began with the movement of sea creatures onto land, and that, in turn, ocean exploration served as a prelude to successful space travel (Clarke 2001: 259).[2] The technological mediation of diving gear proved no impediment to imagining the naturalness of human bodies underwater; indeed, technology was often viewed as an extension of the body in evolutionary arguments. A 1955 how-to book on diving explained, "Instead of being a man or woman inside your equipment, you make your equipment a part of you" (Sweeney 1955: 43). In a 1962 speech, Cousteau announced to the first World Congress on Underwater Activities that "a new species of human being is evolving, *Homo aquaticus*" (Matsen 2009: 16).

The idea that humans could seize control of their own evolution by altering human bodies appealed to Cousteau and others harboring the ambition for people to live and work on the seafloor. During the 1960s Cousteau directed a series of experiments placing divers in seafloor habitats to test the efficacy of saturation diving. Because human bodies absorb nitrogen in deep dives and must spend time decompressing as they ascend to avoid decompression sickness (often called "the bends"), the hope was that, by having divers live at depth, they could spend more time doing useful work relative to time spent in decompression. At the same time as Cousteau's Conshelf program, there were American projects, one undertaken by the inventor-entrepreneur Edwin Link and also the US Navy Sealab program. By the mid-1960s, with the safety demonstrated of underwater habitats placed in depths recommended for recreational divers, habitats began to be constructed by local diving clubs, university engineering students, and private industries. By the late 1970s, over sixty-five habitats were built in seventeen countries in depths from five meters to three hundred meters, used by over eight hundred aquanauts (Miller and Koblick 1995). Many of these ocean-floor visitors, and those who followed their exploits in the media, were inspired by a vision of the undersea as a frontier akin to the nineteenth-century American West, a place that promised food, wealth from extracting minerals and other valuable resources, a site for new undersea industries, and even new living space for the expanding global population (Rozwadowski 2012).

Diving, habitats, and even experimental deep diving limited human travelers to hundreds of meters below the ocean's surface. To go deeper and range far from one's starting point required underwater vehicles that could protect human bodies from the effects of pressure. The story of submarines belongs, of course, to military history, but there is a modest chapter that relates to vertical ocean travel, dating from the imaginative voyage of Jules Verne's *Nautilus*. Most submarines were built by governments for military purposes. Perhaps most notably for its ability to remain submerged for long periods of time the first nuclear-powered submarine, the USS *Nautilus*, was launched in 1954. Yet, the popular enthusiasm and amateur participation in undersea exploration that characterized diving extended to submarines. In 1950 an ex-US marine living in upstate New York built a 3.96-meter submarine in his garage, equipping it with both propellers and tracks for crawling on the bottom, so that it might be used for military reconnaissance landings, salvage, or treasure hunting ("Miniature Sub" 1950).[3] Some Aerojet engineers created an underwater unicycle in a home basement shop in California that could be used alone or with a fiberglass pod enclosure. The latter, though designed with military use in mind, generated a dozen civilian orders upon being listed in the US Divers catalog ("New Ways to Go Under" 1953). In 1960 a Miami ironworker built and tested a 4.88-meter submarine over a Florida reef with the intent of both treasure hunting himself and developing a commercial version ("A Backyard Baby Sub" 1960). These examples have in common that they were reported in the popular American weekly *Life* magazine, which enthusiastically covered diving, habitat experiments, and underwater exploration generally in the 1950s and 1960s, marking these as topics that both attracted the attention of *Life* editors and entertained millions of readers in the United States and beyond.

In the post-Second World War period, private aerospace companies hoping for government contracts for "inner space" exploration and anticipating imminent industrial uses of the seafloor began designing and constructing submersibles that could dive very deep. An early example was the bathyscape *Trieste*, designed by the Swiss inventor August Piccard, manufactured in Italy, and purchased by the US Navy, which used it for a record-breaking 1960 dive to the deepest part of the ocean in the Mariana Trench, an achievement that was chronicled in the book *Seven Miles Down* (Piccard and Dietz 1961). In the mid-1960s, Ocean Dynamics, created by General Dynamics, built the *Star* series of small submersibles for in-house ocean exploration and also for lease to other users, while Lockheed built *Deep Quest* and Westinghouse *Deepstar 4000*. The resulting fleet of small submersibles had longer useful lives than habitats but were never mass-produced for industry as anticipated. A few, such as Woods Hole's famous *Alvin*, had their working lives extended several times over and were featured in the writings of scientist-travelers who discovered deep-sea hydrothermal vent communities, excavated ancient shipwrecks, or explored other parts of the seafloor and water column (Bass 1975; Crane 2004; Van Dover 1996).

The human foray into the ocean's third dimension began in the context of the work of salvage and underwater construction, but expanded dramatically in the twentieth century to encompass play alongside work. Millions of people, including civilians, both women as well as men and also children, entered the undersea to spear-fish, dive on wrecks, and explore. Scuba diving and deep-diving submersibles also created new kinds of underwater work: science, archaeology, photography, and filmmaking, all characterized by the practice of representing and communicating narratives about vertical ocean travel through books, articles, films, and other media. The undersea realm required technology for human access, but motives for going underwater were often tied to the imaginary associated with the action of entering the ocean's depths: romance, adventure, danger, mystery. Imagination in turn shaped changing perceptions of the undersea. In part thanks to direct, visual experience by divers, enthusiasm for extraction as the primary posture toward the ocean gave way to concern for depletions and the active creation of new cultural views of the underwater realm. For example, as spear fishers denuded areas of abalone and other desirable food fish, some divers responded by eschewing spear-guns in lieu of cameras. The failure of underwater habitats to take hold as human undersea domiciles reinforced the role for people of travelers, visitors, and outsiders rather than residents of the ocean.

SAIL TRAINING

While vertical ocean travel involved novel technologies and brand new motives for entering the depths, a very old tradition of cultural engagement with the sea survived into the twentieth century, evolving into the modern sail training industry. Characterized by a dynamic combination of recreation, adventure, education, and employment, sail training combined traditional maritime technology (although often using modern materials) with selected aspects of traditional maritime culture. Ocean cruises for pleasure emerged from the opulent steamships of the late nineteenth century, whose amenities such as electricity and gourmet meals transformed the experience of wealthy transatlantic passengers by distracting them from the ocean. While the cruise industry firmly embraced middle-class travelers in the twentieth century, the experience for passengers remained focused on shipboard social activities and spaces insulated from the sea (Brinnin 1971). Adventurer-seekers turned to alternatives aboard sailing vessels plying the last ocean trading routes where steam could not yet compete, such as between shallow river ports around the Chesapeake Bay accessible by nimble coasting schooners with centerboards or the long-haul nitrate fertilizer and grain trades around Cape Horn and to Australia (Brooks 1988; Newby 1956). For example, Sterling Hayden, a high school dropout who later became a decorated war hero, went to sea as a mate on a schooner at age sixteen and worked on steamships and other schooners before skippering a square-rigger. He used his subsequent, storied Hollywood acting career to support his sailing obsession, including his schooner *Wanderer*, which lent its name as the title of his 1963 autobiography (Hayden 1963; Krebs 1986). The British travel writer, Eric Newby, based his 1956 memoir *The Last Grain Race* on his 1938 voyage aboard the four-masted barque *Moshulu*, which he joined at age eighteen under inspiration from sea tales told by a family friend (Newby 1956).

While Hayden, Newby, and others like them imbibed in a tradition of reflexive writing and voyaging that had been forged by explorers, novelists, and scientists, new technologies proffered the alternate media of film for twentieth-century ocean travelers, including Irving Johnson who is often credited as the founder of modern sail training. A native of landlocked Hadley, Massachusetts, the youthful Johnson dreamed of adventures under sail before his inaugural 1929 voyage from Germany to Chile around Cape Horn in the 105-meter, four-masted barque *Peking*. He documented his first voyage on a square-rigger, and also his preparations back home, involving climbing and standing on the top of telephone poles, in a film titled *Around Cape Horn*, which includes footage of him working aloft at sea, climbing up and sliding down the outward edges of square sails, and working on deck during fierce storms.[4] Johnson met his future wife, Electa, or Exy, while serving as mate aboard the schooner *Wander Bird*, whose captain took paying customers on transatlantic crossings under sail. The pair developed the model of character-building sail training starting in 1933 by taking young men and women on voyages aboard their series of vessels named *Yankee* (Figure 6.3). Eighteen-month voyages, seven circumnavigations in all by 1958, alternated with equal periods based in Gloucester, Massachusetts, conducting shorter trips along the Eastern Seaboard and lecturing, writing articles and books, and partnering with *National Geographic* to make two films, all to raise money to support the voyages. The Johnsons raised their two children largely at sea alongside the young people they taught to sail, and left a lasting legacy by directly inspiring a number of ongoing programs, including the Sea Education Association, whose first vessel, the schooner *Westward*, was built in imitation of the *Yankee*, and also indirectly through the mates and

FIGURE 6.3 Irving and Exy Johnson at the wheel of the schooner *Yankee* with their son in 1938. © Mary Evans/SZ Photo/Scherl. Image No. 105118813.

captains they trained, who went on to start numerous other programs under traditional sail (MacLean 2015; Narvaez 1991).[5]

Among the motives for choosing to sail on a traditionally-rigged vessel was rising nostalgia for a grand maritime past that resonated with appreciative readers of the yearning, romantic tone of John Masefield's 1902 poem "Sea Fever": "I must go down to the seas again, for the call of the running tide / Is a wild call and a clear call that may not be denied" (1923: 27–8). Masefield, who sailed on naval and merchant vessels in the 1890s, contributed the generic appellation "tall ship" to represent a general category of sailing vessel for a culture that no longer needed to distinguish between ships, barques, schooners, and other rigs. Nostalgia in part explains the choice by the naturalist Robert Cushman Murphy to ship out on the whaling brig *Daisy* in 1912. During the voyage, this ardent hunter and member of the Boone and Crockett Club enacted the ultimate big game fantasy by convincing a Norwegian gunner to let him shoot a whale, one of many aspects of the experience he chronicled in his 1947 account, *Logbook for Grace* (Kroll 2008).

The end of the Second World War inadvertently provided more opportunities for experiencing traditional maritime culture and technology, as a number of sailing vessels survived the war and were mostly returned not to commercial service but to an array of uses offering the possibility of sailing or experiencing dockside their by-then firmly antiquated maritime technology. The success of the German Flying P Line in the early twentieth century, whose fast and sturdy four-masted, square-rigged barques all began with the letter P, meant that a number of traditionally-rigged vessels were available for maritime revivalists to preserve after the war essentially ended the age of commercial sail (Grasso 2009). The *Padua*, which went to Russia as war reparation, was renamed *Krustenshtern* and used as a sail training ship, while the *Passat*, *Pamir*, and *Peking* also survived the war and returned for a time to merchant service. The German naval training ship, *Horst Wessel*, was taken by the United States after the war, renamed the USS *Eagle*, and continued in use as a sail training ship to build character and discipline through exposure to traditional maritime work and technology. Dozens of countries developed national sail training programs in the second half of the twentieth century that provided traditional sail training focused on maritime technology, leadership, discipline, and personal development (Sail Training International 2019).

Not all sail training employed old vessels that were preserved after their initial uses became obsolete. Replica and modern tall ships were constructed, restored, or converted, such as the schooner *Pride of Baltimore* (a replica of a Baltimore clipper commissioned in 1977), the barque *Picton Castle* (a fishing trawler and minesweeper converted in the 1990s to a barque), the US Brig *Niagara* (a museum exhibit reconstructed to sail in 1990), and the replica slaving schooner *Amistad* (a replica completed in 2000 of the schooner *La Amistad* whose cargo of slaves revolted in 1839), to name just a few. After the postwar nadir, the numbers of traditionally-rigged sailing vessels began to increase and their missions to widen (Parrott 2003).

Starting in the 1960s, scholar-sailors began trying to unlock the secrets of traditional Pacific navigation by studying with expert navigators from Oceania as well as through oral histories and by conducting experimental voyaging on traditional and replica vessels and modern sailing craft (Gladwin 1995; Lewis [1972] 1994). In 1975 the Polynesian double-hulled voyaging canoe, *Hōkūle'a*, was launched to initiate a program to revive voyaging and rediscover the culture's special relationship with the sea. Movement is a feature of the histories of most Pacific islanders, whose origin stories begin with the discovery and settlement of their island in a narrative that typically features arrival from a distant location, usually from the west (Hau'ofa 1993). With help from the Micronesian navigator Mau Piailug, Hawaiians recovered knowledge of navigation, reevaluated their relationship to their island home, and connected with other voyaging cultures throughout Oceania, some that still practice traditional navigation and others that have lost the tradition. In 2017 *Hōkūle'a* completed a three-year circumnavigation that extended its

FIGURE 6.4 *Hōkūle`a*, a double-hulled Hawaiian voyaging canoe, arriving in Honolulu from Tahiti in 1976. © Phil Uhl via Wikimedia Commons (public domain).

program's mission from voyaging and navigational knowledge to include also an explicit environmental focus that recognized the island properties of planet Earth (Polynesian Voyaging Society 2019) (Figure 6.4).

Travelers who embark on restored or replica tall ships or voyaging canoes recover, practice, and teach historical maritime skills and knowledge through activities that respect history and perhaps imbibe in nostalgia, and yet they equally seek contemporary meanings for their efforts. In 1947, for example, the Norwegian explorer and writer Thor Heyerdahl led a voyage aboard a sailing raft christened *Kon-Tiki* to support his theory that migrants to Polynesia arrived from South America. His team constructed the vessel from balsa logs and other materials native to Peru, using information about Indigenous crafts from historical records. They succeeded at reaching the island of Raroia in the Tuamotu island group after a 101-day voyage. Heyerdahl published an internationally best-selling book (Heyerdahl 1950) and directed an award-winning documentary film after his return and, although his theory was debunked, the *Kon-Tiki* remains preserved at a Norwegian museum.[6]

While *Kon-Tiki* reflected curiosity about the human relationship with the globe, other traditional sail initiatives embraced explicitly environmental missions. In 1969 the sloop *Clearwater*, designed with features of eighteenth-century Dutch sailing sloops that dealt effectively with the strong tides, variable winds, and shallow areas found on the Hudson River, began a program of ecological education and environmental advocacy. The vessel also provides opportunities for volunteers and apprentices to learn sailing and vessel maintenance as well as environmental education (Duffy 2018). The Clearwater program has inspired numerous similar initiatives, some of which also employ traditional sailing vessels, such as the schooner *SoundWaters* in Long Island Sound, the schooner *Adventuress* in the Puget Sound, and the ketch *Roter Sand* on the St. Lawrence River, which visits the Caribbean and northern waters as well (Ecomaris 2019; Sound Experience 2016; SoundWaters 2017). In 2010 a strikingly unique eighteen-meter sail-powered catamaran, named *Plastiki* in homage to Heyerdahl's raft, crossed the Pacific Ocean in 128 days and was chronicled in both a book and a documentary. Made entirely of recyclable materials, including 12,500 discarded plastic bottles serving as floatation, *Plastiki* was built and sailed by the British explorer David de Rothschild and a small crew to raise awareness of the threat of plastic waste to the ocean (Rothschild de 2011). The world's last remaining wooden whaling ship, the *Charles W. Morgan*, embarked in 2014 on its "38th Voyage" with a message of environmental awareness alongside the layers of meanings associated with maritime heritage that the vessel had accrued through its exhibition and interpretation since it was preserved after an eight-decade career of whaling (Mystic Seaport 2019; Smith 2016). In 2011 international sail training embraced protection of the global marine environment through the creation of the Sail Training International Blue Flag Scheme, extending environmental awareness and action into tall ship programs around the world that otherwise pursue mainly traditional maritime and leadership missions (Blue Flag 2014).

Sailing technology, and the associated practices and knowledges of navigation, provided the means for early modern expansion, with ships serving to spread ideas, people, and goods around the globe. In cultural terms, what were traditional sailing vessels in the twentieth century, once their original purposes were superseded? Play joined work as a primary activity and motive for traveling under sail, but the choice to face the unpredictable ocean environment with traditional sail suggests something more complex than the binary of work or play. Sail training required its own professionalization because it involves mastery of complex if traditional technology, highly coordinated operation of the rig, and the choice to face the dangers inherent in seagoing. As one captain-author put it, calling attention to the importance of imaginative engagement with the ocean, "Sailing ships have defied obsolescence by offering an extraordinary experience in a sometimes ordinary world" (Parrott 2003: 2). Media joined print as a means for communicating those experiences of voyaging, while new meanings accrued for ocean travel (which had traditionally been oriented toward resource extraction and trade) as people set sail for historical preservation and reenactment, environmental awareness, leadership and teamwork training, academic credit, scientific research, and self-knowledge.

NONHUMAN OCEAN TRAVELERS

A global perspective reminds us that the ocean, though it covers about three-quarters of the earth's surface, provides volumetrically 99 percent of the planet's living space. Daily or seasonal migration characterizes the lives of marine animals from tiny zooplankton to giant whales. Other marine life moves involuntarily as a result of human activities. Ships have transported marine species from and to far-distant coasts in significant numbers, such as when gold-seekers abandoned a fleet in San Francisco's harbor in 1849, and with increasing frequency as global shipping expanded in the twentieth century (Carlton 1979). A valuable consequence of considering the ocean's true residents—which humans are not (yet)—among ocean travelers is the reminder to consider all the parts of the ocean, including the undersea realm, in our histories.

People have deliberately moved aquatic animals for much of human history, and purposeful introductions of marine species expanded in the twentieth century as scientists gained confidence, often misguided, in their ability to manage fisheries. Chesapeake Bay and Japanese oysters were exported commercially to San Francisco Bay starting in 1869, while programs in Europe and North America early in the twentieth century hatched cod and transplanted young flatfish from crowded nursery grounds so they could grow more quickly to market size (Booker 2013; Carlton 1979; Rozwadowski 2002). The post-Second World War period brought optimism about the prospect of farming shellfish, seaweed, algae, finfish, and even whales in the sea (Rozwadowski 2012).

Meanwhile, recognition dawned that ships carrying cargo across oceans and around the globe inadvertently transported marine fauna between the shores of different continents and the waters of different seas. Since the 1849 gold rush, San Francisco Bay has become home to perhaps the greatest number of introduced marine species, more than one hundred brought from the western and southwestern Pacific and the Atlantic (Carlton 1985). Before the late nineteenth century, hitchhikers were mainly fouling or boring organisms that attached themselves to the hulls of wooden ships. The first recorded arrival was a barnacle from the Atlantic, documented in 1853. Atlantic hydroids were noticed by the 1850s, no doubt carried by the many wooden vessels that were abandoned by gold-seekers to rot in the bay. The shipworm *Teredo navalis* arrived around 1913 and immediately set to work boring into wooden piers and other structures, promoting the formation by 1920 of the San Francisco Bay Marine Piling Committee to address the one of the world's most expensive ever problems of failing harbor infrastructure (Nelson 2016). An Australasian isopod that arrived during the second half of the nineteenth century began boring into clay banks around the bay, weakening them enough to result in massive erosion by wave action (Carlton 1979).

In the twentieth century, metal replaced wood in shipbuilding, anti-fouling paints and coverings were created, and ballast water replaced stones or other solid materials to keep lightly laden vessels low enough in the water to remain stable. As a result the common mechanism for unintended introductions of marine creatures became by the twentieth century transfer through ballast water that was taken up in one port and discharged in another. Whereas wooden vessels had moved boring or fouling organisms, ballast water could move not only certain adult organisms but also the larval stages of far more types of organisms, including hydroids, polychaetes, bivalves, barnacles, isopods, amphipods, bryozoans, ascidians, and algae. The earliest probable ballast water transfers that took hold in their new homes were an Asian diatom moved to the North Sea in 1903 and an Asian crab transported to Germany in 1912. In the early 1930s a North American blue crab made its way to Europe likely as larvae in ballast water. Scientists first discussed the probability of movement of species via ballast water in the 1950s but did not directly examine ballast tanks until two decades later, after the debates prompted by a proposed sea-level canal across the Panamanian isthmus (Carlton 1985).

The 1960s sea-level canal plan generated discussion of potential ecological effects of bringing together two oceans and called attention to the field of so-called "invasion biology" (Elton 1958; Keiner 2017). In response to transported species that have decimated fisheries, damaged infrastructure, endangered human health, and disrupted ecosystems, people have devised international regulations on the treatment of ballast water, requiring exchange of water in the high seas to reduce the likelihood of coastal species from one continent colonizing distant coastal waters (Davidson and Simkanin 2012). Other reactions play out at a more grassroots level, such as the strategy advocated by the creators of the Eat the Invaders website (Eat the Invaders n.d.). Meanwhile, critics question the efficacy of the militaristic and xenophobic metaphors embedded in considering transported species as "invaders" locked in a struggle against humans. Rather, they argue, people should recognize that these species depend on human activities and thrive in the disrupted environments people create (Larson 2005). More recently scientists observing the arrival of three hundred Japanese marine species associated with tsunami debris on the North American West Coast—including a species of shipworm that, if it establishes itself there, is likely to cause significant damage to human coastal structures—recognize natural mechanisms for transport of marine species as rivaling human introductions for distance and scale (Gilman 2016).

Introduced species can wreak havoc because of the suddenness of their arrival in evolutionary terms. On the other hand, some marine species have learned over long spans of time to follow seasonal shifts in water temperature and circulation that affect distribution of their food and survival of their young. North Pacific humpback whales, for example, migrate from cold waters off Alaska that serve as feeding grounds to warmer waters around Hawaii where mothers give birth and raise their calves before teaching them the route to the northern feeding grounds. Separate populations of humpbacks in the Southern Hemisphere travel between Antarctic feeding grounds and tropical seas. Possibly the longest whale migration takes the eastern Pacific gray whale population from the Bering, Chukchi, and Okhotsk seas to the lagoons of the Baja peninsula in northwestern Mexico. Some non-whale species, including salmon, sea turtles, and European eels similarly follow long migratory routes tied to their reproductive cycles. Humans have long exploited all of these populations, but changing perceptions of marine megafauna have inspired new modes of interaction. Global tracking of individual sea turtles and sharks as they trek short and extremely long distances connects human observers to animals whose histories, experiences, and travels have become public knowledge (for example, Sea Turtle Conservency 1996–2020; and Ocearch n.d.).

While long oceanic migrations result from evolutionary-scale interactions of species with their environment, recent research suggests that whales may also be shaped by cultural processes that have until now been assumed as unique to humans. Killer whales learn specific techniques used by their social group for obtaining food, while bottlenose dolphins can open new niches by inventing novel ways to catch fish, then form social networks around these feeding lifestyles. About half the population of Cape Cod humpback whales adopted a particular method of feeding within a decade of its introduction by one individual. Male humpbacks in a breeding population all sing the same song. Those songs change gradually over time, although there is an observed instance of revolutionary change, when a song introduced to whales off eastern Australia from the western Australian population was adopted by the entire group within a year. Both patterns suggest social learning. Killer whales travel and forage in matrilineal groups that each maintain a distinct dialect even though groups frequently interact socially with other groups. If culture is behavior or information that is socially learned and shared within a social community, then, as researchers Hal Whitehead and Luke Rendell have proposed, cetaceans emerge as perhaps the most striking case of nonhuman culture (Mann 2017; Norris 2002; Whitehead and Rendell 2014).

Characteristics of the marine environment may promote the evolution of social behavior among cetaceans. Distribution of food resources is uneven throughout the ocean and marine ecosystems undergo major changes on timescales varying from months to decades. The mobility of cetaceans helps them cope both with a changing environment and patchy food distribution. Sharing information, including intergenerationally, might favor groups capable

FIGURE 6.5 Endangered southern right whale sighted by a whale watcher off Patagonia. © Wikimedia Commons (public domain).

of learning and communicating. There is evidence from the southern right whale population that disruption of the population through whaling eliminated some cultural knowledge of migration routes (Figure 6.5). This example raises the question of human culpability, not just for decreasing the number of whales but also perhaps for decimating their culture.

While it may be premature (although not illogical) to contemplate the binary (or continuum) of work–play for whale culture, the binaries of technology–imagination and extraction–addition bear special reflection in the context of the cultural history of nonhuman ocean travelers. Whale culture has become apparent through the mediation of technologies and knowledge systems associated with contemporary science. Technologies fitted to the animals themselves and also embedded in the marine environment relay information via satellites and make it available over the internet to researchers, civilian scientists, students, and interested web searchers. As important as technology has been for discovering new knowledge about whale populations, however, cultural conceptions of these animals have contributed alongside observations and measurements to shifting understandings of cetaceans. In the 1960s, the film *Flipper* and other popular media dramatically revised Western cultural perception of dolphins from "herring-hogs" that stole fish from human fishers to creatures with the potential to communicate with humans (Burnett 2010; Lilly 1961, 1967). Similarly, whales transformed from giant swimming commodities to "minds in the water," reflecting the title of a popular book summarizing the emerging understanding of whales as possessing intelligence on par with humans (McIntrye 1975). Historians have illustrated how recordings of humpback songs intersected in the 1970s with interest in communicating with potential alien life, encouraging researchers to perceive of dolphin communication as a potential key for future interaction with life from other planets (Burnett 2012). Today's emerging glimpses of whale culture are beholden not only to technoscience but also rely heavily on insights derived from human cultural constructions of whales created decades before insights flowed from current science. The new glimpses of whale culture represent additions to the oceanic imaginary, cultural conceptions that exist in tension with the former posture of viewing marine mammals through the lens of extraction. It remains challenging to decenter humans as the beneficiaries of ocean resources, as is clear from the continued framing of marine mammalian intelligence with reference to human brains and our preoccupation with their potential to communicate with us.

Humans face a potentially greater imaginative challenge from scientific studies showing that fish feel pain, experience joy and fear, learn, problem solve, recognize individuals of their own kind and among humans, and otherwise exhibit evidence of sentience (Balcombe 2017). The possibility that fish, the most exploited—and the most overexploited—group of vertebrates on the planet, have culture lends heft to the call by the marine ecologist and activist Carl Safina for the embrace of a "sea ethic" (2002–3). Safina's sea ethic extends to the ocean Aldo Leopold's "land ethic," articulated in his 1949 book, *A Sand County Almanac*. The land ethic recognized the right of the natural world to exist regardless of its usefulness for people. Leopold's moral principle exerted a profound effect on the environmental movement of the 1960s, but his terrestrial focus did nothing to distract environmental activists from their land orientation. Safina's invocation of a sea ethic not only couches the human relationship with the ocean in moral terms but it also has implications for ocean travel.

The cultural history of ocean travel by people and animals seems to both overlap and diverge. Compared to the sophisticated technologies that have enabled human travel into the sea's depths, sail training may appear as a low-tech harnessing of wind energy, that is until one recalls that large square-rigged vessels were the most sophisticated machines of the early modern period. Human requirements for technology to mediate interactions with the ocean differ fundamentally from the case for cetaceans, fish, and other organisms, which substitute biology for technology to thrive in the sea (Rozwadowski and Van Keuren 2004). Another difference appears to be cetaceans' and other animals' apparent lack of need to filter their experiences of ocean travel through various forms of media—although we cannot, of course, be sure that their cultures do not include communication of stories in some format that functions similarly. Nor do we have confident insight into whether and how the work–play binary that so powerfully divided human experience of ocean travel before and after the turn of the twentieth century operates for oceanic animal cultures; it seems likely that the present human conflation of these categories in our contemporary interactions with the ocean achieves a balance that other species have always practiced. Most strikingly, whereas land territory is home for people, the ocean remains a destination for humans, not a home. Every human foray across or into the ocean is travel, a visit to a place that is home to whales, fish, plankton, microbes, and many other creatures. Recognition of our role as travelers rather than residents might suggest the propriety of a more respectful posture to the ocean than even to land.

CHAPTER SEVEN

Representations

On Undersea Filmmaking

JON CRYLEN

The two of us, my pilot and I, descend through the deepening blue in our little humming bubble of air and light, and the pounds per square inch build up outside. Soon the noonday sun of the surface world has faded, leaving a deep ultramarine twilight. It is the most beautiful color I have ever seen. In some ways it is my favorite moment of the dive, suspended between worlds, saying goodbye to all you've ever known, and surrounded by infinite blue. It's a hue that not only suggests the ocean's vast scale but beckons the mind to a transcendent state—a sense of cosmic unity with the ocean, with ancient time and the history of life, back to the first organisms.

(Cameron 2004: 9–10)

So the deep-sea explorer and filmmaker James Cameron describes a typical submersible descent in the book companion to his film *Aliens of the Deep* (2005). His account is not unique. Comparing underwater descent to a passage between worlds is a familiar trope of first-person accounts of ocean exploration, as is the purportedly transformative nature of the experience, which seems to awaken in divers a feeling of oneness with the cosmos.[1] But in the context of the cinema, the details of this passage suggest an experience (specifically, the trademarked IMAX Experience) that viewers might ideally undergo while engulfed in a rich, high-resolution image and a sea of crisp digital surround sound—seemingly present among the explorers onscreen. Just as the fading of the light conjures for Cameron a sense of transport to a world independent of the surface, so the dimming of the houselights signals for movie viewers a moment of transit into another world by proxy, transforming the theater into its own "humming bubble of air and light" and offering a view onto a simulated sea. Enveloped in the "ultramarine twilight" on a large screen that exceeds one's field of vision, one may appreciate the seeming infinity of the sea as if one were in it, and even experience the same sense of unity with life in its origins that Cameron reports, so that when the lights rise, one may leave the theater feeling a blissful affinity with the greater chain of being.

Although the range of modes of representing and visualizing the ocean from the dawn of the twentieth century is quite vast, encompassing, for example, underwater photography, naturalist illustrations of aquatic life, bathymetric maps, sonar images, spectrograms of humpback whale phonations, and video games set undersea, I begin with Cameron's giant-screen scene-setting to suggest that the past dozen decades of representations of the marine world have, from a cultural standpoint, been predominantly cinematic. This has been particularly true since the early 1950s, when underwater films began to proliferate in the United States and Europe, as their production largely correlates with the Cold War boom in state funding for oceanography (especially in the United States) and the commercial availability of scuba gear (which was not invented until the 1940s). Within the industrialized West, cinematic and televisual narratives of ocean exploration and marine life have arguably played a greater hand than any other facet of culture in shaping common understanding of the sea—its inhabitants, its uses for humans, the dangers it faces (e.g., overfishing, ocean warming, and acidification), and the threats it poses to civilization (sea-level rise). Ask anyone what comes to mind when they think of the ocean, and there is a good chance they will reference a filmmaker-explorer such as Cameron or Jacques-Yves Cousteau—on account of the long-running series *The Undersea World of Jacques Cousteau* (1966–76), easily the figure most synonymous with ocean exploration—or a range of popular Hollywood movies or television documentaries. The reasons, we might gather, involve the relative remoteness of the ocean, particularly below its surface, from the direct experience of most people who are not recreational divers or marine scientists, and the cinema's unique ability to substitute for direct experience in registering the submarine world in motion. Moreover, popular motion pictures, on account of their (largely) fixed content and ability to be seen by different audiences in different places at different times, can easily become a shared reference point in the cultural imaginary of the sea. Even if public aquariums also afford people a shared social experience of marine phenomena, the intimate particulars of what they see is left to chance in a way that with recordings is not; moving images standardize the experience of observing life elsewhere.

Within the robust subfield of environmental media studies, ocean movies constitute a fairly new line of inquiry, one consisting of a growing but still fragmentary body of articles, book chapters, and academic theses and dissertations. Here, rather than provide a historical survey of ocean filmmaking or a focused discussion of representative films or filmmakers, which the reader can find elsewhere (see, for instance, Adamowsky 2015; Beattie 2008; Bellows and McDougall 2000; Cahill 2019; Cubitt 2005; Grimm 2001; Hauser 2009; Hayward 2005; Huggan 2013; Kennerson 2008; Marchessault 2017; Mitman 1999; Past 2009; Shell 2005; Starosielski 2013; Taves 1996; Telotte 2010; Thompson 2007), I instead offer a broad way of conceptualizing ocean movies in general—as they have existed since their origins and continue to be made today. Specifically, I propose that undersea films are characterized by the following: first, a careful aesthetic-technical constructedness that, akin to an aquarium, refashions the ocean for display rather than transparently represents the ocean as it is "out there"; second, a negotiation of reason and wonder, of science and spectacle, that films (particularly documentaries) bear out through a variety of visual techniques, such as time manipulation, magnification, and the use of computer-generated imagery (CGI); and finally, a reliance, particularly in deep-sea filmmaking, on what Keith Benson, Helen Rozwadowski, and David K. Van Keuren (2004: xiii) call "technology writ large"—the large-scale exploratory apparatuses that enable ocean cinema to be made. While the ensuing discussion focuses primarily on live-action documentaries shot undersea (the dominant mode of ocean filmmaking), and the third trait above refers to this mode of filmmaking exclusively, I hope the reader finds the first and second categories helpful for thinking through the whole range of moving images of the sea—whether animated films, popular fiction films, experimental works, or interactive media forms.

A CINEMATIC AQUARIUM: CONSTRUCTING SUBMARINE SPACE ONSCREEN

Undersea films not only bring distant seas to spectators but also remake the ocean for display. In this respect there is a strong analogy between cinema and aquariums, such that we might speak of the film screen (or, domestically, the television set) as a cinematic aquarium. Whether in an aquarium or on film, the ocean never comes to viewers neutrally, as it really is "out there." Rather, the ocean these media depict is an idealized, visually transparent one. As Susan G. Davis writes, not only do public aquariums

> bring marine life to eye level (and more or less hold it there), but aquarium technology clarifies the environment by settling, scrubbing, filtering, stabilizing, and chemically purifying it. Manuals on aquarium building are handbooks in perceptual play, covering how to keep water transparent, how to use light, the absence of light, and perspective to create the illusion of more space.
>
> (1997: 100)

FIGURE 7.1 Cartoon announcing undersea photography. © Universal History Archive/UIG/Getty Images.

These words could analogously describe filmmaking. In its own way, film technology also settles, scrubs, filters, stabilizes, and purifies the sea; the range of devices used as well as the changing practices, institutions, and broad structures of knowledge and representation associated with them all play a hand in remaking the sea for display.

How the ocean looks and sounds on film is deeply indebted to prior representations. Existing films, photographs, television programs, sound recordings of marine life, and home and public aquariums play a great a hand in shaping the norms that govern the construction of believable, realistic, and "natural" undersea space—how the ocean *should* appear—as Nature itself has. This is all the more the case because direct experience of the undersea world has historically been off-limits to nearly everyone except scientists, recreational divers, and the military; even fledgling ocean filmmakers may initially be better acquainted with representations of the sea than with the sea itself. Even though it would be foolish to deny an indexical relationship between reality and filmic representation—that a live-action film image is in some sense a direct imprint of the aquatic scene before the camera (animation is another matter)—the thoroughly constructed nature of recorded sounds and images arguably trumps this relationship. As film historian Rick Altman puts it, *"there is no such thing as direct representation of the real; there is only representation of representation. Anything that we would represent is always constructed as a representation by previous representations"* (2004: 17, emphasis in the original). Thus, whatever ocean film and photography appear to reveal about marine life or other aspects of the seas in the present nonetheless is conditioned by prior representational conventions—conventions that also influence how viewers, even if only unconsciously, interpret them.

One major convention—perhaps the most important one—that ocean movies are both indebted to and deviate from is the 500-year-old system of linear perspective that, as theorists of film and photography have long held, inheres in camera technology. Live-action films, in short, grant viewers a mathematically structured but apparently realistic illusion of three-dimensional space that harks back to techniques developed in Renaissance painting. Moreover, certain theorists, such as Jean-Louis Baudry (1970s–1980s), have held that this system of perspective is ideologically loaded, producing a transcendental, Cartesian subject—"'centering' [...] the single individual as the locus of consciousness and coherence, giving the impression of mastery" over the world they view onscreen (Elsaesser and Hagener 2010: 67–8). To be sure, as scholar Margaret Cohen argues, underwater optics "spectacularly defy" the conventions of linear perspective that the lens perpetuates: "While linear perspective creates substantial depth of field, the poor visibility underwater radically diminishes the ability to perceive distance. The furthest the eye can see in the clearest of water, distilled water, is only 250 feet" (2014: 3, 8). Additionally, "we are not only nearsighted underwater, but prone to confusion. The denser medium of water magnifies objects" (8). On account of such differences, Cohen shows, underwater optics historically align with artistic modernism, resonating with visual effects important to surrealism, and shaped an aesthetics of the deep not informed by perspectival conventions, as in the underwater paintings of Zarh H. Pritchard (Cohen 2014). That said, despite how images recorded underwater differ perceptually from those made on land, the perspectival qualities of the lens still remediate those differential optics. Additionally, distortion-correcting lenses, guidelines to help underwater photographers minimize optical warping, and the typical advice in underwater photography guides to shoot in the clearest possible water aim to ensure that the aquatic world conforms as closely as possible to the visual realism of perspective—as if to shore up an "impression of mastery" against the qualities of underwater optics that undercut it.

In part because of the differences between below- and above-water optics, the construction of undersea space is fraught with difficulties uncommon to terrestrial filmmaking. Underwater, continuity editing, or the set of conventions for establishing spatial relations in narrative cinema, tends to break down; relations between images tend to be more impressionistic than adherent to strict visual coding. The shortage of static spatial landmarks (other than, say, coral reefs and sunken ships) and limited visibility in the open sea can conspire to make onscreen space ambiguous. As seafloor and ocean surface seldom occupy the same shot, vertical depth becomes virtually impossible for filmmakers to convey or viewers to discern (barring perhaps a second-nature viewer understanding of color absorption relative to depth). A standard "beautiful" shot—sunlight rippling through the waves, backlighting a majestic school of fish viewed from below—might orient spectators in images of shallower depths, but such devices fail where the sun's rays cannot penetrate, including nearly everywhere undersea at night.

Additionally, ocean space often looks generic. Without dialogue, narration, title cards, or other cues, it can become difficult for viewers to tell where at sea they are supposed to be once the camera penetrates the waves. Images of certain iconic flora and fauna (e.g., swimming penguins, diving polar bears, coral reefs) and other landmarks (ceilings of ice) may, of course, orient viewers via a general geography (e.g., Arctic, Antarctic, or tropical), but such locations may span thousands of kilometers—making it difficult for viewers to spatially or temporally (as in regard to seasonality) contextualize what they see with any precision from image cues alone. Filmmakers often exploit such visual uncertainty for poetic effect; the famed Jacques-Yves Cousteau's *World Without Sun* (1964), for instance, never identifies the location of the underwater habitat the film depicts daily life inside of, and at the film's premiere he even remarked, "As soon as you are specific, the poetry disappears" (quoted in Madsen 1986: 135).

As visibility can be limited underwater, sound becomes a crucial means of defining undersea space, particularly in live-action films. Because most undersea films were made after the arrival of sync sound in the late 1920s to early 1930s, we can speak of their having soundtracks comprising speech (i.e., dialogue and narration), music, and sound effects. Music, as generations of film sound scholars can attest, powerfully shapes how we perceive film images, and undersea musical scores prove fairly diverse. Sometimes the music is sparse and impressionistic, pointing up the deep sea's strangeness as though it were another planet; other times, the images play to sweeping Romantic melodies, synth pop, or environmentalist ballads courtesy of left-leaning songwriters such as Sting and Crosby, Stills & Nash. By contrast, nonmusical sounds may be deceptively simple. Even a casual viewer of undersea films could identify a mix of whooshes, bubbling noises, and an absence of high frequencies as typical of undersea sound. It deserves mention that early undersea sound effects tend to be anthropocentric, referring to divers and their equipment; more complex undersea soundscapes that make extensive use of location sound and of animal vocalizations—communicative or otherwise—are a fairly recent phenomenon traceable to the 1970s, with the rise of the environmental movement and the popularization of humpback whale recordings.[2]

While the analogy with the aquarium helps to address the general constructedness of the sea, one can further distinguish a specific aquarium aesthetic in undersea films: a relatively static, frontal view of underwater events that resembles the view before a tank (whether a home aquarium or a larger, public one), and where separation of dry space and wet space is maintained—a view that stands in contrast to an unfettered, balletic, and mobile view derivative from scuba diving, gear for which did not exist until Cousteau and Émile Gagnan invented the Aqualung in 1943 (Crylen 2018b). In fact, sometimes aquariums were actually involved in the shooting of early "undersea" films, such as those of the pioneering French filmmaker Georges Méliès, several of whose films of the 1890s and 1900s include undersea sequences whose action, on dry-land sets, was shot through fish tanks placed before the camera.[3] Even the first footage actually obtained undersea—by John Ernest Williamson between 1914 and 1932, including for Universal's productions of Jules Verne's *20,000 Leagues under the Sea* (1916) and *The Mysterious Island* (1929)—offer views of the deep resembling those onto aquariums (see Crylen 2021; Elias 2019). Shot from within the "photosphere," a steel underwater camera chamber attached to the bottom of a boat via a flexible, watertight tube, Williamson's films display ocean landscapes and wildlife frontally and at eye level, without ever penetrating forward or backward into that aquatic space. Such views echo the illustrations of aquatic scenes in popular aquarium handbooks that had circulated widely in Europe and the United States since the latter half of the nineteenth century—images that could well have served as Williamson's visual models. Even the crystalline Caribbean waters in which he filmed resemble the artificially clarified environs of a tank. Later films shot from inside submersibles (1960s onward), such as the deep-ocean films I address in the last section of this chapter, also perpetuate this aquarium view on account of the physical separation (the window) between the cameraperson and the aquatic scene, even if, unlike Williamson's chamber, these submersibles are not tethered to the surface and can freely navigate ocean space. Strikingly, in interwar animation, such as Disney's numerous underwater Silly Symphony shorts,[4] one finds the frontal, eye-level view consistently replicated in the underwater background

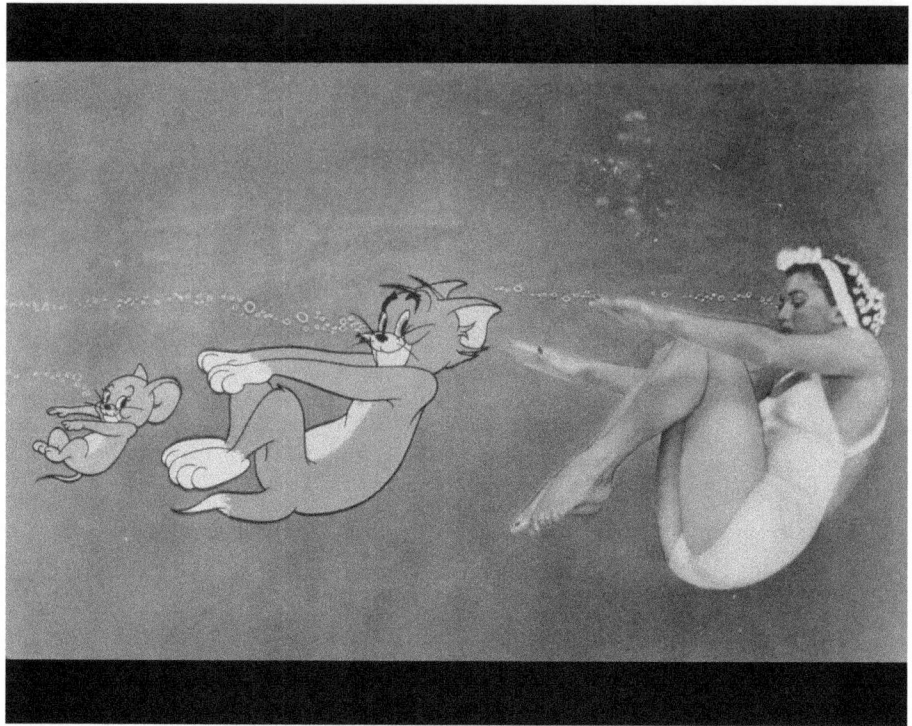

FIGURE 7.2 Esther Williams with Tom and Jerry in *Dangerous When Wet* (dir. Charles Walters, 1953). © Silver Screen Collection/Getty Images.

imagery—visuals likely modeled on nineteenth-century naturalist's drawings and the constructed scenes of public and home aquariums. That vertical views upward toward the surface or downward toward the seafloor are uncommon in animated movies of the pre-scuba period further reinforces the idea of a spectatorial position "outside" the water than immersed within it.

To be sure, other critics have noted the parallels between the cinematic view and the aquarium (Adamowsky 2009, 2015; Hauser 2009; Weigel 2009), sketching out some of the traits I describe above and even extending it to video art and gallery installations. However, as Judith Hamera (2012) points out, the aquarium itself has been bound up with earlier forms of viewing that destabilize it as a discrete apparatus. These "visual affinities," as she terms them, include the window, theater, panorama, and voyage (24–49); that the cinema also shares these affinities bolsters the aquarium analogy's power when it comes to subaquatic films, regardless of a particular visual aesthetic. In cinema, one looks upon the world onscreen as if through a window while at the same time being reminded of the image's artifice by that window's frame (the edges of the screen); with an aquarium, one likewise peers at a scene that, because of the transparency of the glass, appears continuous

FIGURE 7.3 Filming of a scene from Disney's *20,000 Leagues Under the Sea* (dir. Richard Fleishcer, 1954). © Peter Stackpole/Getty Images.

with the space of viewing while understanding the glass as a barrier between environments—a container separating a dry space from a wet one. Theatrically, with the aquarium, viewers were long encouraged to "read the tank as they would read the stage" (32)—as a site of drama and action, and its inhabitants players (much as animals are oft anthropomorphized in films). Similarly, both contemporary documentary narration and the guided aquarium tours hark back to nineteenth-century tradition of the popular scientific lecture, in which, as Rick Altman explains, the lecturer not only explained their visuals but redefined them, shaping viewers' perceptions (2004: 71–2). The view unto both follows from the visual logic of the panorama, one of the nineteenth century's key "rational amusements," and particularly the moving panorama, which unwound steadily on rollers to give viewers the sense of movement through space (Hamera 2012: 35); cinematically, the panoramic view resonates most with widescreen (early 1950s onward) and large-format (e.g., IMAX— late 1960s onward) landscape imagery that allows the viewer's eye to explore the frame. Finally, aquariums invite their spectators to travel in both space and time—to imagine the experience of submarine exploration while encountering the deep time of evolutionary forebears the fish, without any of the associated dangers of exploration; cinema similarly allows viewers illusory transit to distance places and a vicarious experience of other lives. Taken in relation to common traits of aquatic cinema, these shared traits allow one to trace even recent examples to discursive roots in nineteenth-century aquarium culture.

OCEAN IMAGERY: BETWEEN REASON AND WONDER, SCIENCE AND SPECTACLE

Ocean movies have long straddled the divide between art and science. Indeed, from their photographic origins, cinematic images of the sea have been imbricated with scientific inquiry and modes of visualization, with European men of science obtaining much of the earliest pre-cinematic aquatic imagery. The first known underwater photographer, William Thompson (1856), was an amateur naturalist, and the French zoologist Louis Boutan (1893) produced the first undersea photographs by a diver (Deane 2013: 1416–17). Physiologist Etienne-Jules Marey (1890) published a chronophotographic study of aquatic motion in the popular science magazine *La Nature*; his images, shot using a small aquarium, inspired the brothers Auguste and Louis Lumière, two of the world's first filmmakers, to record eels, fish, and frogs in their 1896 film *L'Aquarium* and inaugurated the motion studies of marine life that continue today (Shell 2005: 326).

In part because of the sheer strangeness of much marine life compared to more familiar terrestrial flora and fauna, ocean films, and especially nonfiction ones, tend to operate along two registers of vision—one that gives in to spectacle, awe, and wonder and another that seeks rational mastery over the unknown. Frequently, these registers overlap, perhaps most strikingly in the popular science films of French biologist and educator Jean Painlevé (see Beattie 2008; Bellows and McDougall 2000; Cahill 2012, 2019; Hayward 2005). Made between the 1920s and 1970s, Painlevé's lyrical, surrealism-influenced documentaries of aquatic life led the famous French film critic André Bazin to wax ecstatic in a 1958 essay: "Here, at the farthest reaches of interested and practical research, where the most absolute proscription of aesthetic intention as such reigns, cinematic beauty unfolds like a supernatural grace"—"the miracle of the science film, and its inexhaustible paradox" ([1958] 2009: 21). Though they beautifully encapsulate the experience of viewing a seminal Painlevé work such as *L'Hippocampe* (*The Seahorse*) (1934), Bazin's words could also describe a viewer's reaction to the imagery in many other marine movies—notably, the mid-century films and television shows of Cousteau and his Austrian contemporary Hans Hass; the sundry David Attenborough—hosted BBC Nature programs devoted to the marine realm, such as *Blue Planet* (2001) and *Blue Planet II* (2017–18); and research videos posted to the YouTube and Twitter pages of the Monterey Bay Aquarium Research Institute and other marine science organizations during the past decade. Like Painlevé's, these films tend to elicit a response that oscillates between enthrallment to the strangeness of what one sees and a more sober desire to know, one that informative voiceover narration or title cards generally satisfy (even if, as in Cousteau and Painlevé, the voiceovers are often poetic).

On an optical level, this dual response may to some degree inhere in underwater photography—specifically in the aforementioned tension between underwater optics and the perspectival nature of the camera, with the confusions of the distortions of the former undercutting the position of rational mastery that the apparatus supposedly constructs. But even so, other, specialized visual techniques, common to natural science films, dramatically heighten both a desire to know and a sense of awe. Three crucial such devices are magnification (e.g., close-ups, micro- and macrocinematography), time lapse, and slow motion. All three have been vital to undersea documentaries, including in many of the examples mentioned above. Via these techniques, as film theorists have long held, the camera reveals previously "hidden" aspects of the visible world—hidden because either too small or distant for the human eye to perceive unaided or too fast or slow to be perceived in real time. Microscopic imagery and varied image speed are staples of Painlevé's films; to cite other examples, Cousteau makes remarkable use of microscopic imagery in his underwater habitat documentary *World Without Sun*, and the filmmaker Jeff Orlowski reveals an improbable riot of colors in the macro- and microphotography of corals in *Chasing Coral* (2017) (on which see Gaycken 2018). Not solely provided by specialized optical techniques, cinematographic magnification also takes the form of enlargement on account of screen size—notably in IMAX films. On

FIGURE 7.4 Extreme close-up of coral polyps in Tubbataha, Phillipines. © Alexis Rosenfeld/Getty Images.

a twenty-meter screen, massive visual scale not only defamiliarizes standard photographic images but further heightens the strange and revelatory qualities of enlarged, slowed down, or sped-up phenomena. As documentary scholar Keith Beattie summarizes, writing of marine magnification in both Painlevé's and IMAX films, "image enlargement and enhancement function as a mode of cognition and understanding"—one highly pleasing to the aesthetic sense (Beattie 2008: 150).

Whereas the above techniques simultaneously elicit awe and rational engagement, ocean movies also work more dialectically on the level of the image—splitting reason and wonder along photographic and nonphotographic lines. When it comes to mapping ocean space for the sake of viewer comprehension, for instance, filmmakers avail themselves of sonar graphs, hand-drawn diagrams, bathymetric maps, and other nonphotographic imagery that gives viewers the means to conceptualize ocean space in greater totality than the limits on direct vision underwater permit. Such images not only compensate for what photography cannot do underwater but also, by serving a purely rational, informational function, help foreground the ambiguous, strange, and lyrical qualities that typify undersea cinematography.

Over the past three decades, the primary form of nonphotographic imagery in ocean documentaries has been CGI—in particular, illustrative CGI sequences that generally resemble extended, single-take traveling shots in cinematography. Elaborate visual diagrams of a sort, these CGI images are able to weave together in a single, seemingly continuous shot a range of things that would resist such assemblage photographically, thus allowing viewers to quickly make conceptual sense of a wide range of ocean phenomena, often vast in scale. Indeed, because they enable traversal of spatial (and temporal) gulfs impossible to navigate photographically, such CGI sequences afford viewers a sense of rational mastery over phenomena far *greater* in intricacy and spatiotemporal scale than photography or cinematography can. An absolutely crucial aspect of digital imagery is that it tends to be unusually clean—smoother and less densely detailed than photographic imagery. This lack of detail renders what might in a photorealistic image amount to an information glut into something more easily grasped; consequently, it allows the digitally animated images to function as a purely rational counterpoint to photographic images whose richness of detail allows them to overwhelm the aesthetic sense.

Consider two such CGI sequences from director Stephen Low's IMAX documentary *Volcanoes of the Deep Sea* (2003), both of which quickly traverse spatiotemporal gulfs that cannot be negotiated photographically. In the first sequence, the "camera" begins on the ocean floor and then vaults into space to show the viewer the length of the Mid-Atlantic Ridge (where the film's titular volcanoes are found) in relation to the continents. The earth rotates to reveal a cutout view of the magma and volcanic activity beneath the earth's crust; then the camera plunges back into the ocean to the sea floor, where we suddenly find ourselves billions of years ago, watching as the ridge is formed. A later CGI sequence purports to explain the origins of deep-sea tubeworms and chemosynthetic life (as distinguished from photosynthetic life) by explaining the origins of the solar system. A star explodes; part of it collides with the earth, the earth as we know it forms thanks to this contact; and the view of roiling magma, which dissolves into a film image of a tubeworm-covered chimney, lets us know that these "embers of a dying star," as the narrator describes them, were life's initial spark.

As supplements and counterpoints to photographic images, such digitally animated sequences conform to what Mark J.P. Wolf calls a "subjunctive documentary" style. As Wolf argues, "computer imaging and simulation are concerned with what *could be*, *would be*, or *might have been*" and become ways of rendering things beyond the range of human vision (natural or mechanically extended) and of a conceptual nature into visual analogues (1999: 274, emphasis in original). Like false-color Hubble Space Telescope images of deep space or brain scans in which disparate colors indicate different levels of synaptic activity, these CGI sequences are "not a record of how the subject appears to the observer, but rather how it *might* appear" (277, emphasis in original).[5] The danger of such sequences is that although they helpfully present a range of discrete phenomena holistically in a manner not possible photographically, it can be difficult to tell how much of the imagery we see is purely speculative or to what degree it takes liberties with the empirical bases for what we see.

Additionally, the improbable speeds of the "camera" that visually unifies so many digitally rendered phenomena is characteristic of what Chris Tong (2014) calls "the age of the world zoom," wherein imaging technologies are of a piece not only with planetary consciousness but also with war and surveillance. Rapid zooms from deep space to the ocean floor or across the solar system, even across entire geological epochs, suggest a world in which vision assumes a scope unlimited by time or space. In regard to the ocean, such zooms—which plunge from surface to depth at the same speed as they move among planets—also posit a future when water can be as open to movement as the vacuum of outer space and when the messy, protean qualities of sea water can be abolished so the ocean can be more easily ordered. To be sure, this nonprotean quality is characteristic of not only the CGI in ocean documentaries but of digital animation of the ocean in general. As Melody Jue argues, digital sea water typically behaves as "a passive medium of frictionless navigation without any of the chemical properties that make it such a powerful agent of transfiguration in life and in the imagination" (2014: 246–7). Though digital seas may be eminently navigable, those in undersea documentaries nonetheless retain some opacity. Unlike other digital oceans, such as Google Ocean, that do away with not only the ocean's fluidity but also its opacity and all the life forms within it, those in the above and other examples tend to selectively maintain visual qualities of that characterize the live-action imagery: they suggest an ocean that is not fully known or knowable and may yet yield surprising discoveries.[6] Even as their frictionless quality abets the construction of single-shot diagrams that bring many spatially and temporally disparate elements together at once, then, these digital seas still refer back to the mysterious and startling qualities of the photographic ocean they visually counterpoint.

UNDERSEA CINEMA AND "TECHNOLOGY WRIT LARGE"

Whether as a matter of heroic explorers or cinematic auteurs (e.g., Cousteau, Painlevé, and Cameron), it is tempting to treat ocean filmmaking as an affair of individuals. Doing so, however, overlooks both filmmakers' institutional ties as well as the scale of the science to which many sounds and images of the sea owe their existence. Oceanography, after all, is Big Science—costlier and more technology-heavy than most terrestrial sciences. It is not the domain of independent men and women. No mere recreational diver could photograph the deep-sea anglerfish found in a coffee-table tome; the extreme pressure would crush their body well before they reached depth. Cousteau, that most famous of filmmaker-explorers, might not have been able to make his films without the Irish millionaire who leased him the *Calypso* for a symbolic one franc per year. Further, Cameron, who remains best known for his Hollywood blockbusters, likely could not have funded his own Cousteau-inspired ocean explorations without the wealth and cachet his mainstream successes have brought him.[7] The history of undersea cinema as we know it would be unimaginable without considerable technology and capital to back it.

This is to say that although shooting undersea requires special equipment (hydrophones, distortion-correcting camera lenses, elaborate lighting-rigs, high-speed film stocks, waterproof camera casings) that bear on the aesthetics of submarine imagery, consideration of cinematic technologies alone is inadequate. Ocean films are equally the products of the ships, diving gear, submersibles, underwater habitats, and other apparatuses that have historically made undersea filming possible. Choices about lighting and camera placement become inseparable from not only nonfilmic practice, such as the use of dive tables or the collective labor involved in any submersible expedition, but also the resources (material, institutional, political, and economic) and agendas (state and corporate) needed to develop and maintain the most sophisticated of these machines. Just as aerial filmmaking cannot be thought apart from the history of aviation, for instance, so undersea filmmaking cannot be thought outside the history of twentieth-century marine exploration and oceanographic research.

Nowhere are the problems of undersea cinema's dependence on exploratory technologies more pronounced than in the past two decades' films of the deep sea. Getting to the bottom of the ocean requires the assistance of submersible technologies that can sustain incredible pressures, withstand extreme cold (especially important so riders of manned submersibles don't freeze); navigate the darkness (with its high-wattage lamps); fight strong currents with their propellers; provide their passengers with enough oxygen for descents and ascents that can last several hours each; and obviate the need for long-term, post-dive decompression. In deep-sea films and television programs, such as Low's *Volcanoes of the Deep Sea*, National Geographic's *Alien Deep with Bob Ballard* (2012), and Cameron's various dive documentaries, the narration and human subjects consistently make viewers aware of these facts. Indeed, whenever the submersibles become the focus of the image, they serve as reminders of all of the problems that must be solved before the spectacular deep-sea images we see can be produced—foregrounding the degree to which technology necessarily mediates ocean images. By depicting and discussing these technologies, the films point to their own conditions of possibility in such a way that conveys the sheer *difficulty* of going underwater, of overcoming the power of the ocean environment. In this respect, films aestheticize the means of exploration as an instance of what the scholar David E. Nye (1994) has dubbed the technological sublime.

Consider, again, *Volcanoes of the Deep Sea*. In this documentary, the submersible that conveys the ocean's power is the deep-submergence vehicle (DSV) *Alvin*, owned by the US Navy and housed and operated by the Woods Hole Oceanographic Institution since 1964. Weighing seventeen tons and able to dive to 4,500 meters, it is easily the most storied of all deep-sea submersibles. As the film's narrator apprises us, the *Alvin* "has spent more hours in the deep sea than all of the world's submersibles combined" and been instrumental in collecting data for some two thousand scientific articles. Instrumental in proving the theory of plate tectonics in the early 1970s, *Alvin* was also the submersible to discover hydrothermal vents along the Galapagos Rift (in 1975) as well as the "black smokers" depicted in the film (1978–9) (Reidy, Kroll, and Conway 2007: 213). In presenting the hydrothermal vents from *Alvin*'s perspective, *Volcanoes* amounts to something of a throwback to a significant moment of discovery that occurred three decades prior to the film's release.

In contrast to Low's film's evocation of Cold War oceanography, Cameron's *Aliens of the Deep* pairs old and new exploratory technologies. Early on, the film confronts the viewer with two sleek Deep Rover submersibles armed with 3D HD cameras and equipped with giant acrylic domes rather than the tiny portholes of the *Alvin*. These bubble-like subs offer their riders a 320-degree panoramic view of the deep that, in an IMAX theatrical setting, mirrors the movie spectator's visual relationship. The acrylic spheres, however, cannot withstand the extreme pressures *Alvin* can. As a result, the film's scientists avail themselves of the Soviet *Mir 1* and *2* submersibles, which were designed in the late 1980s to reach depths as great as six thousand meters, a depth as great as the vast majority of the ocean ever gets. Here, screen size becomes a particularly important component of the viewing experience: the giant IMAX display lets viewers see these submersibles as the gargantuan things they are in life; indeed, seen in certain museums, images of them may be continuous in size and apparent heft with the ships and submersibles displayed in exhibition halls.[8]

In a theatrical context, the enormous physical stature of these technologies as they appear on a huge screen impresses on viewers a sense of the sheer techno-scientific prowess that allows them to enter the deep sea—and even then, the films insist, only precariously. This is particularly true in *Aliens of the Deep* and the more recent *Deepsea Challenge 3D* (2014), which chronicle the troubles Cameron and his crew have merely getting the colossally heavy submersibles into the water with a crane; on rough seas they will swing out of control like wrecking balls and destroy the ship deck. Both films also document their crews' efforts to plan for every imaginable contingency. Cameron and company assure the viewer that things *will* go wrong, and both films, especially *Deepsea Challenge*, spend considerable time on the crew's safety drills and efforts to troubleshoot seemingly dozens of technical failures. To be sure, their difficulties testify to technology's precariousness before the overwhelming forces of nature. But once these obstacles are overcome, the technological feats appear even more impressive, becoming emblems of a collective ingenuity and will to power.

In *Deepsea Challenge* the engineering of submersible technology, a process rarely depicted in ocean films, further bolsters the impression of a technological sublime. No extant submersibles, the film tells us, would have been capable of traveling so deep without imploding; the singular nature of the dive—Cameron's plunge to Challenger Deep was only the second manned dive to the deepest part of the world's oceans, and for research purposes he needed to spend significant time on the bottom—calls for a singular submarine.[9] In an unusual instance of the infrastructural imaginary in deep-sea cinema, we actually see a steel diving sphere (the bottom part of the submersible where the diver sits) being forged and heat treated to withstand the pressure imposed by eleven vertical kilometers of sea water—about 1,100 kilograms per square inch, what Cameron likens to "having two Humvees stacked on your thumbnail." The "wow" power of the submersible also speaks to nature in its very design, seeming to prove a dictum Cameron attributes to the physicist Freeman Dyson: "Nature's imagination is so much richer than our own" (Cameron 2004: 10). The strange-looking device, a "vertical torpedo" designed to minimize descent time and maximize time spent at depth, is partly modeled on razorfish, which swim vertically with their heads pointed downward and offer a biological precedent for the seemingly counterintuitive idea of an upright submersible.

Skeptical viewers of these films—particularly Cameron's, which more or less uncritically celebrate exploration rather than question the impulse to explore or the socio-economic arrangements that undergird such resource-intensive uses of science and technology—may notice an irony. The scale of the diving technology involved so overwhelms the human figure that it is difficult to see the latter at the center of the expedition, despite participants' rhetoric about the importance of seeing the ocean floor with one's own eyes. Indeed, seemingly without intending to, *Deepsea Challenge* gives the lie to this notion. For most of his time underwater, Cameron watches the ocean not through the porthole but on a computer screen that blocks it; a video feed from the external HD cameras gives him a more panoramic view than could the window. Only when he touches bottom does he move the screen and look around with his own eyes, a token gesture toward the importance of direct vision.

Deep-sea films' emphasis on manned descents arguably represents an older wave of oceanographic research. As anthropologist Stefan Helmreich writes, "In an age of remotely operated robots [and] Internet ocean observatories [...] presence in 'the field' is increasingly simultaneously partial, fractionated, and prosthetic; it is not just distributed across spaces—multisited—but cobbled together from different genres of experience, apprehension, and data collection. It is multimodal" (Helmreich 2009: 233). Cameron's claims for the importance of an observer's physical presence at the bottom of the sea are overstated and have more to do with a conservative impulse to preserve the human's place at the site of research at a time when remotely operated vehicles (ROVs), autonomous underwater vehicles (AUVs), and other technologies of remote sensing have rendered it increasingly superfluous.[10] The future of undersea representations may therefore lie in images retrieved not by flesh-and-blood explorers but by programmable and remote-controlled machines—images, moreover, likely to be viewed on small, portable screens in a wide range of locations (homes, subways, coffee shops, etc.) rather than in theaters whose screens monumentalize older modes of transit.

CONCLUSION

Cinematic moving images are, I have proposed, the dominant cultural means of visualizing and representing the ocean in the modern era; this chapter has outlined three ways of conceptualizing marine filmmaking. First, motion pictures, like aquariums, technically and aesthetically remake the undersea world for display; they present viewers with something of an ideal ocean, one highly mediated by not only film technology but also by inherited representational codes, that may—perceptually, experientially—differ markedly from the seas as they might encounter them "out there." Second, undersea films have occupied scientific and popular contexts, and they structure a mode of viewing that oscillates between amusement and reason, knowledge seeking and awe. While these dual registers of viewing are often prompted by devices common to science cinema, such as slow-motion, time-lapse, and macroscopic imagery, that reveal aspects of the natural world that are invisible to the naked eye, they also are apparent in the alternation between spectacular photographic imagery that overwhelms the aesthetic sense and nonphotographic CGI that serves a more rational, analytic purpose. Finally, ocean movies, particularly deep-sea films of the past couple decades, are reliant on the vast scientific and technological apparatus of ocean exploration, which in turn the films fashion as a kind of technological sublime that, as well as the sea's natural wonders, elicits awe. However, much of the large-scale science and technology that deep-sea films depend on and depict has the arguably antiquated aim of supporting human physical presence undersea; the future of undersea motion pictures arguably lies in remote image capture and viewing.

Other issues, of course, impinge on ocean films as they have existed and continue into the future. Beyond the aesthetic-technical construction of space, as Nicole Starosielski has argued, undersea films construct power relations and cultural difference (2013: 152). Although ocean films frequently have generally presented the underwater world as civilization's opposite, a timeless, fundamentally nonhuman environment that exists outside the purview of humans' social and political affairs, in doing so they have "often masked the racial, cultural, and gendered dynamics which have historically unfolded across the ocean" (150). Indeed, through the 1960s, as she demonstrates, American movies and television "mediated a broader cultural transition to an internationally governed ocean and the ascendance of the United States as a dominant marine power," in effect representationally displacing coastal communities that have historically depended on the ocean for resources (150). Even if recent films upend the longstanding image of ocean exploration as a predominantly white male pursuit—*Aliens of the Deep*, for instance, commendably gives prominent roles to female scientists, among them the film's de facto African American star Dijanna Figueroa—they can also advance negative stereotypes and cultural prejudices, as in the controversial depiction of Japanese in the anti–dolphin slaughter documentary *The Cove* (dir. Louie Psihoyos, 2009).

More dramatically, of course, is the ongoing mass extinction of ocean life, which film and television have only begun to deal with, both in terms of the effects on wildlife and on human communities whose economies and cultures are closely tied to the sea. Recent films such as *Chasing Coral*, about the disappearance of the world's coral reefs, and *Sonic Sea* (dir. Michelle Dougherty and Daniel Hinerfeld, 2016), about the catastrophic effects of man-made ocean noise on cetaceans and other animals whose perceptual systems are oriented around sound, are strongly conservationist in terms of marine ecology. But one wonders whether their message is too little, too late. Indeed, as anthropogenic ocean warming and acidification take a greater toll on the marine realm's denizens, it is difficult to conceive of the future of cinematic representations of the sea. Will the undersea world depicted be depleted? Dominated by the jellyfish that seem to bloom in times of crisis (Crylen 2018a)? Perhaps, in the face of annihilation, an archival tendency will persevere: movies of the past will stand as records of an ocean that once was. In the nearer term, however, it is likely that the project of representing the sea, cinematically and otherwise, will pivot on the matter of how to visualize extinction in ways that not only clarify the crisis but also excite passionate action.

CHAPTER EIGHT

Imaginary Worlds

The Human–Ocean Relation in Fantastic Futures of Affluence and Formidable Visions of Unsettledness

ARIANE TANNER

INTRODUCTION

It was with an article entitled "Undersea" (1937) that Rachel Carson first stepped into the public eye as poetic scientific writer. Today remembered foremost as the courageous scientist who in the early 1960s revealed the disastrous effects of the pesticide DDT, the recent secondary literature has emphasized that the sea was in fact the biographical and thematic starting point for her broader interests.[1] Indeed, in the 1937 article—which the *Atlantic Monthly* published under the title "Undersea" but that Carson had originally named "The World of Waters," which better conveys what she was doing—the reader was to be submerged in an unfamiliar *Lebensraum* animated by hitherto unknown creatures that spend their lives between waves and currents, coasts and the open sea. Drawing on her profound knowledge of the appearance and characteristics of sea animals, their life cycles, and their predators, Carson employed prose that was both lucid and light-footed, earnest and emphatic, to transform the fathomless waters into a tangible world animated by creatures of the sea that seem now like familiar aliens—creatures that, although they do not share the space of humans, now appear as our near companions in an adjacent life-world (Carson 1937, 1941). Furthermore, almost incidentally, the reader comes to understand that only through consciously engaging with

FIGURE 8.1 Rachel Carson standing seaside, examining specimen in jar. Photograph by Alfred Eisenstaedt/The LIFE Picture Collection/Getty Images.

these "Worlds of Waters" will we be able to preserve its beauty, so admirably represented through Carson's poetic language (Figure 8.1).

The stunning thing about Carson's insights into the complexities of the ocean is hidden in a biographical detail about the author herself: she could not swim (Lepore 2018: 66). As a writer and a biologist she thus exemplifies the crucial role of imagination for the understanding of the ocean: "To sense this world of water known to the creatures of the sea we must shed our human perceptions of length and breadth and time and place, and enter vicariously into a universe of all-pervading water" (1937: 322).

CHARACTERISTICS OF OCEANIC IMAGINATION

Imagining and knowing are profoundly interrelated activities. Since the 1970s the history of science has been shedding light on the soical and material contingencies that inflect scientific practices (see, for example, Latour and Woolgar 1979; Shapin 2010), and has reconsidered the value of such approaches as thought experiments, fallacious hypotheses, and hazardous theorizing. Imagination is indeed a resource for the advance of science, and most especially when direct experience is hard to obtain or lacking altogether. The sea is bound to evoke "imaginary worlds" simply by reason of its sheer magnitude, accounting as it does for 70 percent of our planet's surface (Arthus-Bertrand and Skerry 2013: 22). The conditions of high pressure, the absence of respiratory oxygen, the profound darkness from about two hundred meters, all mitigate against direct accessibility, and so call forth our dreams. In this regard, even deep-sea marine biologists talk about the ocean and its inhabitants' lives as a "black box" (Boetius and Boetius 2011: 11) meaning that human experiences of the (deep) ocean are always "mediated through technologies, knowledge systems, or cultural conceptions of this space – or some combination of these" (Rozwadowski 2012: 583). The use of elaborate techniques such as robotics and sonar point to the fact that human beings are scarcely able to explore this remote space by themselves, and must instead supplement or substitute their physiological conditions. Deep oceans share this characteristic with outer space. As a consequence, imagination is assigned an outstanding role in connection to our knowledge of the oceans, just as essential as technology, and indeed the two exert a powerful mutual influence on each other (Rozwadowski 2010a: 524).

The materiality of the ocean, in the sense of its physico-chemical characteristics and the corresponding human physiological limits, forms the premise for the following survey of the "imaginary worlds" of the oceans in the period 1920–2020. "Imagination," as I use the term in this chapter, does not simply mean everything that exceeds perception and has therefore to be imagined. Rather, the power of imagination lies in its ability to produce "mental pictures" and "sociotechnical imaginaries" (Mattl and Schulte 2014: 10; Jasanoff 2015). The interplay between the reflection of the past and the projection of the future has both reproductive and productive elements, and both movements have their creative, social, and moral aspects.

As I will show, the translation of imaginary practices related to the oceans in such highly industrialized regions as Europe and the United States, primarily took place in association with the idea of resources. Plankton—the billions of tiny, floating organisms (flora and fauna) in watery environments—plays a special role in this story: it represents many aspects of an imagined scientific, technical, and geopolitical solution to the problems faced by the Western world. Around this substance we find imaginary worlds of cornucopian nourishment, endless energy repositories, and a secure future. I will argue that the conceptual translation of plankton into aggregated "biomass" during the 1920s fostered the idea of quantifiable biological marine masses that could serve human needs; the hopes connected to the industrial fabrication of food through algae from the 1940s until the end of the 1960s were based upon these expectations; and this in turn meant that the (predicted) absence of plankton was translated into visions of hunger, scarcity, and war, such as the perfect dystopia depicted in the 1973 movie *Soylent Green* (dir. Richard Fleischer).

The context in which we locate algae from the 1990s onwards expresses the new meaning assigned to biomass: fuel. From feeding the world to keeping the highly industrialized countries rolling, I call the corresponding historical process between the end of the 1960s and the 1980s the "geopolitical shift in oceanic imaginations." This shift is crucial for the recent understanding of the oceanic imaginaries and constituted by two complementary developments. On the one hand, the fact of limited land resources and decolonialization led to the identification of new frontiers in space and in the ocean. On the other hand, expressions of the vulnerability and exhaustion or even destruction of oceanic life increased. The notion that connects the two is that of the "carrying capacity," namely, the question how many people the planetary resources could sustain. This question in turn led to the emergence of new international organizations and other actors enmeshed in new networks of geopolitical power, as well as new ideas of sustainability and environmental protection.

The pictures from space that showed the limits of "the blue planet" were the very same pictures that conveyed its fragility and dignity, allowing a reinspired relationship with the ocean to develop during the 1960s and 1970s. As it became ever more clear that the ocean itself is heavily influenced by global warming, and therefore that marine life and human beings themselves are threatened by profound changes, the ocean reentered the imaginary world with a new and lively force. The proposed new geological epoch, the Anthropocene, bundles different imaginative encounters with the ocean, ranging from ideas of geo-engineering to the fiction of the intelligent self-empowerment of the sea to get rid of (some) humans.

The conclusion of this chapter offers some thoughts about the intimate connection between humans and the ocean, showing that the territorial thinking that was so prominent during the last century, based on a strict nature/culture distinction and paralleled by an equally strict land/water distinction, has dissolved in this time of global warming. Today, above all, the ocean confronts us with the implications of the history of ecological entanglement.

BIOMASS AS IMAGINARY POTENTIAL

The tiny floating organisms that would eventually be identified as the bottom of the marine food chain first excited scientific interest in the middle of the nineteenth century. The so-called Müller gauze, developed by the German physiologist Johannes Müller and implemented together with his student Ernst Haeckel, became the cornerstone of pelagic fishery and therefore of a new branch of science. The net itself was the concrete expression of Müller's idea that imagination proceeds knowledge, and that expertise goes hand in hand with reflection (Rheinberger 1998: 144–5). Haeckel (1862) became especially fascinated by one zooplankton species, the Radiolaria, and published various works intended to substantiate Darwin's idea of gradual evolution. Like many of his contemporaries, he was convinced that these organisms promised direct access to knowledge about the origin of life.

The physiologist and marine biologist Victor Hensen followed another hypothesis while researching the same object. In 1889 he set sail to reveal the metabolism of the sea, seeking to evaluate the distribution of masses of plankton—a term that he himself coined (1887: 1). Employing a physiological analogy, he talked of plankton as the "blood of the sea" (1911: 5), emphasizing its life-supporting function in the ocean, and filtered the water column at selected locations in the Atlantic. The counting of the catches followed a prescribed protocol and took several years. Although his method was severely criticized and his conclusions about the distribution of plankton were not entirely correct, the work of Hensen and other marine scientists who adopted a quantitative methodology succeeded in promoting oceanography to the status of an independent research area and so laid the grounds for a new discipline (biological oceanography) as well as an economic perspective on the biological productivity of the sea (Mills 1989: 2).

Hensen and Haeckel engaged in intense debates about methodology, and questioned each others' expertise. Yet what unites their different approaches is the underlying idea of a tight relation between ocean and land, and a supposition that knowledge and techniques for the visualization of ocean life can lead to better knowledge about human life itself. Both treated plankton as the basis of the marine food chain, and therefore as an important "ecological" (especially for Haeckel) factor in oceanic as well as human welfare (Tanner 2014: 336–41).

During the 1920s this approach in marine biology was strenghtened by the introduction of the concept of "biomass." What was probably the very first notion of "Bio-Masse" (in German) reveals a story that has those characteristics of which historians of science are so fond, where contingency leads to knowledge: it begins with an omission. The German zoologist and limnologist Reinhard Demoll (1927), a specialist in pondlife fertilization experiments, put aside a covered bowl containing some common freshwater amphipoda, and forgot about it for weeks. When he finally remembered the vessel on the windowsill, he lifted the lid to find full-grown amphipods. Demoll turned the accident into an experiment: over the following year the water was pored over and the *Gammarus fossarum*—a zooplankton species—were counted. What he had observed in the unintended experiment on the windowsill was the fact that counting and weighing provided results that overall remained stable. It was in this respect that he coined the term *biomass*; a huge term that emerged, so to speak, out of a little pond, in connection with a species of zooplankton (Figure 8.2).

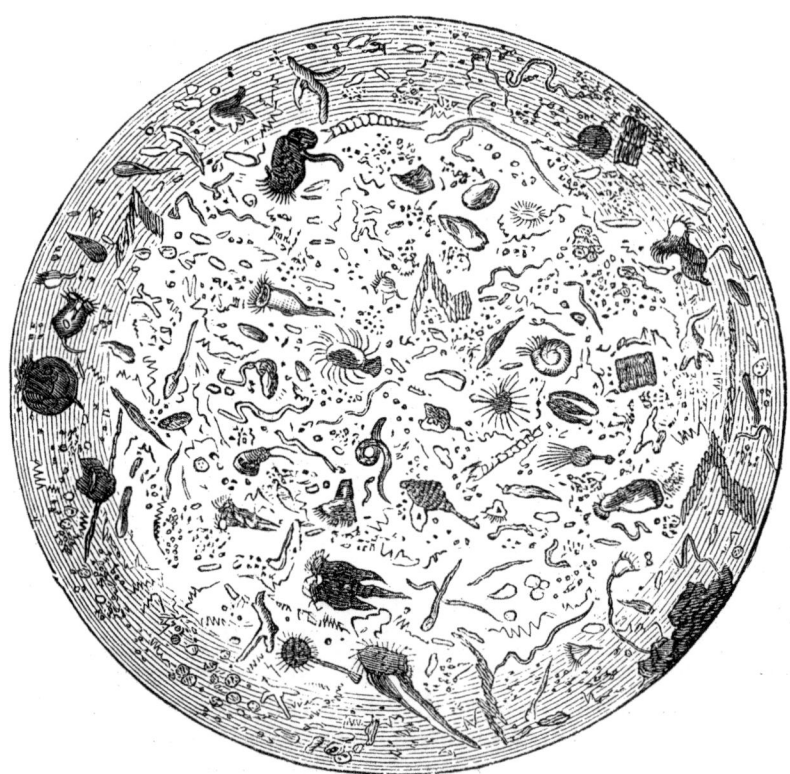

FIGURE 8.2 Antique illustration of life in a water drop.

With questions of fertilization and optimum yield firmly in mind, Demoll defined "bio-mass" as a quantitative indicator of the nutritive storage in a defined area (1927: 462). But in saying that biomass—or the present mass of biological material—is an indicator of the prosperity of the whole, it becomes evident that biomass is connected to other masses as well.

I would like to emphasize several aspects of this little story: first, the fact that this biological mass grew out of sight. This alludes to seventeenth-century discourse about abandoned buckets and pots that would all of a sudden be aswarm with living beings, giving rise to speculation about *generatio spontanea* in water. A fantastic potential for reproduction and rapid renewal has been attributed to biomass. As far as phytoplankton is concerned, these tiniest of watery creatures in the ocean make up to 95 percent "of the vegetation of the sea" (Seavitt Nordenson 2014: 7).

The second important aspect lies in the possibility of quantification: biomass affords of numerical measurement that makes it possible to deal with the different elements participating in the food chain. Hensen had already alluded to the possibility of an analogous treatment for biological aggregates—such as "grass, grain, human beings, and domesticated animals" (1887: 2, my translation)—irrespective of their ontological status. The concept of biomass neutralizes genetic, phenotypical, or any other difference. It is a number for a biological aggregate that can be translated in terms of mass or in terms of energy (Lotka 1925). This allows for mathematical calculation and prognosis of biomasses that we are more accustomed to talking about in terms of "primary producers" and "consumers" (Townsend, Begon, and Harper 2009: 428–40).

Third, the characteristic of an instantaneous tipping between plenty and sparsity, between control and chaotic behavior, is rooted in the notion of "biomass" from the 1920s. This signifies that masses-in-motion always raise questions of regulation and involve the possible unintended achievement of a "critical mass" after which the possibility of control is undermined.[2] On the one hand, this echoes trends in political theory around 1900 in the face of industrialization and urbanization, when the mass of employees and citizens came into the focus of political discourse as a beacon of hope with the potential to realize social reforms, as well as an anarchic force that threatened established political hierarchies and therefore needed strong guidance (Gamper and Schnyder 2006). On the other hand, it resonates with today's discussions of possible "tipping points" of ecosystems in the sense of a sudden collapse after a period of continuously increasing stress.

As a consequence of these three aspects—reproductivity, quantification, regulation—the concept of biomass inherently encourages the development of ideas of optimum control and administration of all the biological "masses" that are involved in the production cycle, and evokes technocratic visions and ideas of total operationalization. Questions emerge about feasibility, optimum use, and establishing balance as well as of the perfect loop between increase, throughput, feedback, and regulation. With dreams of potential resources and fantastic accretion, but also fear of loss of control, marvelous futures go hand in hand with apocalyptic doomsaying—all mediated through the ocean.

UTOPIA ON YOUR PLATE

The statistical, qualitative, and quantitative work on plankton fostered the idea of food chains (Elton 1927) beginning in the ocean and ending on land with human beings. Alister Hardy, for example, worked on the possible catch of herrings, evaluating their nutrition (1924), while others spoke of "The farmer of the sea" who could not only expand his traditional working area by acquiring new bases for nutrition but also transfer his agricultural knowledge into oceanic areas (Herdman 1920: 289). The idea of harvesting the sea was fostered after the Second World War and its disastrous consequences, in particular the malnutrition of millions of people. In this period, as the historian Warren Belasco has described, several discourses supported the industrial plankton project: pessimistic prognoses were heavily influenced by a neo-Malthusian perspective that expected that the world's food capacities would not keep up with the development of the human population. Even the optimists raised profound concerns that agriculture could not provide enough food, because of topographically restricted soil resources and the dearth of innovation (Belasco 1997: 608).

Economic prognosis is strongly based in "imagined futures" (Beckert 2016). In reference to resources of the ocean, these imagined futures include estimated stocks that would outweigh investments and so promise entrepreneurial incomes. Given that the access to the resources in the world's oceans is bound up with specific and intractable problems, such economic imagined futures remain highly speculative and even utopian.

In the 1950s the focus fell upon one species of phytoplankton, *Chlorella*, which seemed to fulfill the technocratic and optimistic dreams of general advancement. The fast-growing fresh-water algae was expected to have a photosynthetic rate twenty times greater than the mean rate of the terrestrial crop. It even promised to leverage the second law of thermodynamics, since *Chlorella* seemed to produce more output than it needed input. Sustained by an inexhaustible resource—sunlight—algae plants were supposed to grow "with less than nothing" (Stimson 1956: 264) and could also be situated in the desert and would not compete with agricultural land; the supposed twentyfold production could be harvested daily and independent of the season; and the metabolic loop would be perfect in that there were no waste products (Figure 8.3). Sterility and manageability seemed unbeatable arguments for algae cultures in comparison to people-intensive, energy-sapping work outside on damp fields in capricious

FIGURE 8.3 Melvin Calvin inspects *Chlorella* tanks in his laboratory, Berkeley, 1961. © Bettmann/Getty Images.

weather. The arguments in favor of raising phytoplankton on a grand scale to gain food were convincing, promising, and a good fit for the science magazines that popularized the idea (Belasco 1997: 619).

Most importantly, *Chlorella* promised to produce a very high level of proteins. This last factor, the percentage of proteins, provided a strong argument for the cultivation of algae, because the level of provision of proteins appeared in the statistics of the Food and Agricultural Organization (FAO) as an indicator for malnutrition (FAO 1948: 2). The focus, therefore, was not only on the condition of the existing world population but also on the nourishment of future generations. In this prospect, Lionel A. Walford's monograph *Living Resources of the Sea* found a prominent place in the discourse about a growing world population that needed increased yields from the sea, a world to which "scientific research will show the way" (1958: 3). In an arithmetically perfect harmony, the algae was broken down into its nutritive substances on the one hand, and the human needs were listed on the other. Product and consumer matched in a technocratic way. The energy-consuming metabolic transformations between phytoplankton and herring were to be considerably shortened. It seemed possible to fight hunger on a global scale. Where scarcity loomed, plenty was promised.

Two strands of the "utopia out of biomass" scenario are particularly worthy of mention: first, and most importantly, is the continuous—and presumably fantastic—productivity of the algae in clean, enclosed, and perfectly controlled artificial environments. In this respect phytoplankton served as an analogy for the future of technological innovation itself (Belasco 2006: 201–7; Prehoda 1967: 202). Second, the new highly regulated environment of the cultivated algae gave rise to a new role of stewardship to mankind. In 1952, Francis Joseph Weiss, biochemist and author of the book *Chemical Agriculture*, predicted: "Thus the algae, which started out as pilot plants of Nature, are now serving as pilot plants of Man, who will doubtless get equally important results – and far more speedily" (1952: 17). The grand narrative of evolution that started out with tiny watery organisms was to be transferred into humanity's hands.

By the end of the 1960s, after two decades of test tubes, ponds, and experiments with algae the pioneers had to admit that their project had failed: major problems had emerged due to variations in temperature; the difficulty in evaluating the appropriate depth of the algae pond, or the light intensity, or the correct rhythm of stirring and cropping; the unstable aggregations of protein; not to mention the insurmountable difficulties in keeping the mixture sterile. Moreover, it turned out that industrially cultivated *Chlorella* devoured astronomical amounts of energy in the form of fresh water, oxygen, and carbon dioxide. A pound of dry phytoplankton cost 1 dollar and 12 cents, while the same quantity of soy cost 6 cents (Belasco 2006: 211). In addition to the soy, efficient fertilizers, and hybrid forms of corn that economically outclassed the algae project, food habits in the Western world emerged as huge obstacle. Only very small amounts of algae would be eaten in Europe and the United States, and only when hidden in ice cream or chicken soup, while the raw product was described as too brittle and its flavor unsatisfactory. Utopia foundered on traditional dinnertime habits (Belasco 2006: 207–13). Even the cooking experiments by the (wives of the) Japanese algae engineers (Milner 1953: 31) or Demoll's ironic menu card, from algae soup to algae gateau, could not shift that impediment (1957: 136).

Algae food did find an application in health food stores and during journeys in space (Wharton, Smernoff, and Averner 1988); it thus became reserved to a small segment of the world's population, while in the latter application phytoplankton retained its original promise as a possibly perfect material for closed cycles, guaranteeing oxygen and food under isolated conditions. Further, exactly when the enthusiasm for industrial phytoplankton-experiments had imploded, a dystopian version of the perfect metabolic loop found its way into a movie.

THE PERFECT METABOLIC CYCLE IS DYSTOPIAN

The 1973 movie *Soylent Green* is a radical interpretation of the utility of biomass. Based on Harry Harrison's novel *Make Room! Make Room!* (1966), the plot of the film emphasizes the problem of food in a state of overpopulation. In a fantastical future set in 2022, the world finds itself on the edge of environmental collapse: forty million people live in New York, the climate conditions are almost unbearably hot, the landscape is destroyed, vegetables or meat fetch exorbitant prices that even the rich cannot afford. Only very few people have an income, and most are homeless, forced to sleep on the stairs inside dilapidated buildings. The imagined technocratic future is represented by the pervasive "Soylent Corporation" that provides the population with plankton chips, the very final nutritional resource. Every Tuesday, we learn, the Soylent Corporation promotes special chips with a particular taste, which people run for, having after all nothing better to do. One Tuesday they find out that the so-called Soylent Green has run out, which causes a riot. The crowd, the furious, hungry, and enraged mass of people, is confronted with the brute force of the police and reduced to a physical mass that has to be removed (Figure 8.4).

While the older lead character, disillusioned by the world, elects to die in a euthanasia hospital surrounded by images of unspoiled nature, the younger one, Thorn, follows the trucks that leave the building, where he learns what "Soylent Green" really is made of: the allegedly endless source of plankton has been replaced by what is indeed the very last nutrient resource … dead human bodies, as part of the biomass, have been supplying the industrial production of the Soylent Corporation. Following this terrible insight, Thorn is discovered and has to flee. The last sequence of the film shows him wounded, in a overcrowded church that serves as refuge. His very last words, which became a cult reference point, are: "Soylent Green is people!"

The movie *Soylent Green* thus follows the reasoning to its logical conclusion: the interpretation of biomass as a potential energy reservoir came along with the possibility of the operationalization of the different masses in circulation as well. Technocratic and engineering approaches are to be evaluated solely in terms of their feasibility, to fulfill dreams about the ideal regulation of the masses involved in the societal metabolism. *Soylent Green* is the dystopian answer to the questions raised by idealized conceptions of closed cycles of resource usage (Höhler 2014b: 438–9), which contain the possibility of total recycling. Combined with a capitalist system

FIGURE 8.4 *Soylent Green* (dir. Richard Fleischer, 1973), film still. Photograph by MGM Studios/Courtesy of Getty Images.

premised on the unending exploitation of resources without consideration of environmental limits, we end up in a dictatorship of monopolists.

THE GEOPOLITICAL SHIFT IN OCEANIC IMAGINATIONS

In the 1970s the economist Colin Clark wrote about the massive protein stores in the ocean, but pointed to the problem of costs in harvesting. Notwithstanding, following the idea of the so-called Asian diet, Clark speculated about a possible future wherein 146 billion people could be nourished (1970: 195). He later adjusted that number, but still postulated a possible food supply for 47 billion people if policymakers would only channel innovation through funding and taxes (1977: 153). Another path, referred to by Clark, was followed by authors who proposed to speed up the production of plankton, and therefore of fish, through warming the sea water with nuclear energy (Clark 1970: 170). Clark's thinking reveals a mix of demasking the "myth of overpopulation"—which was the title of one of his books—and a strong predilection for the technological fix boosted by political regulation.

In contrast to these visions, the late 1960s and the 1970s were generally characterized by a neo-Malthusian discourse of overpopulation that favored isolationist tendencies. One famous example of this tendency was the 1967 publication of the Paddock siblings' *Famine 1975! America's Decision, Who Will Survive?* The oil price crises of 1973 and 1979 made it clear that the economics of the Western world was not self-sustaining, and depended on politically unstable nations. This last aspect in particular prompted the search for alternative fuel resources. Around 1980, biomass became the *terminus tecnicus* for quantifying reservoirs of potentially usable energy sources from renewable origins. Several anthologies with headings such as *Biomass for Energy* or *Energy from Biomass* were published, and in one of these the editors plainly stated that having survived starvation, epidemics, and war, the world sees itself confronted with a new problem: the energy crisis (Cheremisinoff, Cheremisinoff, and Ellerbusch 1980: 1).

So the earlier scheme, in which the Western world could perfect the techniques for raising marine biomass to ensure its own freedom through feeding the rest of the world, turned into a project of securing the energy needs of the industrialized countries. The question "Food or Fuel from Algae?" had been posed as early as the 1950s (Milner 1954), and by the 2000s the answer seemed clear: definitely fuel. Between 2005 and 2012 the fuel-from-algae enterprises experienced a boom, the rhetoric of these projects reflecting the photosynthetic wonder machine of the 1950s. But almost all of them had to scale back their enormous promises of billions of gallons of fuel and specialize on the production of very specific ("pharmazeutical") material in small amounts. In recent years the food-or-fuel discussion has cast disrepute on the use of biomass such as maize, soy, or vegetable oil as a fuel resource. At the same time, there was renewed interest in the idea of algae for food or protein storage (UN Environment Programme [UNEP] 2009).

Although the industrial algae projects had failed by the end of the 1960s, the ocean was still conceived of as cornucopian. As Sabine Höhler explains, around 1970 the sea became a substitutional space—as did outer space—in a period of rising consciousness of the limited land (Höhler 2014b: 440). What she referred to as the "Age of Capacity" denotes exactly that shift from a territory-oriented expansionism (from 1860 to 1970, the colonial age) to a global geopolitics (Höhler 2015b: 5). Space exploration and imaginations of the ocean's endless resources went hand in hand. Technologies that were developed during the first half of the twentieth century promised to attain resources that formerly had been beyond our reach (see Höhler in this volume). In particular, the extraction of ores, the promise of manganese nodules, and the possibility of drilling for oil at formerly unimaginable depths seemed to come into the realm of practicability (Sparenberg 2015a). The sea was still referred to as a place of endless storage, but now in connection to non-biotic material.

Cyberneticists and futurists followed an engineering approach and spoke of unforeseen treasures in the deep, forecasting that by mining rare ores on the sea bottom using machines fueled by nuclear power, human development would no longer be limited by the availability of the rarest elements on the earth's surface, as posited in "Liebig's law" (Marfeld 1972: 13; Prehoda 1967: 145–8). New technologies and anticipated new material sources mutually affirmed each other, raising in turn new questions of property rights (Hull 1967; Wooster 1969). The sea mirrored not only the prospective gains in welfare but also the new potential economic and political power.

Interestingly, the discussions on the global commons that took place in the 1970s did not perceive the three-dimensionality of the oceans. The regulations concerning sea miles and the proprietorship of sea shelves were limited to territorial concepts of access. Visions and practices of (colonial) exploration and new landfalls pervaded in the international politics of sea law around 1970 (Höhler 2014a: 59–61). In so doing, international regulations displayed a perfect fit with the early diving films from the 1920s and 1930s, showing divers walking the seabed, an activity that was enabled by the developments in equipment as well as older ideas of exploring new frontiers (Torma 2013: 30, 35).

Envisioned resources or substitutional spaces used to be at the core of the so-called imaginary war (Kaldor 1990). As the historian of science Naomi Oreskes explains, together with outer space, the deep-sea environment, also called "inner space," played a key role during the Cold War. She names scientists and military strategists involved in framing the "theater" for which the ocean provided the stage, and "in which nuclear weapons might be stored, transported, disguised, detected, and, ultimately (in the worst case), exchanged" (2014b: 383). On the other hand, Matthew Grant and Benjamin Ziemann make the insightful point that the "Cold War" was a war against the imagination because it suppressed every alternative scenario: "the Bomb" seemed mandatory to secure freedom, and the possibilty of universal destruction was a necessary corollary of present-day security and future well-being (2016: 2–4). As Kaldor remarks, however, while the strategies themselves belong to the realm of imagination, the "preparations for an imaginary war are real enough" (1990: 212). Analogously, one could state that presumed oceanic resources belong to the imaginatory realm (even if some quantities do exist), but the preparations for reaping them are real—or, in other words, they constitute an economic investment.

The modes in which perceptions of the ocean have been integrated into geopolitical views are elaborated by the sociologist John Hannigan (2016), who defines four recent discursive framings that he calls "Oceanic frontiers," "governing the Abyss," "sovereignty games," and "saving the oceans." Even where they are not embedded into territorial thinking, they retain close relations with the relevant institutions, organizations, international players, regulations, and policies. In recent times, capitalist thinking has expanded across the ocean too (Steinberg 2001): entrepreneurship has come to supersede claims of national or international sovereignty on the oceans. The geopolitical shift mentioned above is still operative today. The spaces of the ocean are becoming more and more mapped, regularized, explored, and exploited.

The conceptualization of the ocean as a frontier, as Helen Rozwadowski remarks, has been weighing upon it since the 1960s: "The stubborn persistence in viewing the ocean in terms of its economic resources has contributed to massive global overfishing, depletion of other marine resources, and cascades of unintended ecosystem effects" (2012: 597). As Carmel Finley (2011) writes, the concept of the "maximum sustainable yield," characteristic of the thinking of the 1940s and 1950s, was fundamentally misleading, and even after its reformation still provided a basis for international policies and subsidies that have led to global overfishing. Again, this is a logic that remains widespread today. As has aptly been remarked, "The only way to end overfishing is to fish less" (Rosenberg 2003: 105).

With the rise of the capitalist economy "a major transformation in the temporal orientation of actors took place" (Beckert 2016: 33). This change in cognitive orientations is crucial for an understanding of capitalist dynamics, because expectations of the future shape present decisions and guide our imagination of what is to happen (33–6). In this respect, the simplest image can gain a totally new meaning: for example, the prognosis that the melting of the Arctic ice could cut the passage from Rotterdam to Tokyo from 23,000 kilometers to 16,000 kilometers awakens economic desires that outstrip any worries about climatic change (Arthus-Bertrand and Skerry 2013: 212). The so-called run on the Arctic expressed these desires: although it is not yet decided who shall be allowed to use which parts of this space and volume or in which way, the corresponding "imaginaries" of the different groups and actors are vividly reported by Philip Steinberg, Jeremy Tasch, and Hannes Gerhardt in *Contesting the Arctic* (2015). This example shows how the human–ocean relation, for decades thought of in terms of inexhaustible marine resources, develops in parallel with our views about profound changes in the earth system overall.

A SENSE OF FRAGILITY

The unilateral perception of the ocean as a "frontier" (or in terms of any other terrestrial concept) was not mandatory, not even around 1970. Describing the emergence of the visual culture of "planet Earth," Sheila Jasanoff observes that the NASA space programs did not fall upon minds that were entirely unprepared but rather resonated with the growing environmental consciousness, the new pictures being taken to express our sense of interconnectedness

(2001: 309–10). Pictures of our planet from space on the one hand elicited metaphors of our "spaceship earth" that needed to be wisely managed, and on the other hand gave rise to perceptions of our "one earth only" that was genuinely fragile and in need of protection (Höhler 2015b: 3). Thus these photographs from space caught the spirit of the "Limits to Growth" (Meadows et al. 1972) as well as the idea of this being the only living space in the whole cosmos (Lovelock 1979). Strikingly, the iconic name "blue marble" referred to the color of the ocean.

The twofold perception—of limited space that needed expansion and of fragile space that needed protection—is also hidden in the figure of the "aquanaut." The science fiction author and diver Arthur C. Clarke, for example, "presented a vision of a new human relationship with the ocean, one that integrated science, recreation, industry, government, and spirituality" (Rozwadowski 2012: 580). While highly technical books such as *Living and Working Under the Sea* (Koblick and Miller 1984) can be interpreted as a extension of terrestrial life into the sea, the picture they sketch would be incomplete without all the photographs and filmic documentation of the biological diversity, multifaceted habitats, and variegated marine forms obtained during these experiments. In a related manner, Hans Hass's film *Menschen unter Haien* (Men Among Sharks) (1947) was basically an effort to abolish prejudice against sharks, seeking to replace this with understanding and respect for the living form. The BBC series *Blue Planet* (and *Blue Planet II*) continued the tradition of enlightening the public about the oceans and their inhabitants. The framing of the films, which are technically highly sophisticated, is explicitly intended to awaken environmental consciousness about the oceans.

In retrospect, there is good reason to think that between 1979 and 1989 there was sufficient knowledge available about climate and environmental change for this to have been "the decade we almost stopped climate change" (Rich 2018). In recent times, the West has been confronted with the legacy of its capitalist and industrialist past, which has led and continues to lead to massive emissions of greenhouse gases that boost global warming. The Intergovernmental Panel on Climate Change (IPCC) addressed oceanic issues in their very first Scientific Assessment of Climate Change in 1990, treating it as a (not-yet-quantifiable) carbon dioxide sink and as part of the world that was warming; at the same time, for example, it mentioned our "incomplete understanding" of "the oceans which influence the timing and patterns of climate change" (IPCC 2010: xii) (Figure 8.5). Today it is widely known that the ocean plays a key role for all planetary systems: the acidification and (plastic) pollution of water destroys marine life and severs food chains, while the polar ice sheets are melted by the warming seas, with the predictable consequences of coral reef die-offs, rising sea levels, and weather extremes such as hurricanes, droughts, and floods. The drastic drop in biodiversity, the loss of biomass, and the unknown decline in

FIGURE 8.5 NASA ocean data shows "climate dance" of plankton, 2014. NASA Goddard Space Flight Center. Wikimedia Commons (public domain).

the amount of plankton (Jackson 2008), are all by now as alarming as they are uncontested. Metaphors such as "boundaries" and "tipping points"—whether soon to be passed or already exceeded—foster the perception of global endangerment.

The concept of the Anthropocene bundles together all the recent changes in planetary parameters in comparison to the conditions that have been generally typical since the last ice age ended circa 11,000 years ago. With the Anthropocene, natural scientists have proposed the study of "the geology of mankind," starting with the Industrial Revolution in Europe (Crutzen 2002). Humanists debate whether a concept as universal as the Anthropocene can be meaningfully posited if the greenhouse gas emissions that are causing the "present crisis of climate change" (Chakrabarty 2009: 201) are so strongly bound to industrialization in Western countries (Malm and Hornborg 2014); and critics ask whether we should not differentiate between an Anthropocene narrative and a sociopolitical narrative (Simon 2020). Indeed, the Anthropocene as a tool for reflection embraces all parts of the world, connects the planetary scale to human history, and relates the present to the deep past and to the future.

In the final section I analyze perceptions of the ocean in the Anthropocene, these being characterized on the one side by intense capitalist activity geared to acquiring fossil resources, and on the other side by a strong consciousness of the endangered planet.

OCEANIC IMAGINATIONS IN THE TIME OF THE ANTHROPOCENE

In recent decades it has become possible to measure the oceanic warming and acidification (Tyrrell 2011). This new knowledge has brought to consciousness that the ocean is not static but rather is a dynamic system that plays a vital and life-sustaining role within the world climate system:

> This shift in understanding – from the ocean as deep, dark, vast, and mostly inaccessible and not (except to mariners and fishermen) terribly important to the ocean as a vast abode of life, both familiar and strange, and a place on which all life, both marine and terrestrial, depends – is one of the most important cultural and scientific shifts of the twentieth century.
>
> (Oreskes 2014b: 384)

The important role of fiction, imagination, and the arts in finding societal answers has been repeatedly emphasized (Emmett and Lekan 2016). As the very notion of the Anthropocene tacitly implies that the present period could be the last on earth to be observed by humanity, it also evokes an apocalyptic imagination. There is even a genre of science fiction devoted to images of a world devoid of human beings (Horn 2014: 11–12; Weisman 2007). The four examples can be labeled *technological fix*, *escapism*, *adaptation*, and *nature's revenge*. Fictions are not boundless: they are interventions in the imaginary realm of culture and therefore help shape it at the same time as they express it (Horn 2014: 23–4). The examples will be followed by some reflections on the anthropomorphization of the ocean.

One mooted answer to the frightening changes brought about by global warming in all parts of the planetary system is the idea of the "technological fix." Science and technology, so it is thought, will save the world. In so far as marine environments are concerned, the metaphor of "the biological pump" gained influence around 1990. CO_2 was to be "pumped" through phytoplankton from upper water layers to certain depths where the lower temperatures and the higher pressures would inhibit its dissemination for hundreds of years. Large-scale experiments between 1993 and 2009 aimed at amplifying this natural process and promised a cheap way to mitigate climate change (Strong, Cullen, and Chisholm 2009). In the plans for these projects we observe the translation of a biological object (phytoplankton) into a logistical one (carbon carrier), although the initiators emphasize they do not seek to act invasively but rather in the sense of strengthening a biological process that was ongoing anyway. At root, though, the ocean here is thought of as a regulatable space. However, experiments did not provide the expected results but rather showed the deeply interconnectedness and complexity of the biological, chemical, and physical aspects of the ocean (Tanner 2019).

Analysts of the Anthropocene state that the proposals for large-scale geo-engineering date back to the Western imperial and economic thinking of the nineteenth century. The reemerging discourse on scarcity, connected with a strong belief in the power of technology, constrains all questions to receive this kind of answer. The ideological dimension of such climate solutions is manifest in their tacit assumption of the continued leadership of Western countries (Baskin 2015).

The shadow side of the technological fix is escapism. If everything seems to be a step closer to catastrophe, the Western world needs an alternative planet, or at least a complementary space as in the case of the movie *Red Planet* (dir. Anthony Hoffman, 2000). Anthony Hoffman's movie deals with the attempted establishment of an atmosphere on Mars using a species of algae, prior to human colonization. Sabine Höhler remarks that Mars forms the backdrop for a bundle of images: escapism, technological hubris, dreams of perfect metabolic loops. The striking thing here is that Earth—presumably abandoned—"acts as standby" (Höhler 2017b). We find the same cognitive disposition in two other fictional works: T.C. Boyle's novel *The Terranauts* (2016) about the American tests with "biosphere II" during the 1990s, and the film *The Martian* (dir. Ridley Scott, 2015). In each case, the final aim is to come back to earth and optimize its biosphere, giving the whole experiment a touch of pseudo-escapism; but to reach that goal a great deal of knowledge, technology, and physical work is required—or as the protagonist of *The Martian* puts it: "I'm gonna have to science the shit out of this." This forward-and-backward movement between space and earth, artificial and "real time" biosphere, is also evident in the framing of NASA's NEEMO 21 mission in 2016: its sixteen-day stays in the ocean, when they went for so-called spacewalks at the bottom of the sea, was meant as training for manned missions to Mars (Figure 8.6).[3]

Adaptation seems to be a middle ground between technocratic control and escapism. The figure of the "aquanaut" (with its obvious analogy to space exploration) provides some insights in this respect: it stands not only for technological experiments and the expansion of the human domain, but also for a physiological test of the possibilities and limitations of bodily adaptation to oceanic milieus. The aquanaut is a living human experiment in becoming a quasi-fish, both in the sense of adaption to watery environments and in the

FIGURE 8.6 NASA NEEMO 22, aquanaut crew, 2017. NASA Analogs via Wikimedia Commons (public domain).

sense of "going back to where we came from." The fascination of amphibian life forms is mostly expressed in the fantasy literature about mermaids, but remains alive even today, as proven by the multiple Oscar-winning movie *The Shape of Water* (dir. Guillermo del Toro, 2017). From a scientific—but also a mystical—point of view, the saltiness of our bodily fluids and the little webs of skin between our fingers were interpreted as evidence of anatomical features that humans had lost in the course of evolution—as Sir Alister Hardy, author of a natural history entitled *The Open Sea* (1958), speculated, "Was man more aquatic in the past?" (1960).

Besides such unproven theories about man's oceanic past, concrete questions remain about the limits of possible adaptation to rising sea levels. The historian John Gillis claims that "Today half of the world's population resides within 120 miles of the sea. By 2025 it is estimated that this could reach 75 percent" (2012: 187). He raises questions about how we are to "live with coasts" that are eroding and endangered by floods and extreme weather. His warning, that only rich people with spare time can afford to live on houseboats and therefore easily adapt (2012: 194–5), must be extended to projects such as Dubai's para-national social constructs, the artificial floating islands for billionaires.

In other examples of imaginary worlds, the agency is transferred entirely to the natural realm itself, namely, the ocean. One topos in this respect—nature as actant—is the *deluge*: as the French historian Alain Corbin puts it in his history of the discovery of the coasts, in the Christian tradition the ocean used to be perceived as a deluge only temporarily subdued (1988). Many films have addressed the motif of drastic rises in sea level and disastrous inundations. As Eva Horn observes, these stagings of catastrophes go together with a new understanding of eschatological history that sees either the deluge or the end of the world itself as initiated by an almighty God: the modern metaphor of the "tipping point" conveys the idea of vicious natural feedback loops as well as that of the abrupt loss of human empowerment (2014: 15–20).

In Frank Schätzing's novel *Der Schwarm* (The Swarm) (2004) a marine creature takes control, and only marine biologists and whale observers realize it is a multifaceted entity composed of thousands of protozoans. The organism wages a form of biological warfare "in revenge" for the unthinking behavior of humanity (Nitzke 2012: 168–72): the final collapse of the European continental shelf into the sea is thus the result of nature's agency guided by a new form of self-organized intelligence. In a similar vein we should also consider representations of failed attempts to communicate with an intelligent being that supposedly supersedes the human intellect. In the case of *The Swarm* this being is hostile, whereas in the case of *The Abyss* the sublime marine creature that the researchers discover finally comes to their rescue. A mystical bright pink light announces the presence of an unknown creature that, when first encountered, has a protean watery form. The spiritual work the researchers must perform to gain its sympathy remains on a rather materialistic level (touching the watery form with a fingertip), but in the end their friendly stance to the undersea aliens results in an escape from the deep ocean. The key is, however, that in both storylines—of catastrophic revenge and spiritual awakening—knowledge about the nature of nature itself is reserved to the few.

Such fictions about natural disasters also function as biopolitical playgrounds. The answer to the question "Who survives?" is a judgment that raises ethical problems. Narratives of catastrophe always debunk the political possibilities for action (Horn 2010: 118). The paradox of the new epoch called the Anthropocene, as Bruno Latour says, is the fact that mankind is poised in the center, only to disappear in the next moment (2017: 207–11). But the concentration on the "Anthropos" may in any event be mistaken: eventually the hour will strike in which we must think of "being human" in a different mode, to accept hybrid existences on earth, or "Gaia" (Latour 2017). Some kind of sensitivity to other forms of life—of "making kin," as Donna Haraway (2015) puts it—will be mandatory if we are to conceive of a future on our planet.

CONCLUSION

The Pacific Ocean could encompass all of the other oceans combined (D'Arcy 2012: 196); the sea accounts for 99 percent of Earth's biosphere (Gass 2013). Imaginations that are projected into that vast realm can thus hardly be surpassed in their scope and ambition—only outer space offers us a larger canvass for our dreams.

I began this chapter by referring to Rachel Carson's writing, in which she expresses deep ethical identification with marine creatures, and highlights the fundamental interrelations between onshore and offshore life. As has aptly been remarked, "nature's end" is where the "environment" starts (Sörlin and Warde 2009), and there is now, in essence, no space anywhere on the surface of this planet, including the ocean floors, where human actions have not left traces. Yet we, being irreducibly intertwined with our environment, cannot step outside this picture. The concept of biomass as a tool for the management of food chains strengthened the idea of the interdependencies between land and sea, between humans and marine organisms. The consequence of the tightening of this relationship is that the idea of the ocean as "the other," "the alien," or the "grand void" has definitively become obsolete. Especially in recent times, in that period that has been labeled the Anthropocene, we have experienced the consequences of global warming, induced by human-made greenhouse gas releases principally over the last seventy years. The two strands of imagination of the human–ocean relation are today converging: one characterized by questions of resources and of access and control, and promising a better future for everybody or the aggrandizement of the power of the few; the other characterized by worries about vulnerability and "tipping points" in the functioning of the marine environment conceived now as a vital part of the earth system. The ocean today confronts us with the history of the world's industrial civilizations.

This observation resonates with the famous fictional ocean in Stanisław Lem's 1961 science fiction novel *Solaris*: an unknown entity, covering a remote planet, is called "the ocean." It is a formless and fluid entity, exhibiting bizarre, ever-changing, and uncategorizable excrescences. The planet has given its name to an entire research field called "Solaristics," initiated a century earlier to search for intelligent life in space. But the scientists who remain engaged in that once-splendid research topic today find themselves in a deteriorating psychological and physical condition, haunted by encounters with dead relatives and lost children in their space station, specters seemingly of flesh and blood who plague the scientists with questions about their unresolved pasts, burdensome memories, and conflicting biographies. The strange oceanic entity, with its vast yet inhuman intelligence, is the source of these troubling mental occurrences. One interpretation of Lem's ocean would emphasize the process of anthropomorphizing. An alternative interpretation would emphasize the immanent interconnections between the history of humanity and that of the oceans, attributing the latter a role as the memory of mankind.

By adopting the framework of so-called Wet Ontologies (Steinberg and Peters 2015) we transcend perceptions of the ocean that are restricted to seeing it as (im)material space defined in territorial terms, and instead come to appreciate it as volume that affects us socioculturally. This newly posited ontology not only allows us to "think with the ocean" in confronting the new challenges that face us and our planet, but also enables a new reading of "The Ocean in Us," as Epeli Hau'ofa proposed in 2000. Hau'ofa offered a postcolonial critique of the narrative of the Grand Pacific as "passage" to and from imperial metropoles, stating that this region has always had and still has its own history. But he did not posit this framework of analysis to claim ethnical exclusivity but, on the contrary, to lay emphasis on the many different regional experiences with the ocean in order to show what spans the whole globe. Thus, in these times of the Anthropocene, "The Ocean in Us" presents itself as a Western adaption of an anti-colonial statement, and simultaneously as a planetary expression of an empirical reality—the ocean—on which we depend and that feeds our imaginations. "The ocean is not merely our omnipresent, empirical reality; equally importantly it is our most wonderful metaphor for just about anything" (Hau'ofa 2000: 40). Alienation gained a new quality in the twenty-first century: what was once the Other is now inseparably—Us.

NOTES

Preface

1 This phrase is the title of a Walcott poem "The Sea Is History" (Walcott 2007).

Introduction

1 See, for example, their newsletters and attached list of publications, for example, Working Group on the "Anthropocene" (n.d.).
2 John Gillis speaks of a second discovery of the sea (2012). Helen Rozwadowski of a third discovery of the sea (2018).
3 See, for example, Deering Estate (2012, 2015); there are other terminologies as well, but all describe the fact that the ocean changes its environmental conditions in the third dimension.
4 One could, as Johanna Sackel proposed to me, think of a third approach, the scientific approach. I think that either a romantic and/or environmental attitude can be part of scientific cultures. A cultural history perspective emphasizes human notions/attitudes. To connect science and romantic views, I use the concept of "Romantic biology," but the differentiation of science, environmentalism, and romanticism would need further investigation.
5 I owe thanks to Ariane Tanner for this point.
6 Promising are Island Studies; see, for example, *Island Studies Journal* (2005–17).
7 This touches on a general problem of how humans see "livestock" in the sea and on land (Croney 2014).

Chapter 1

1 The Ocean Literacy campaign's institutional network includes the National Oceanic and Atmospheric Administration (NOAA), the National Geographic Society, USC Sea Grant, Centers for Ocean Sciences Education Excellence (COSEE), the College of Exploration, and the National Marine Educators' Association (Ocean Literacy Network n.d.).
2 The resolution of the acronym ASDIC is contested since archival traces of such a committee have not been found. It is probable that the name was meant to camouflage ongoing British Naval work on active sound detection.

3 Wegener's continental drift theory of 1912 contended that the earth's continents, once a single landmass, had drifted away from one other over geological time, a process that the oceanic ridges gave an indication of.

Chapter 2

1 I speak of skilled mariners, as distinct from those who also travel by sea either as passengers, emigrants, or as captives, and who constitute the many diasporas of modernity. Despite efforts to change the gender balance at sea—and some improvement—seafaring remains a resolutely male-dominated occupation. Statistical data collected by the European Maritime Safety Agency (EMSA) to 2015 indicates that only 2.15 percent of officers and 3.51 percent of ratings in the EU labor market are women (EMSA 2017).
2 Anthropogenic climate change, ocean acidification, and plastics pollution are among the many ways that the sea is emphatically *not* "the same," yet to the seafarer, the practices of piloting and navigation are principally unchanged. Electronics assist, but do not yet replace, ancient skills.
3 In July 1880, the British SS *Jeddah* of the Singapore Steamship Company left Penang for Jeddah, on the Arabian Sea. She carried nearly one thousand pilgrims bound for Mecca. On August 10, she was reported lost with all hands excepting the English captain, his wife, and several European officers who escaped in a lifeboat. The SS *Scindia* picked up the boat carrying the *Jeddah* officers. Meanwhile, the *Jeddah,* reported lost, was towed into Aden by the SS *Antenor*. Subsequent hearings concluded that the *Jeddah*, though damaged by bad weather, was in no danger of sinking. The captain and officers were punished by suspension or revocation of their licenses and both the incident and trial were reported and discussed in newspapers throughout the Anglophone world. See Norman Sherry, "The Pilgrim-Ship Episode" in Conrad (1996: 319–58).
4 The craft of the mariner is the "compleat, whole, or perfect knowledge" of navigation, seamanship, and the work of the sea (Cohen 2010: 40). It values collective effort, and is "flexible and pragmatic […] ready to utilize any expedient that fits the situation, be it patient waiting, following prior wisdom, bold gestures, or creative jury-rigging" (58). However, craft is also "amoral, instrumentalizing" (26), having "potential to be used for good, bad, or amoral action outside the law" (88), being "a capacity that can serve vice as well as virtue" (96). As such, it serves heroic mariners as well as pirates and their possible descendants, capitalist multinational corporations (see also Hayes 2008).
5 For a recent critical study of the long history of containers and the cultural consequences of the shipping container, see Klose (2015). Other, less critical, books on containerization in shipping, mostly from a US perspective, include Levinson (2016), and Donovan and Bonney (2006).
6 Many classification societies still exist today: Det Norske Veritas (DNV; Denmark), Lloyd's Register (LR; United Kingdom), Germanischer Lloyd (GL; Germany), Bureau Veritas (BV; France), and eventually, the American Bureau of Shipping (ABS, United States).
7 For artists who sometimes successfully negotiate this dangerous space, see especially Sekula, Buchloh, and centrum voor hedendaagse kunst Witte de With (1995); Sekula et al. (2010); Inselmann et al. (2007); and Farquarson and Clark (2013).
8 "Robots and Memories," and the closing sentiment of this chapter, come from Noah Luff, formerly a student in my "Maritime Culture" seminar at the California State University Maritime Academy, and now a third mate somewhere on the world's

ocean. I thank him and his fellow students at Cal Maritime, who for the past five years have immensely enriched my thinking about oceanic matters, for their work and their insights.

Chapter 4

1 With this environmental perspective, this chapter falls in line with a growing historiography analyzing the complex relations between elements, ocean life, and human activity in and on the seas, see Bolster (2006); Gillis and Torma (2015); Máñez and Poulsen (2016).
2 This perspective is not exclusive to oceans, see Müller and Stradling (2019).
3 The arts and literature provide other ways of *knowing* the ocean, so do the blue humanities (Gillis 2013).

Chapter 5

1 The documentary *Island Solider* gives an excellent contemporary account of Micronesian soldiers from Kosrae fighting for the US military and feeds into critical discussions about Pacific militarism and postcolonial dependencies. For a review, see Kihleng, Yow Mulalap, Leota-Mua, and Diaz (2019).
2 With the end of the Cold War, Western interests in Oceania subsided considerably, making room for other nations who have had interests in the region before or who became newly attracted to Pacific markets and political opportunities. Recent decades thus saw increasing aid flowing in from mainly Asian countries such as Japan, South Korea, China, the Philippines, but also from Israel. The young independent states of Micronesia, for example, have long become frustrated with US promises and illusions and willingly access new international waters in politics.
3 In 1971, island politicians installed the South Pacific Forum to discuss common economic and social development, including matters of decolonization, shipping, aviation, trade, telecommunications, fish resources, and the nuclear question.

Chapter 6

1 "Oceanography is Fun" declared the title of a chapter of Elizabeth Shor's history of Scripps Institution of Oceanography, which covered expeditions in the 1950s and 1960s (Noble Shor 1978: 373).
2 Published as a novel in 1957, *The Deep Range* was based on a short story of the same name published in *Argosy* magazine in April 1954. See Wernher von Braun, "Introduction," in Clarke (1960: 7–8).
3 Three years later an Alabama dentist constructed a 5.2-meter submarine in his basement then tested it in a local quarry ("A Homemade Sub" 1953).
4 *Around Cape Horn* (Mystic Seaport, 1985; from original 16-mm footage shot by Irving Johnson 1929).
5 The Johnson's first book was *Westward Bound on the Schooner Yankee* (Johnson 1936).
6 The film *Kon-Tiki* was released in 1950 and the following year won the Oscar for Best Documentary. The raft is on display at the Kon-Tiki Museum in Oslo, Norway.

Chapter 7

1 Claire Nouvian offers a particularly dramatic description of this sense of oneness: "It is impossible not to experience profound, primitive emotions that surprise the senses and stimulate the mind and touch a fragile zone within, at once infantile and animal. Anyone who has had the chance to spend time in the nether realm of darkness has expressed, in one way or another, this shock that carries us back to our aquatic origins [...] once immersed several hundred meters below the surface, face to face with raw, untamed life, a truly primal emotion seizes hold of us [...]. A deep dive allows one to understand this on a level deeper than the intellectual. It's an experience that should be offered to every human being, a baptism as an adult that lets us renew our intimate connections with the chain of the living" (2007: 26).

2 On undersea soundtracks, particularly those of the 1950s, see Chapman (2016), who shows how normative conventions governing how undersea space should sound took hold in both fiction films and documentaries of the mid-twentieth century. The legacy of these conventions include ideas about the "acceptable" range of frequencies to emphasize or suppress to "territoralize" the underwater environment, even though these conventions differ markedly from how human hearing actually operates underwater. Where animal vocalizations are concerned, cetacean communications—whale and dolphin "speech" and "song"—became staples of marine-themed movies and their underwater soundscapes in the 1970s, shortly after the New York Zoological society released the LP *Songs of the Humpback Whale* (1970), recorded by marine biologist Roger Payne and US Naval hydrophone engineer Frank Watlington, and the formal "discovery" of whale song by Payne and the naturalist Scott McVay in an August 1971 *Science* article.

3 The most famous of these films is easily *Le Voyage dans la lune* (1902); others include the topical reenactment *Visite sous-marine du Maine* (1898), *Le Royaume des fées* (1903), *La Voyage à travers l'impossible* (1904), and *La sirène* (1904).

4 The Disney shorts are *Frolicking Fish* (dir. Burt Gillett, 1930), *King Neptune* (dir. Burt Gillett, 1932), *Water Babies* (dir. Wilfred Jackson, 1935), *Merbabies* (dir. Rudolf Ising and Vernon Stallings, 1938), *The Whalers* (dir. David Hand and Dick Heumer, 1938), and *Sea Scouts* (dir. Dick Lundy, 1939), which together one might regard as a series of experiments in aquatic animation leading up to the protracted undersea sequence in the feature-length *Pinocchio* (1940).

5 In a similar vein, Elizabeth Kessler writes that Hubble images "appear to present the universe as one *might* see it, thus previewing what we imagine space explorers and tourists may experience when manned space travel extends humanity's reach beyond the earth's orbit" (Kessler 2012: 4, emphasis in original).

6 For Stefan Helmreich, Google Ocean realizes a cultural fantasy of making the ocean totally transparent: "This is not the dark deep," he writes, "but a clear fishbowl—though with no fish; sea life does not swim in this space" (2011: 1226).

7 Cameron's notable Hollywood hits include *Aliens* (1986), *Terminator* (1984), *Terminator 2: Judgment Day* (1991), *Avatar* (2009), and *Titanic* (1997); at the time of writing, the last two of these rank first and second, respectively, in all-time worldwide box office grosses. Not coincidentally, he has made all of his deep-sea diving films in the time since *Titanic*. Besides *Aliens of the Deep*, these documentaries include *Ghosts of the Abyss* (2003), his film of the *Titanic* shipwreck;

    Deepsea Challenge 3D (dir. John Bruno, Ray Quint, and Andrew Wight, 2014); and a TV documentary about the wreck of the German battleship *Bismark* titled *Expedition: Bismarck* (dir. James Cameron and Gary Johnstone, 2002). For better or worse, Cameron's celebrity and documentary output have made him the most recognizable ocean explorer since Cousteau.

8. Between May and October 2015, for instance, *Deepsea Challenge* played in 3D at the Mariners' Museum and Park in Newport News, Virginia, coinciding with an exhibit called Extreme Deep that allowed visitors to "step inside a full scale mockup of the interior of *Alvin* and use a joystick to explore a worm colony; operate *Alvin*'s robotic arm to pick up lava rocks and clams from the sea floor; examine other-worldly creatures; and so much more" ("Extreme Deep" 2015). In some cases, the submersibles onscreen become continuous with spacecraft on display, continuing the aforementioned dialectic between inner and outer space. *Aliens of the Deep*, for instance, played in the IMAX Dome at the Kansas Cosmosphere and Space Center in Hutchinson, Kansas, during September 2010.
9. The other ship to reach the ocean floor, the bathyscaphe *Trieste* in 1960, spent over eight hours between descent and ascent and a mere twenty minutes on the seafloor. *Deepsea Challenger* spent merely two-and-a-half hours on descent and three hours filming and collecting samples from the bottom.
10. Not unlike Cameron, marine biologist Jon Copley, a scientific adviser on *Blue Planet II*, affirms that although ROVs can live-stream images from the bottom of the Pacific into the comfort of one's living room, there remains "something special about immersing yourself in the environment you are trying to understand"—a *je ne sais quoi* about human presence in the deep, however anachronistic or empirically unnecessary in terms of observation (quoted in Wong 2018: 35).

Chapter 8

1. Lepore (2018) remarks critically that a new edition of Carson's writings does not include her early books on the sea, despite the current state of research.
2. In civil nuclear physics the attainment of critical mass is explicitly desired, because it marks the point at which the fission process becomes self-sustaining.
3. "The first steps in exploring Mars. It is time to put people on the red planet. Fly NASA," Commander Reid Wiseman, quoted in Kernagis (2016).

BIBLIOGRAPHY

Adamowsky, Natascha (2009), "Approaches to an Aesthetics of the Mysterious—with Reference to Marine Research of the 19th Century," in Viola Weigel (ed.), *Under Water above Water: From the Aquarium to the Video Image*, 8–17, Bielefeld: Kerber Verlag.
Adamowsky, Natascha (2015), *The Mysterious Science of the Sea, 1775–1943*, London: Routledge.
Aiken, Conrad (1927), *Blue Voyage*, New York: Charles Scribner's Sons.
Alaimo, Stacy (2014), "Oceanic Origins, Plastic Activism, and New Materialism at Sea," in S. Iovino and S. Oppermann (eds.), *Material Ecocriticism*, 186–203, Bloomington: Indiana University Press.
Alcalay, Glenn (2002), *Utrik Atoll: The Sociocultural Impact of Living in a Radioactive Environment An Anthropological Assessment of the Consequential Damages from Bravo*, Montclair, NJ: Department of Anthropology, Montclair State University.
Alkire, William H. (1977), *An Introduction to the Peoples and Cultures of Micronesia*, Menlo Park, CA: "Cummings."
Allen, Oliver E. (1994), "The Man Who Put Boxes on Ships," *Audacity: The Magazine of Business Experience*, no. 2: 13–23.
Altman, Rick (2004), *Silent Film Sound*, New York: Columbia University Press.
Amstutz, Marc R. (2018), *International Ethics: Concepts, Theories, and Cases in Global Politics*, 5th edn., Lanham, MD: Rowman & Littlefield.
Anable, David (1970), "Lethal Wastes, Legal Void: Dumping at Sea Makes Waves," *Christian Science Monitor*, August 27.
Anderson, Katharine and Helen Rozwadowski, eds. (2017), *Soundings and Crossings: Doing Science at Sea 1800–1970*, Sagamore Beach, MA: Science History Publications/USA.
"Appeal on Seabed Dumping," (1970), *The Times (London)*, August 21.
Arison, H. Lindsey (2014), *European Disposal Operations: The Sea Disposal of Chemical Weapons*, Createspace Independent Publisher.
Armitage, David, Alison Bashford, and Sujit Sivasundaram, eds. (2018), *Oceanic Histories*, Cambridge: Cambridge University Press.
Arrighi, Giovanni (2010), *The Long Twentieth Century: Money, Power and the Origins of our Times*, London: Verso.

Arthus-Bertrand, Yann and Brian Skerry (2013), *Der Mensch und die Weltmeere*, Munich: Knesebeck.

Aust, M.O. and J. Herrmann (2013), "Summary of the Situation of Dumped Nuclear Waste in the North-East Atlantic Ocean: Layman's report for OSPAR-RS," London: OSPAR Commission.

Avango, Dag and Per Högselius (2013), "Under the Ice: Exploring the Arctic's Energy," in Miyase Christensen, Annika E. Nilsson, and Nina Wormbs (eds.), *Media and the Politics of Arctic Climate Change: When the Ice Breaks*, 128–56, New York: Palgrave Macmillan.

"A Backyard Baby Sub" (1960), *Life*, 49 (20) November 14: 68.

Baine, Emily (2004), "Mitigating the Possible Damaging Effects of Twentieth Century Ocean Dumping of Chemical Munitions," Washington, DC: US Department of the Army.

Balcombe, Jonathan (2017), *What A Fish Knows: The Inner Lives of Our Underwater Cousins*, New York: Scientific American/Farrar, Straus and Giroux.

Baldacchino, G. and E. Clark (2013), "Guest Editorial Introduction: Islanding Cultural Geographies," *Cultural Geographies*, 20 (2): 129–34.

Bane, Theresa (2014), *Encyclopedia of Imaginary and Mythical Places*, Jefferson, NC: McFarland & Company.

Barada, Bill (1959), *Underwater Adventure*, Los Angeles: Trend Books.

Barada, Bill (1965), *Let's Go Diving: Illustrated Diving Manual*, Santa Ana, CA: US Divers Company.

Barnett, Jon and W. Neil Adger (2003), "Climate Dangers and Atoll Countries," *Climatic Change*, 61 (3): 321–37.

Barr, Susan and Cornelia Lüdecke, eds. (2010), *The History of the International Polar Years (IPYs)* (From Pole to Pole, 1), Berlin: Springer.

Baskin, Jeremy (2015), "Paradigm Dressed as Epoch: The Ideology of the Anthropocene," *Environmental Values*, 24: 9–29.

Bass, George F. (1975), *Archaeology Beneath the Sea*, New York: Walker and Company.

Bazin, André ([1958] 2009), "On Jean Painlevé," in *What Is Cinema?*, trans. Timothy Barnard, 21–3, Montreal: Caboose.

Bearden, David M. (2007), *CRS Report for Congress: US Disposal of Chemical Weapons in the Ocean: Background and Issues for Congress*, Washington, DC: US Government Printing Office.

Beattie, Keith (2008), "Natural Science Film: From Microcinema to IMAX," in *Documentary Display: Re-Viewing Nonfiction Film and Video*, 129–50, London: Wallflower Press.

Beaver, Wilfred N. (1920), *Unexplored New Guinea: A Record of the Travels, Adventures and Experiences of a Resident Magistrate*, London: Seely, Service & Co.

Beckert, Jens (2016), *Imagined Futures: Fictional Expectations and Capitalist Dynamics*, Cambridge, MA: Harvard University Press.

Behm, Alexander (1913), "Einrichtung zur Messung von Meerestiefen und Entfernungen und Richtungen von Schiffen oder Hindernissen mit Hilfe reflektierter Schallwellen," *Kaiserliches Patentamt*, Patent No. 282009 from July 22, 1913.

Belasco, Warren (1997), "Algae Burgers for a Hungry World? The Rise and Fall of Chlorella Cuisine," *Technology and Culture*, 38 (7): 608–34.

Belasco, Warren (2006), *Meals to Come: A History of the Future of Food*, Berkeley: University of California Press.

Bellows, Andy Masaki and Marina McDougall, eds. (2000), *Science Is Fiction: The Films of Jean Painlevé*, Cambridge, MA: MIT Press.

Benson, Keith R., Helen M. Rozwadowski, and David K. Van Keuren (2004), "Introduction," in Keith R. Benson, Helen M. Rozwadowski, and David K. Van Keuren (eds.), *The Machine in Neptune's Garden: Historical Perspectives on Technology and the Marine Environment*, xiii–xxviii, Sagamore Beach, MA: Science History Publications.

Berger, Michele (2015), "Coastal Populations Grow — And Will Continue To — As Sea Levels Rise," The Weather Channel, March 12. Available online: https://weather.com/science/environment/news/coastal-populations-grow-sea-levels-rise (accessed March 20, 2019).

Bergstrom, Dana M. and Steven L. Chown (1999), "Life at the Front: History, Ecology and Change on Southern Ocean Islands," *Trends in Ecology & Evolution*, 14 (12): 472–7.

Beyer, Robert T. (1999), *Sounds of Our Times: Two Hundred Years of Acoustics*, New York: Springer.

Biggs, Duan, Christina C. Hicks, Joshua E. Cinner, and C. Michael Hall (2015), "Marine Tourism in the Face of Global Change: The Resilience of Enterprises to Crises in Thailand and Australia," *Ocean & Coastal Management*, 105: 65–74.

Bitterli, Urs (1980), *Die Entdeckung und Eroberung der Welt: Dokumente und Berichte 2: Asien, Australien und Pazifik*, Munich: C. H. Beck.

Bjerknes, Vilhelm, Johan Wilhelm Sandström, Theodor Hesselberg, and Olak Martin Devik (1910/11), *Dynamic Meteorology and Hydrography*, 2 vols, Washington, DC: Carnegie Institution of Washington.

Blue Flag (2014), "To Train the Sailors of Tomorrow." Available online: http://www.blueflag.global/sail-training-international/ (accessed March 20, 2019).

Boetius, Antje and Henning Boetius (2011), *Das dunkle Paradies: Die Entdeckung der Tiefsee*, Munich: Bertelsmann.

Boisson, Philippe (1999), *Safety at Sea: Policies, Regulations & International Law*, Paris: Veritas.

Bolster, W. Jeffrey (2006), "Opportunities in Marine Environmental History," *Environmental History*, 11 (3): 567–97.

Bolster, W. Jeffrey (2012), *The Mortal Sea: Fishing the Atlantic in the Age of Sail*, Cambridge, MA: Belknap Press of Harvard University Press.

Bond George, F. and Helen A. Siiteri (1993), *Papa Topside: The Sealab Chronicles of Capt. George F. Bond, USN*, Annapolis, MD: Naval Institute Press.

Booker, Matthew (2013), *Down By the Bay: San Francisco's History Between the Tides*, Berkeley: University of California Press.

Borgese, Elisabeth Mann (1970), "Introduction to the Report of Pacem in Maribus I," Elisabeth Mann Borgese Fond, Dalhousie University, Halifax/Canada, MS-2-744, Box 128, Folder 1.

Borgese, Elisabeth Mann (1976), *The Drama of the Oceans*, New York: Abrams.

Borgese, Elisabeth Mann (1993), "The International Ocean Institute Story," in Elisabeth Mann Borgese, Norton Ginsburg, and Joseph R. Morgan (eds.), *Ocean Yearbook No. 10*, 1–12, Chicago: University of Chicago Press.

Borgese, Elisabeth Mann and Arvid Pardo (1975), *The New International Economic Order and the Law of the Sea*, Malta: International Ocean Institute.

Boyle, T.C. (2016), *The Terranauts*, London: Bloomsbury.

Brassey, Anne (1878), *Around the World in the Yacht "Sunbeam,"* New York: Henry Holt & Co.

Bridges, Lloyd and Bill Barada (1960), *Mask and Flippers: The Story of Skin Diving*, Philadelphia: Chilton Company Publishers.
Brinnin, John Malcolm (1971), *Sway of the Grand Saloon: A Social History of the North Atlantic*, New York: Delacorte Press.
"Britain Voices Concern on Nerve Gas" (1970), *New York Times*, August 7.
Brooks, Kenneth F., Jr. (1988), *Run to the Lee*, Baltimore: Johns Hopkins University Press.
Burnett, D. Graham (2010), "A Mind in the Water: The Dolphin as Our Beast of Burden," *Orion*, May/June: 38–51.
Burnett, D. Graham (2012), *The Sounding of the Whale: Science and Cetaceans in the Twentieth Century*, Chicago: University of Chicago Press.
Cahill, James Leo (2012), "Forgetting Lessons: Jean Painlevé's Cinematic Gay Science," *Journal of Visual Culture*, 11 (3): 258–87.
Cahill, James Leo (2019), *Zoological Surrealism: The Nonhuman Cinema of Jean Painlevé*, Minneapolis: University of Minnesota Press.
Calmet, D.P. and J.M. Bewers (1991), "Radioactive Waste and Ocean Dumping," *Marine Policy*, 15 (6): 413–30.
Cameron, James (2004), "Introduction," in Joseph MacInnis (ed.), *James Cameron's Aliens of the Deep*, 9–11, Washington, DC: National Geographic.
Campe, Sabine (2009), "The Secretariat of the International Maritime Organization: A Tanker for Tankers," in Frank Biermann and Bernd Siebenhüner (eds.), *Managers of Global Change: The Influence of International Environmental Bureaucracies*, 143–68, Cambridge, MA: MIT Press.
Carlisle, Rodney P. (1981), *Sovereignty for Sale: The Origins and Evolution of the Panamanian and Liberian Flags of Convenience*, Annapolis, MD: Naval Institute Press.
Carlisle, Rodney P. (2013), "Danzig: The Missing Link in the History of Flags of Convenience," *The Northern Mariner/Le Marin Du Nord*, 23 (2): 135–50.
Carlton, James T. (1979), "Introduced Invertebrates of San Francisco Bay," in T. John Conomos (ed.), *San Francisco Bay: The Urbanized Estuary*, 427–44, San Francisco: American Association for the Advancement of Science (AAAS).
Carlton, James T. (1985), "Transoceanic and Interoceanic Dispersal of Coastal Marine Organisms: The Biology of Ballast Water," *Oceanography and Marine Biology: Annual Review*, 23: 313–71.
Carlton, James T. (2019), "Assessing Marine Bioinvasions in the Galápagos Islands: Implications for Conservation Biology and Marine Protected Areas," *Aquatic Invasions*, 14 (1): 1–20.
Carrier, Rick and Barbara Carrier (1955), *Dive*, New York: Wilfred Funk.
Carrington, Damian (2014) "Earth Has Lost Half of Its Wildlife in the Past 40 Years, Says WWF," the *Guardian*, September 29. Available online: https://www.theguardian.com/environment/2014/sep/29/earth-lost-50-wildlife-in-40-years-wwf (accessed October 16, 2020).
Carson, Mike T. (2014), *First Settlement of Remote Oceania: Earliest Sites in the Mariana Islands*, Cham: Springer.
Carson, Rachel (1937), "Undersea," *Atlantic Monthly*, September: 322–5.
Carson, Rachel (1941), *Under the Sea-Wind: A Naturalist's Picture of Ocean Life*, New York: Simon & Schuster.
Carson, Rachel (1951), *The Sea around Us*, Oxford: Oxford University Press.
Carson, Rachel ([1952] 1961), *The Sea Around Us*, New York: Oxford University Press.

Chakrabarty, Dipesh (2009), "The Climate of History: Four Theses," *Critical Inquiry*, 35 (2): 197–222.
Changnon, Stanley A., ed. (2000), *El Niño 1997–1998: The Climate Event of the Century*, Oxford: Oxford University Press.
Chaplin, Joyce E. (2013), *Round the Earth: Circumnavigation from Magellan to Orbit*, New York: Simon & Schuster.
Chapman, David (2016), "The Undersea World of the Sound Department: The Construction of Sonic Conventions in Sub-aqua Screen Environments," *New Soundtrack*, 6 (2): 143–57.
Charette, Matthew and Walter Smith (2010), "The Volume of Earth's Ocean," *Oceanography*, 23 (2): 112–14.
Chasek, Pamela S. (2010), *Earth Negotiations: Analyzing Thirty Years of Environmental Diplomacy*, Tokyo: United Nations University Press.
Cheremisinoff, Nicholas P., Paul N. Cheremisinoff, and Fred Ellerbusch (1980), *Biomass: Applications, Technology, and Production*, New York: Dekker.
Chircop, Aldo (2012), "Elisabeth Mann Borgese's Humanist Conception of Marine Technology Transfer," in Holger Pils and Karolina Kühn (eds.), *Elisabeth Mann Borgese und das Drama der Meere*, 112–21, Hamburg: Mare.
Christianson, Scott (2010), *Fatal Airs: The Deadly History and Apocalyptic Future of Lethal Gases that Threaten Our World*, Santa Barbara, CA: Praeger.
"Christ of the Depth" (1954), *Life*, 37 (11) September 13: 151–2.
Cioc, Mark (2002), *The Rhine: An Eco-Biography, 1815–2000*, Seattle: University of Washington Press.
Cioc, Mark (2009), *The Game of Conservation: International Treaties to Protect the World's Migratory Animals*, Athens: Ohio University Press.
Clark, Colin (1970), *Die Menschheit wird nicht hungern: Programm zur Ernährung der Weltbevölkerung*, Bergisch Gladbach: Gustav Lübbe Verlag.
Clark, Colin (1977), *Population Growth and Land Use*, 2nd edn., London: Macmillan.
Clarke, Arthur C. (1960), *Challenge of the Sea*, New York: Holt, Rinehart Winston.
Clarke, Arthur C. (2001), *The Ghost from the Grand Banks; and The Deep Range*, New York: Aspect/Warner Books.
Cohen, Jeffrey J. and Linda T. Elkins-Tanton (2017), *Earth*, New York: Bloomsbury Academic.
Cohen, Margaret (2010), *The Novel and the Sea*, Princeton, NJ: Princeton University Press.
Cohen, Margaret (2014), "Underwater Optics as Symbolic Form," *French Politics, Culture & Society*, 32 (3): 1–23.
Cohen, Margaret (2018), "Adventures in Toxic Atmosphere," in Will Abberley (ed.), *Underwater Worlds: Submerged Visions in Science and Culture*, 72–89, Newcastle Upon Tyne: Cambridge Scholars Publishing.
Committee on Merchant Marine and Fisheries (1980), *Dredge Spoil Disposal and PCB Contamination: Hearings before the Committee on Merchant Marine and Fisheries*, Washington, DC: US Government Printing Office.
Committee to Frame a World Constitution (1948), *The Preliminary Draft of a World Constitution*, Chicago: University of Chicago Press.
Connery, Christopher (2006), "There Was No More Sea: The Supersession of the Ocean, from the Bible to Cyberspace," *Journal of Historical Geography*, 32 (3): 494–511.
Conrad, Joseph (1988), *The Mirror of the Sea; and, A Personal Record*, ed. Zdzisław Najder, Oxford: Oxford University Press.

Conrad, Joseph (1996), *Lord Jim: Authoritative Text, Backgrounds, Sources, Criticism*, ed. Thomas C. Moser, 2nd edn., New York: W.W. Norton & Co.
Conway, Erik M. (2006), "Drowning in Data: Satellite Oceanography and Information Overload in the Earth Sciences," *Historical Studies in the Physical and Biological Sciences*, 37: 127–51.
Corbin, Alain (1988), *Le territoire du vide: L'Occident et le plaisir du rivage, 1750–1840*, Paris: Aubier.
Corbin, Alain (1994), *The Lure of the Sea: The Discovery of the Seaside in the Western World 1750–1840*, London: Penguin Books.
Corner, James (1999), "The Agency of Mapping: Speculation, Critique and Invention," in Dennis Cosgrove (ed.), *Mappings*, 213–52, London: Reaktion Books.
Cortés, Sandra, Lucía del Carmen Molina Lagos, Soledad Burgos, Héctor Adaros, and Catterina Ferreccio (2016), "Urinary Metal Levels in a Chilean Community 31 Years after the Dumping of Mine Tailings," *Journal of Health and Pollution*, 6 (10): 19–27.
Council on Environmental Quality (1970), *Ocean Dumping: A National Policy*, Washington, DC.
Cowen, Deborah (2014), *The Deadly Life of Logistics: Mapping Violence in Global Trade*, Minneapolis: University of Minnesota Press.
Cowley, J. (1989), "The International Maritime Organisation and National Administrations," *Institute of Marine Engineers Transactions*, 101 (Part 3).
Crane, Kathleen (2004), *Sea Legs: Tales of a Woman Oceanographer*, New York: Basic Books.
Croney, Candace C. (2014), "Bonding with Commodities: Social Constructions and Implications of Human–Animal Relationships in Contemporary Livestock Production," *Animal Frontiers*, 4 (3): 59–64.
Crosby, Alfred W. (1986), *Ecological Imperialism: The Biological Expansion of Europe, 900–1900*, Cambridge: Cambridge University Press.
Crosby, Alfred W. (1994), *Germs, Seeds, and Animals: Studies in Ecological History*, Armonk, NY: M. E. Sharpe.
Crutzen, Paul. J. (2002), "Geology of Mankind," *Nature*, 415 (6867): 23.
Crylen, Jon (2015), "The Cinematic Aquarium: A History of Undersea Film," PhD thesis, University of Iowa.
Crylen, Jon (2018a), "Cinema Cnidaria, or Marine Movies in an Age of Mass Extinction," *Media Fields Journal*, 13. Available online: http://mediafieldsjournal.org/cinema-cnidaria-or-marine-movi (accessed December 15, 2018).
Crylen, Jon (2018b), "'Living in a World Without Sun': Jacques Cousteau, *Homo aquaticus*, and the Dream of Dwelling Undersea," *Journal of Cinema and Media Studies*, 58 (1): 1–23.
Crylen, Jon (2021), "Aquariums, Diving Equipment, and the Undersea Films of John Ernest Williamson," in James Leo Cahill and Luca Caminati (eds.), *Cinema of Exploration: Essays on an Adventurous Film Practice*, 143–57, New York: Routledge.
Cubitt, Sean (2005), "*The Blue Planet*: Virtual Nature and Natural Virtue," in *EcoMedia*, 43–60, New York: Rodopi.
Czub, Michal et al. (2018), "Deep Sea Habitats in the Chemical Warfare Dumping Areas of the Baltic Sea," *Science of the Total Environment*, 616–17: 1485–97.
D'Arcy, Paul (2012), "Oceania: The Environmental History of One-Third of the Globe," in John R. McNeill and Erin Stewart Mauldin (eds.), *A Companion to Global Environmental History*, 196–221, Chichester: Wiley-Blackwell.

Dalla Valle, Gustav, Benjamin S. Holderness, Charles M. Smithline, Arthur Stanfield, and Harry Vetter (1963), *Skin and Scuba Diving*, New York: Sterling Publishing Co.
Davidson, Ian C. and Christina Simkanin (2012), "The Biology of Ballast Water 25 Years Later," *Biological Invasions*, 14: 9–13.
Davis, Susan G. (1997), *Spectacular Nature: Corporate Culture and the Sea World Experience*, Berkeley: University of California Press.
Davis, W. Jackson and John VanDyke (1982), *Evaluation of Oceanic Radioactive Dumping Programs*, Santa Cruz: University of California Press.
Dawson, Kevin (2006), "Enslaved Swimmers and Divers in the Atlantic World," *Journal of American History*, 92 (4): 1327–55.
De Bont, Raf (2015), *Stations in the Field: A History of Place-based Animal Research, 1870–1930*, Chicago: University of Chicago Press.
Deane, Robert (2013), "Underwater Photography," in John Hannavy (ed.), *Encyclopedia of Nineteenth-Century Photography*, 1416–17, New York: Routledge.
Deering Estate (2012, 2015), "Marine Conservation Science & Policy: Ocean Zones." Available online: https://www.rsmas.miami.edu/_assets/pdf/outreach/1.1-ocean-zones.pdf (accessed October 16, 2020).
DeLoughrey, Elizabeth (2013), "The Myth of Isolates: Ecosystem Ecologies in the Nuclear Pacific," *Cultural Geographies*, 20 (2): 167–84.
Demoll, Reinhard (1927), "Betrachtungen über Produktionsberechnungen," *Archiv für Hydrobiologie*, 18: 460–3.
Demoll, Reinhard (1957), *Früchte des Meeres*, Berlin: Springer-Verlag.
DeSombre, Elizabeth R. (2006), *Flagging Standards: Globalization and Environmental, Safety, and Labor Regulations at Sea*, Cambridge, MA: MIT Press.
Det Norske Veritas (n.d.), "ORE BRASIL - DNV GL Vessel Register." Available online: http://vesselregister.dnvgl.com/VesselRegister/vesseldetails.html?vesselid=30616 (accessed August 19, 2018).
Devanney, Jack (2006), *The Tankship Tromedy: The Impending Disasters in Tankers*, Tavernier, FL: CTX Press.
Diaz, Vicente (2001), "Deliberating 'Liberation Day': Identity, History, Memory, and War in Guam," in T. Fujitani, Geoffrey M. White, and Lisa Yoneyama (eds.), *Perilous Memories: The Asia-Pacific War(s)*, 155–80, Durham, NC: Duke University Press.
Dietrich, Chris R.W. (2017), *Oil Revolution: Sovereign Rights and the Economic Culture of Decolonization*, Cambridge: Cambridge University Press.
Disco, Nil and Eda Kranakis (2013), "Toward a Theory of Cosmopolitan Commons," in Nil Disco and Eda Kranakis, *Cosmopolitan Commons: Sharing Resources and Risks across Borders*, 13–53, Cambridge, MA: MIT Press.
Dixon, Conrad (1996), "The Rise of the Engineer in the Nineteenth Century," in Gordon Jackson and David M. Williams (eds.), *Shipping, Technology, and Imperialism: Papers Presented to the Third British-Dutch Maritime History Conference*, 231–41, Farnham: Ashgate.
Dodds, Klaus (2010), "Flag Planting and Finger Pointing: The Law of the Sea, the Arctic and the Political Geographies of the Outer Continental Shelf," *Political Geography*, 29: 63–73.
Doel, Ronald E. (2003), "Constituting the Postwar Earth Sciences: The Military's Influence on the Environmental Sciences in the USA after 1945," *Social Studies of Science*, 33 (5): 635–66.
Doel, Ronald E., Tanya J. Levin, and Mason K. Marker (2006), "Extending Modern Cartography to the Ocean Depths: Military Patronage, Cold War Priorities, and the

Heezen-Tharp Mapping Project, 1952–1959," *Journal of Historical Geography*, 32: 605–26.

Donovan, Arthur and Joseph Bonney (2006), *The Box That Changed the World: Fifty Years of Container Shipping; an Illustrated History*, East Windsor, NJ: Commonwealth Business Media.

Dorsey, Kurk (2014), *Whales and Nations: Environmental Diplomacy on the High Seas*, Seattle: University of Washington Press.

Draft Minutes of the 15th Session of the Planning Council (1978), Divonne-les-Bains, April 22, Projects in Course, in Elisabeth Mann Borgese fond, Dalhousie University, Halifax/Canada, MS-2-744, Box 38, Folder 10.

Drogin, Bob (2009), "Mapping an Ocean of Life Forms on the Move," *Los Angeles Times*, August 2.

Duffy, Thom (2018), "Aboard the Clearwater: Five Decades of Environmental Activism Rooted In Music," Billboard, June 13. Available online: https://www.billboard.com/articles/news/8460369/clearwater-environmental-activism-pete-seeger (accessed March 20, 2019).

Du Pontavice, E. (1973), "Pollution," in L.J. Bouchez and L. Kaijen (eds.), *The Future of the Law of the Sea: Proceedings of the Symposium on the Future of the Sea*, 104–53, Dordrecht: Springer Netherlands.

Dugan, James (1965), *Man Under the Sea*, New York: Collier Books.

Earle, Sylvia A. (1999), *Dive! My Adventures in the Deep Frontier*, Washington, DC: National Geographic Society.

Earle, Sylvia A. and Al Giddings (1980), *Exploring the Deep Frontier: The Adventure of Man in the Sea*, Washington, DC: National Geographic Society.

Eat the Invaders (n.d.), "Home." Available online: http://eattheinvaders.org/ (accessed October 18, 2020).

Ecomaris (2019), "Ecomaris." Available online: https://ecomaris.org/ (accessed March 20, 2019).

Edwards, Paul N. (2010), *A Vast Machine: Computer Models, Climate Data, and the Politics of Global Warming*, Cambridge, MA: MIT Press.

Edwards, Paul N. (2017), "Knowledge Infrastructures for the Anthropocene," *Anthropocene Review*, 4 (1): 34–43.

Egan, Dan (2017), *The Death and Life of the Great Lakes*, New York: W.W. Norton & Co.

Egerton, Frank N. (2014), "History of Ecological Sciences, Part 51: Formalizing Marine Ecology, 1870s to 1920s," *Ecological Society of America Bulletin*, 95 (4): 347–420.

Eilperin, Juliet (2011), *Demon Fish: Travels Through the Hidden World of Sharks*, New York: Pantheon Books.

Elias, Ann (2019), *Coral Empire: Underwater Oceans, Colonial Tropics, Visual Modernity*, Durham, NC: Duke University Press.

Ellis, Erle C. (2018), *Anthropocene: A Very Short Introduction*, Oxford, New York: Oxford University Press.

Elsaesser, Thomas and Malte Hagener (2010), *Film Theory: An Introduction through the Senses*, New York: Routledge.

Elton, Charles (1927), *Animal Ecology*, New York: Macmillan.

Elton, Charles (1958), *The Ecology of Invasions by Animals and Plants*, New York: Wiley.

Emmett, Robert and Thomas Lekan, eds. (2016), *Whose Anthropocene? Revisiting Dipesh Chakrabarty's Four Theses*, Munich: RCC Perspectives.

Epstein, Charlotte (2008), *The Power of Words in International Relations: Birth of an Anti-Whaling Discourse*, Cambridge, MA: MIT Press.

Esposito, Maurozio (2013), *Romantic Biology, 1890–1945*, New York: Routledge.

European Maritime Safety Agency (EMSA) (2017), "Seafarer Statistics in the EU - Statistical Review," September 7. Available online: http://www.emsa.europa.eu/publications/technical-reports-studies-and-plans/item/3094-seafarer-statistics-in-the-eu-statistical-review-2015-data-stcw-is.html (accessed March 20, 2019).

European Marine Observation and Data Network (2018), "Links between Dredge Spoil Dumping and the Marine Environment." Available online: http://www.emodnet-humanactivities.eu/blog/?p=558 (accessed March 15, 2019).

"Extreme Deep: Mission to the Abyss" (2015), *Mariners' Museum and Park*. Available online: http://www.marinersmuseum.org/extremedeep (accessed December 15, 2018).

Farbotko, Carol (2005), "Tuvalu and Climate Change: Constructions of Environmental Displacement in the Sydney Morning Herald," *Geografiska Annaler: Series B, Human Geography*, 87 (4): 279–93.

Farbotko, Carol (2010), "Wishful Sinking: Disappearing Islands, Climate Refugees and Cosmopolitan Experimentation," *Asia Pacific Viewpoint*, 51 (1): 47–60.

Farbotko, Carol (2012), "Skilful Seafarers, Oceanic Drifters or Climate Refugees? Pacific People, News Value and the Climate Refugee Crisis," in Kerry Moore, Bernhard Gross, and Terry Threadgold (eds.), *Migrations and the Media*, 119–42, New York: Peter Lang.

Farbotko, Carol and Heather Lazrus (2012), "The First Climate Refugees? Contesting Global Narratives of Climate Change in Tuvalu," *Global Environmental Change*, 22(2): 382–90.

Farquarson, Alex and Martin Clark, eds. (2013), *Aquatopia: The Imaginary of the Ocean Deep*, Nottingham: Nottingham Contemporary and Tate Gallery St Ives.

Fink, Leon (2011), *Sweatshops at Sea: Merchant Seamen in the World's First Globalized Industry, from 1812 to the Present*, Chapel Hill: University of North Carolina.

Finley, Carmel (2011), *All the Fish in the Sea: Maximum Sustainable Yield and the Failure of Fisheries Management*, Chicago: University of Chicago Press.

Food and Agricultural Organization (FAO), ed. (1948), *The State of Food and Agriculture 1948: A Survey of World Conditions and Prospects*, Washington, DC.

Friends of the Earth Norway (2015), "Dumping of Mine Tailings in the Ocean." Available online: https://naturvernforbundet.no/getfile.php/13123052-1496922755/Bilder/Forurensing/Norway-s%20international%20activity%20-%20tailings%20dumping%202015-3.pdf (accessed March 15, 2019).

"Front Cover" (1955), *Sports Illustrated*, May 23: front cover.

Foulke, Robert (1997), *The Sea Voyage Narrative*, New York: Twayne Publishers.

Fujitani, Takashi, Geoffrey M. White, and Lisa Yoneyama, eds. (2001), *Perilous Memories: the Asia-Pacific War(s)*, Durham, NC: Duke University Press.

Furphy, J.S., F.D. Hamilton, and O.J. Merne (1971), "Seabird Deaths in Ireland, Autumn 1969," *Irish Naturalists' Journal*, 17 (2): 34–40.

Gamper, Michael and Peter Schnyder, eds. (2006), *Kollektive Gespenster: Die Masse, der Zeitgeist und andere unfassbare Körper*, Freiburg: Rombach Verlag.

"Gas Wells Moved" (1960), *Pensacola News Journal*, March 9.

Gass, Scott (2013), "How Big is the Ocean?," Ted-Ed, June 24. Available online: https://www.youtube.com/watch?v=QUW_Zv_jJb8 (accessed February 17, 2018).

Gaycken, Oliver (2018), "Febrile Ocean: How to See Climate Change Underwater," *Docalogue*. Available online: https://docalogue.com/january-chasing-coral (accessed March 13, 2019).

George, Rose (2013), *Ninety Percent of Everything: Inside Shipping, the Invisible Industry That Puts Clothes on Your Back, Gas in Your Car, and Food on Your Plate*, New York: Metropolitan Books/Henry Holt and Co.

Gerber, Lear R. and Sascha K. Hooker (2004), "Marine Reserves as a Tool for Ecosystem-Based Management: The Potential Importance of Megafauna," *BioScience*, 54 (1): 27–39.

Geyer, Martin H. and Johannes Paulmann, eds. (2001), *The Mechanics of Internationalism: Culture, Society and Politics from the 1840s to the First World War*, Oxford: Oxford University Press.

Gillis, John R. (2012), *The Human Shore: Seacoasts in History*, Chicago: University of Chicago Press.

Gillis, John R. (2013), "The Blue Humanities," *Humanities*, 34 (3): 10–13. Available online: https://www.neh.gov/humanities/2013/mayjune/feature/the-blue-humanities (accessed April 10, 2019).

Gillis, John R. and Franziska Torma, eds. (2015), *Fluid Frontiers: New Currents in Marine Environmental History*, Knapwell: White Horse Press.

Gilman, Nils (2015), "The NIEO: A Reintroduction," *Humanity: An International Journal of Human Rights, Humanitarianism, and Development*, 6 (2): 1–16.

Gilman Sarah (2016), "The Clam That Sank A Thousand Ships," *Haikai Magazine*, December 5. Available online: https://www.hakaimagazine.com/features/clam-sank-thousand-ships/ (accessed March 20, 2019).

Gilpatric, Guy (1957), *The Compleat Goggler*, New York: Dodd, Mead and Company.

Gladwin, Thomas (1995), *East is a Big Bird: Navigation and Logic on the Puluwat Atoll*, Cambridge, MA: Harvard University Press.

Glasby, Geoffrey P. (2002), "Deep Sea Mining: Past Failures and Future Prospects," *Marine Georesources and Geotechnology*, 20 (2): 161–76.

Golding, William (1954), *Lord of the Flies*, London: Faber.

Goldman, Francisco (1997), *The Ordinary Seaman*, New York: Atlantic Monthly Press.

Goldsmith, Michael (2015), "The Big Smallness of Tuvalu," *Global Environment Special Issue*, 8 (1): 134–51.

Goodwin, Charles (1995), "Seeing in Depth," *Social Studies of Science*, 25: 237–74.

Grant, Matthew and Benjamin Ziemann, eds. (2016), *Understanding the Imaginary War: Culture, Thought and Nuclear Conflict, 1945–90*, Manchester: Manchester University Press.

Grasso, Glenn (2009), "The Maritime Revival: Anti-modernism and the Maritime Revival, 1870–1940," PhD diss., University of New Hampshire.

Greig, Nordahl (1927), *The Ship Sails On*, trans. A.G. Chater, New York: Alfred Knopf. (First published in Norway in 1924 as *Skibet Gaar Videre*.)

Grider, John (2014), "'Tis a Shameful Confession': Steam Power and the Pacific Maritime Labor Community," *The Northern Mariner/Le Marin Du Nord*, 24 (2): 111–33.

Griffiths, Alison (2007), *Shivers Down Your Spine: Cinema, Museums, and the Immersive View*, New York: Columbia University Press.

Grimm, Charles "Buckey" (2001), "Carl Louis Gregory: Life through a Lens," *Film History*, 13 (2): 174–84.

Grotius, Hugo ([1609] 2004), *The Free Sea* ("Mare Liberum," *De Indis*, ch. 12, Leiden), ed. David Armitage, Indianapolis, IN: Liberty Fund.

Hadley, Malcolm (2005), "Nature to the Fore: The Early Years of UNESCO's Environmental Programme, 1945–1965," in UNESCO (ed.), *Sixty years of Science at UNESCO, 1945–2005*, 201–32, Paris: UNESCO Publishing.
Haeckel, Ernst (1862), *Die Radiolarien: (Rhizopoda Radiaria) Eine Monographie, Mit einem Atlas von fünf und dreissig Kupfertafeln*, Berlin: Georg Reimer.
Hamblin, Jacob D. (2005), *Oceanographers and the Cold War: Disciples of Marine Science*, Seattle: University of Washington Press.
Hamblin, Jacob D. (2008), *Poison in the Well: Radioactive Waste in the Oceans at the Dawn of the Nuclear Age*, New Brunswick, N.J: Rutgers University Press.
Hamera, Judith (2012), *Parlor Ponds: The Cultural Work of the American Home Aquarium, 1850–1970*, Ann Arbor: University of Michigan Press.
Hanauer, Eric (1994), *Diving Pioneers: An Oral History of Diving in America*, San Diego, CA: Watersport Publishing.
Hanlon, Christopher (2016), "Under the Atlantic," in Julia Straub (ed.), *Handbook of Transatlantic North American Studies*, 283–96, Berlin: De Gruyter.
Hanlon, David (1998), *Remaking Micronesia: Discourses Over Development in a Pacific Territory, 1944–1982*, Honolulu: University of Hawai'i Press.
Hannigan, John (2016), *The Geopolitics of Deep Oceans*, Cambridge: Polity.
Haq, Gary and Alistair Paul (2011), *Environmentalism since 1945*, London: Routledge.
Haraway, Donna (2015), "Anthropocene, Capitalocene, Plantationocene, Chthulucene: Making Kin," *Environmental Humanities*, 6: 159–65.
Hardin, Garrett (1968), "The Tragedy of the Commons," *Science*, 162 (3859): 1243–8.
Hardy, Alister C. (1924), "The Herring in Relation to Its Environment Part I," *Fishery Investigations*, 7 (3): 2–53.
Hardy, Alister C. (1958), *The Open Sea: Its Natural History*, London: Collins.
Hardy, Alister C. (1960), "Was Man More Aquatic in the Past?," *The New Scientist*, 7 (174), March 17: 642–5.
Harris, Michael (1999), *Lament for an Ocean: The Collapse of the Atlantic Cod Fishery: A True Crime Story*, updated trade paperback edn., Toronto: McClelland & Stewart.
Harrison, Harry (1966), *Make Room! Make Room!*, Garden City, NY: Doubleday & Co.
Hart, John (2008), "Looking Back: The Continuing Legacy of Old and Abandoned Chemical Weapons," *Arms Control Today*, 38 (2): 55–9.
Hass, Hans ([1957] 1958), *Wir Kommen aus dem Meer*, Berlin: Ullstein Verlag; trans. Alan Houghton Brodrick, *We Come from the Sea*, London: Jarrolds.
Hassan, D. (2006), *Protecting the Marine Environment from Land-based Sources of Pollution: Towards Effective International Cooperation*, Aldershot: Ashgate.
Hau'ofa, Epeli (1993), "Our Sea of Islands," in Eric Waddell, Vijay Naidu, and Epeli Hau'ofa (eds.), *A New Oceania: Rediscovering Our Sea of Islands*, 2–16; Suva: University of the South Pacific School of Social and Economic Development.
Hau'ofa, Epeli (1994), "Our Sea of Islands," *Contemporary Pacific*, 6 (1): 147–61.
Hau'ofa, Epeli (2000), "The Ocean in Us," in Antony Hooper (ed.), *Culture and Sustainable Development in the Pacific*, 32–43, Canberra: Asia Pacific Press.
Hauser, Stephan E. (2009), "The Sub-aquatic Picture Cosmos: A Brief History of the Aquarium and Underwater Film from 1890 to the Present Day," in Viola Weigel (ed.), *Under Water above Water: From the Aquarium to the Video Image*, 18–35, Bielefeld: Kerber Verlag.
Haward, M.G. and J. Vince (2008), *Oceans Governance in the Twenty-first Century: Managing the Blue Planet*, Cheltenham: Edward Elgar Publishing.
Hayden, Sterling (1963), *Wanderer*, New York: Knopf.

Hayes, Peter (2008), "Pirates, Privateers and the Contract Theories of Hobbes and Locke," *History of Political Thought*, 29 (3): 461–84.

Hays, Samuel P. (1998), "The Limits-to-Growth-Issue: A Historical Perspective," in Samuel P. Hays (ed.), *Explorations in Environmental History: Essays*, 3–23, Pittsburgh: University of Pittsburgh Press.

Hayward, Eva (2005), "Enfolded Vision: Refracting *The Love Life of an Octopus*," *Octopus: A Visual Studies Journal*, 1 (Fall): 29–44.

Heffernan, Patrick H. (1981), "Conflict over Marine Resources," *Proceedings of the Academy of Political Science*, 34 (1): 168.

Heidbrink, Ingo (2011), "A Second Industrial Revolution in the Distant Water Fisheries? Factory-Freezer Trawlers in the 1950s and 1960s," *International Journal of Maritime History*, 23 (1): 179–92.

Heine, Jorge (2013), "From Club to Network Diplomacy," in Andrew F. Cooper, Jorge Heine, and Ramesh Takur (eds.), *The Oxford Handbook of Modern Diplomacy*, 54–69, Oxford: Oxford University Press.

Helcom (2018), "Sea-Dumped Chemical Munitions." Available online: http://www.helcom.fi/baltic-sea-trends/hazardous-substances/sea-dumped-chemical-munitions (accessed December 13, 2018).

Hellwarth, Ben (2012), *Sealab: America's Forgotten Quest to Live and Work on the Ocean Floor*, New York: Simon & Shuster.

Helmreich, Stefan (2009), *Alien Ocean: Anthropological Voyages in Microbial Seas*, Berkeley: University of California Press.

Helmreich, Stefan (2011), "From Spaceship Earth to Google Ocean: Planetary Icons, Indexes, and Infrastructures," *Social Research*, 78 (4): 1211–42.

Hensen, Victor (1887), "Über die Bestimmung des Plankton's oder des im Meere treibenden Materials an Pflanzen und Thieren," *Fünfter Bericht der Kommission zur wissenschaftlichen Untersuchung der deutschen Meere in Kiel für die Jahre 1882 bis 1886*, Kiel: Schmidt & Klaunig.

Hensen, Victor (1911), *Das Leben im Ozean nach Zählung seiner Bewohner: Übersicht und Resultate der quantitativen Untersuchungen*, Kiel: Verlag von Lipsius & Tischer.

Herdman, William A. (1920), "Oceanography and the Sea-Fisheries," *Scientific Monthly*, 11 (4): 289–96.

Heyerdahl, Thor (1950), *Kon-Tiki: Across the Pacific in a Raft*, Chicago: Rand McNally & Company.

Hobsbawm, Eric (1994), *The Age of Extremes: The Short Twentieth Century 1914–1991*, London: Michael Joseph.

Hofmann, Rebecca (2016), "Situating Climate Change in Chuuk: Navigating 'Belonging' Through Environmental and Social Transformations in Micronesia," Munich: Ludwig-Maximilians-Universität.

Hofmann, Rebecca and Uwe Lübken (2018), "Laboratorien der ökologischen Moderne? Umwelt, Wissen und Geschichte (auf) der kleinen Insel," *Aus Politik und Zeitgeschichte*, 68 (32-3): 4–9.

Höhler, Sabine (2002a), "Depth Records and Ocean Volumes: Ocean Profiling by Sounding Technology, 1850–930," *History and Technology*, 18 (2): 119–54.

Höhler, Sabine (2002b), "Profilgewinn: Karten der Atlantischen Expedition (1925–1927) der Notgemeinschaft der Deutschen Wissenschaft," *NTM International Journal of History and Ethics of Natural Sciences, Technology and Medicine*, 10 (4): 234–46.

Höhler, Sabine (2008), "Spaceship Earth: Envisioning Human Habitats in the Environmental Age," *Bulletin of the German Historical Institute*, 42: 65–86.
Höhler, Sabine (2014a), "Exterritoriale Ressourcen: Die Diskussion um die Tiefsee, die Pole und das Weltall um 1970," *Jahrbuch für europäische Geschichte*, 15: 53–82.
Höhler, Sabine (2014b), "Science und Fiction des Unerschöpflichen in Zeiten neuer Wachstumsgrenzen," *Geschichte und Gesellschaft*, 40 (3): 437–51.
Höhler, Sabine (2015a), "Inventorier la Terre," in Kapil Raj and H. Otto Sibum (eds.), *Modernité et globalisation*, Histoire des sciences et des saviors 2, 167–81, Paris: Éditions du Seuil.
Höhler, Sabine (2015b), *Spaceship Earth in the Environmental Age, 1960–1990*, London: Pickering & Chatto.
Höhler, Sabine (2017a), "Local Disruption or Global Condition? El Niño as Weather and as Climate Phenomenon," in Sebastian Grevsmühl (ed.), "Global Environmental Images," special issue of *GEO Geography and Environment*, 4 (1). Available online: http://doi.org/10.1002/geo2.34/pdf.
Höhler, Sabine (2017b), "Survival: Mars Fiction and Experiments with Life on Earth," *Environmental Philosophy*, 14 (1): 83–100.
Höhler, Sabine and Nina Wormbs (2017), "Remote Sensing: Digital Data at a Distance," in Jocelyn Thorpe, Stephanie Rutherford, and L. Anders Sandberg (eds.), *Methodological Challenges in Nature-Culture and Environmental History Research*, 272–83, London: Routledge.
Holland, Geoff and David Pugh, eds. (2010), *Troubled Waters: Ocean Science and Governance*, New York: Cambridge University Press.
Holm, Poul (2012), "World War II and the 'Great Acceleration' of North Atlantic Fisheries," *Global Environment*, 10: 66–91.
Holm, Poul, Tim D. Smith, and David J. Starkey (2001), *The Exploited Seas: New Directions for Marine Environmental History*, St. John's, Newfoundland: International Maritime Economic History Association.
Holm, Paul, Tim D. Smith, and David J. Starkey (2017), *The Exploited Seas: New Directions for Marine Environmental History*, Liverpool: Liverpool University Press.
Holzer, Kerstin (2003), *Elisabeth Mann Borgese: Ein Lebensporträt*, 2nd edn., Frankfurt: Fischer.
"A Homemade Sub" (1953), *Life*, 34 (19) May 11: 73–6.
Hong, Gi Hoon and Young Joo Lee (2015), "Transitional Measures to Combine Two Global Ocean Dumping Treaties into a Single Treaty," *Marine Policy*, 55: 47–56.
Hook, Leslie (2012), "China: Risk of Conflict over Resources in Deep Water," *Financial Times*, November 5.
Horn, Eva (2010), "Enden des Menschen: Globale Katastrophen als biopolitische Fantasie," in Reto Sorg and Stefan Bodo Würffel (eds.), *Utopie und Apokalypse in der Moderne*, 101–18, Munich: Wilhelm Fink.
Horn, Eva (2014), *Zukunft als Katastrophe*, Frankfurt: S. Fischer Verlag.
Hsü, Kenneth J. (1992), *Challenger at Sea: A Ship That Revolutionized Earth Science*, Princeton, NJ: Princeton University Press.
Huggan, Graham (2013), "Lives Aquatic: Underwater with the Cousteaus," in *Nature's Saviours: Celebrity Conservationists in the Television Age*, 65–104, New York: Routledge.
Hull, Edward Whaley Seabrook (1967), "The Political Ocean," *Foreign Affairs*, 45 (3): 492–502.

"Iceland Calls for a Parley To Bar Pollution of Seabed" (1970), *New York Times*, August 21.
Inselmann, Andrea, Don Doe, Dylan Graham, Sally Smart, and Herbert F. Johnson Museum of Art (2007), *Dangerous Waters*, Ithaca, NY: Herbert F. Johnson Museum of Art, Cornell University.
International Atomic Energy Agency (IAEA) (1999), *Inventory of Radioactive Waste Disposal at Sea*, Vienna: IAEA.
International Labour Office (ILO) and Seafarers International Research Centre (2004), *The Global Seafarer: Living and Working Conditions in a Globalized Industry*, Geneva: ILO.
Intergovernmental Panel on Climate Change (IPCC) (2010), *Climate Change*. Available online: https://www.ipcc.ch/report/ar1/wg1/ (accessed October 18, 2020).
International Maritime Organization (IMO) (2018), "IMO Takes First Steps to Address Autonomous Ships," *IMO*, May 25. Available online: http://www.imo.org/en/MediaCentre/PressBriefings/Pages/08-MSC-99-MASS-scoping.aspx (accessed March 20, 2019).
International Union for Conservation of Nature (IUCN) (n.d.), "World Database on Protected Areas." Available online: https://www.iucn.org/theme/protected-areas/our-work/world-database-protected-areas (accessed October 16, 2020).
Iovino, S. and S. Oppermann, eds. (2014), *Material Ecocriticism*, Bloomington: Indiana University Press.
Island Studies Journal (2005–17) "Journal Archive." Available online: https://www.islandstudies.ca/ (accessed October 16, 2020).
Jackson, Jeremy B. C. (2008), "Ecological Extinction and Evolution in the Brave New Ocean," *Proceedings of the National Academy of Sciences of the United States of America*, 105 (suppl. 1) (August 12): 11458–65.
Jackson, Jeremy B.C. et al. (2001), "Historical Overfishing and the Recent Collapse of Coastal Ecosystems," *Science*, 293 (530): 629–38.
Jameson, Fredric (1994), *The Political Unconscious: Narrative as a Socially Symbolic Act*, Ithaca, NY: Cornell University Press.
Jasanoff, Sheila (2001), "Image and Imagination: The Formation of Global Environmental Consciousness," in Clark A. Miller and Paul N. Edwards (eds.), *Changing the Atmosphere: Expert Knowledge and Environmental Governance*, 309–37, Cambridge: MIT Press.
Jasanoff, Sheila (2015), "Future Imperfect: Science, Technology, and the Imaginations of Modernity," in Sheila Jasanoff and Sang-Hyun Kim (eds.), *Dreamscapes of Modernity: Sociotechnical Imaginaries and the Fabrication of Power*, 1–33, Chicago IL: Chicago University Press.
Johnson, Irving (1936), *Westward Bound on the Schooner Yankee*, New York: W.W. Norton & Company.
Jonsson, Albritton Frederik (2012), "The Industrial Revolution in the Anthropocene," *Journal of Modern History*, 84 (3): 679–96.
Jónsson, Hannes (1982), *Friends in Conflict: the Anglo-Icelandic Cod Wars and the Law of the Sea*, London: C. Hurst.
Juda, Lawrence (1996), *International Law and Ocean Use Management: The Evolution of Ocean Governance*, London: Routledge.
Jue, Melody (2014), "Proteus and the Digital: Scalar Transformations of Seawater's Materiality in Ocean Animations," *Animation: An Interdisciplinary Journal*, 9 (2): 245–60.
Kaldor, Mary (1990), *The Imaginary War: Understanding the East-West Conflict*, Oxford: Blackwell.

Kaldor, Mary (2003), *Global Civil Society. An Answer to War*, Cambridge: Polity Press.
Kehrt, Christian (2014), "'Dem Krill auf der Spur': Antarktisches Wissensregime und globale Ressourcenkonflikte in den 1970er Jahren," *Geschichte und Gesellschaft*, 40 (1): 403–36.
Kehrt, Christian and Franziska Torma, eds. (2014), "Lebensraum Meer," special issue of *Geschichte und Gesellschaft, Zeitschrift für Historische Sozialwissenschaft*, 40 (3).
Keiner, Christine (2017), "A Two-Ocean Bouillabaisse: Science, Politics, and the Central American Sea-Level Canal Controversy," *Journal of the History of Biology*, 50 (4): 835–87.
Kempf, Wolfgang (2009), "A Sea of Environmental Refugees? Oceania in an Age of Climate Change," in Elfriede Hermann, Karin Klenke, and Michael Dickhardt (eds.), *Form, Macht, Differenz: Motive und Felder ethnologischen Forschens*, 191–205, Göttingen: Universitätsverlag Göttingen.
Kennerson, Elliott Doran (2008), "Ocean Pictures: The Construction of the Ocean on Film," MFA thesis, Montana State University, Bozeman.
Kernagis, Dawn (2016), "Mission Day 7–8: Remembering Where We Are," IHMC [Blog], July 28. Available online: https://www.ihmc.us/mission-day-7-8-remembering/ (accessed October 18, 2020).
Kessler, Elizabeth A. (2012), *Picturing the Cosmos: Hubble Space Telescope Images and the Astronomical Sublime*, Minneapolis: University of Minnesota Press.
Kihleng, Emelihter, Clement Yow Mulalap, Jacki Leota-Mua, and Vicente Diaz (2019), "*Island Soldier*: By Nathan Fitch, Review," *The Contemporary Pacific*, 31(1): 248–61.
Kiste, Robert and Suzanne Falgout (1999), "Anthropology and Micronesia: The Context," in Robert C. Kiste and Mac Marshall (eds.), *American Anthropology in Micronesia: An Assessment*, 11–51, Honolulu: University of Hawai'i Press.
Klose, Alexander (2015), *The Container Principle: How a Box Changes the Way We Think*, trans. Charles Marcrum, Infrastructures, Cambridge, MA: MIT Press.
Knauft, Bruce M. (1990), "Melanesian Warfare: A Theoretical History," *Oceania*, 60: 250–311.
Krebs, Albin (1986), "Sterling Hayden Dead at 70: An Actor, Writer and Sailor," *New York Times*, May 24. Available online: https://www.nytimes.com/1986/05/24/obituaries/sterling-hayden-dead-at-70-an-actor-writer-and-sailor.html (accessed March 20, 2019).
Krige, John (2014), "Embedding the National in the Global: US-French Relationships in Space Science and Rocketry in the 1960s," in Naomi Oreskes and John Krige (eds.), *Science and Technology in the Global Cold War*, 227–50, Cambridge, MA: MIT Press.
Kroll, Gary (2008), *America's Ocean Wilderness: A Cultural History of Twentieth-Century Exploration*, Lawrence: University Press of Kansas.
Kupper, Patrick (2003), "Die ,1970er Diagnose': Grundsätzliche Überlegungen zu einem Wendepunkt der Umweltgeschichte," *Archiv für Sozialgeschichte*, 43: 325–48.
Kurlansky, Mark (1998), *Cod: A Biography of the Fish that Changed the World*, New York: Penguin Books.
Kurlansky, Mark (1999), *Cod: A Biography of the Fish That Changed the World*, London: Vintage.
Langston, Nancy (2017), *Sustaining Lake Superior: An Extraordinary Lake in a Changing World*, New Haven, CT: Yale University Press.
Larson, Brendon M. H. (2005), "The War of the Roses: Demilitarizing Invasion Biology," *Frontiers in Ecology and the Environment*, 3 (9): 495–500.

Latour, Bruno (1986), "Visualization and Cognition: Thinking with Eyes and Hands," *Knowledge and Society: Studies in the Sociology of Culture Past and Present*, 6: 1–40.
Latour, Bruno (1990), "Drawing Things Together," in Michael Lynch and Steeve Woolgar (eds.), *Representation in Scientific Practice*, 19–68, Cambridge, MA: MIT Press.
Latour, Bruno (2017), *Kampf um Gaia: Acht Vorträge über das neue Klimaregime*, Suhrkamp: Berlin-Verlag.
Latour, Bruno and Steve Woolgar (1979), *Laboratory Life: The Social Construction of Scientific Facts*, Beverly Hills, CA: Sage.
Lausche, Barbara J. (2008), *Weaving a Web of Environmental Law*, Bonn: Erich Schmidt Verlag.
Lear, Linda (1997), *Rachel Carson: Witness for Nature*, New York: Henry Holt.
LeCain (2016), "Heralding a New Humanism: The Radical Implications of Chakrabarty's 'Four Theses,'" in Robert Emmett and Thomas Lekan (eds.), "Whose Anthropocene? Revisiting Dipesh Chakrabarty's 'Four Theses,'" *RCC Perspectives: Transformations in Environment and Society*, (2): 15–20.
Lee, Martin ([1981] 1983), *Ocean Dumping: A Time to Reappraise?*, Washington, DC: US Government Printing Office.
Lehman, J. (2018), *Oceans Ventured: Winning the Cold War at Sea*, London: W.W. Norton.
Lem, Stanisław (1977), *Solaris*, 4th edn., Frankfurt: Suhrkamp.
Lepore, Jill (2018), "The Shorebird: Rachel Carson and the Rising of the Seas," *The New Yorker*, March 26: 64–72.
Lessenich, Stephan (2016), *Neben uns die Sintflut: Die Externalisierungsgesellschaft und ihr Preis*, Munich: Carl Hanser Verlag.
Levering, Ralph B. and Miriam L. Levering (1999), *Citizen Action for Global Change: The Neptune Group and Law of the Sea*, Syracuse, NY: Syracuse University Press.
Levinson, Marc (2016), *The Box: How the Shipping Container Made the World Smaller and the World Economy Bigger*, 2nd edn., Princeton, NJ: Princeton University Press.
Lewis, David ([1972] 1994), *We the Navigators: The Ancient Art of Landfinding in the Pacific*, 2nd edn., ed. Derek Oulton, Honolulu: University Press of Hawaii.
Liebers, Arthur (1962), *The Complete Book of Water Sports*, New York: Coward McCann.
Lilly, John (1961), *Man and Dolphin: Adventures of a New Scientific Frontier*, Garden City, NY: Doubleday.
Lilly, John (1967), *The Mind of the Dolphin: A Nonhuman Intelligence*, Garden City, NY: Doubleday.
Linnér, Björn-Ola (2003), *The Return of Malthus: Environmentalism and Post-war Population-Resource Crises*, Isles of Harris: White Horse Press.
Löhr, Isabella and Andrea Rehling (2014), *Global Commons im 20. Jahrhundert: Entwürfe für eine globale Welt*, Munich: De Gruyter/Oldenbourg.
Lotka, Alfred James (1925), *Elements of Physical Biology*, Baltimore, MD: Williams & Wilkins.
Lovelock, J.E. (1979), *Gaia: A New Look at Life on Earth*, Oxford: Oxford University Press.
Lowry, Malcolm (2005), *Ultramarine (Tusk Ivories)*, New York: Overlook Press.
Lüdecke, Cornelia (2004), "The First International Polar Year (1882–83): A Big Science Experiment with Small Science Equipment," *Proceedings of the International Commission on History of Meteorology*, 1 (1): 55–64.

Macekura, Stephen J. (2015), *Of Limits and Growth: The Rise of Global Sustainable Development in the Twentieth Century*, Cambridge: Cambridge University Press.

Marriam-Webster (2019), s.v. "Voyage." Available online: https://www.merriam-webster.com/dictionary/voyage (accessed March 20, 2019).

McIntosh, Malcolm (1987), *Arms Across the Pacific: Security and Trade Issues Across the Pacific*, London: Pinter.

MacLean, Eleanore (2015), "He Couldn't Have Done It Without Her: Exy Johnson's Seafaring Legacy," *Sea History*, 152 (Autumn): 16–20.

Maclellan, Nic (2014), *Banning Nuclear Weapons: A Pacific Islander Perspective*, Australia: International Campaign to Abolish Nuclear Weapons (ICANW).

Madsen, Axel (1986), *Cousteau: An Unauthorized Biography*, New York: Beaufort Books.

Mahrane, Yannick, Marianna Fenzi, Céline Pessis, and Christophe Bonneuil (2012), "De la nature à la biosphère: L'invention politique de l'environnement global, 1945–1972," *Vingtième Siècle: Revue d'histoire*, 113 (1): 2127–41.

Malm, Andreas and Alf Hornborg (2014), "The Geology of Mankind? A Critique of the Anthropocene Narrative," *Anthropocene Review*, 1 (1): 62–9.

Máñez, Kathleen Schwerdtner and Bo Poulsen, eds. (2016), *Perspectives on Oceans Past: A Handbook of Marine Environmental History*, Dordrecht: Springer Netherlands.

Mann, Janet (2001), "Cetacean Culture: Definitions and Evidence," *Behavioral and Brain Sciences*, (24): 309–82.

Mann, Janet, ed. (2017), *Deep Thinkers: Inside the Minds of Whales, Dolphins, and Porpoises*, Chicago: University of Chicago Press.

Manovich, Lev (2001), *The Language of New Media*, Cambridge, MA: MIT Press.

Marchessault, Janine (2017), "Invisible Ecologies: Cousteau's Cameras and Ocean Wonders," in *Ecstatic Worlds: Media, Utopias, Ecologies*, 53–84, Cambridge, MA: MIT Press.

Marfeld, A.F. (1972), *Zukunft im Meer: Bericht - Dokumentation - Interpretation zur gesamten Ozeanologie und Meerestechnik*, Berlin: Safari-Verlag.

Marx, Robert F. ([1978] 1990), *The History of Underwater Exploration*, New York: Dover Publications.

Masefield, John (1923), *The Collected Poems of John Masefield*, London: William Heineman.

Matsen, Brad (2009), *Jacques Cousteau: The Sea King*, New York: Pantheon Books.

Mattl, Siegfried and Christian Schulte (2014), "Vorstellungskraft," *Zeitschrift für Kulturwissenschaften*, 2: 9–11.

Maurer, Hans (1933), *Die Echolotungen des "Meteor": Deutsche Atlantische Expedition auf dem Forschungs- und Vermessungsschiff "Meteor", ausgeführt unter der Leitung von Professor Dr. A. Merz † und Kapitän z. S. F. Spiess, 1925–1927; Wissenschaftliche Ergebnisse, herausgegeben im Auftrage der Notgemeinschaft der Deutschen Wissenschaft von Dr. A. Defant*, Berlin: de Gruyter.

McCormick, John (1991), *Reclaiming Paradise: The Global Environmental Movement*, Bloomington: University of Indiana Press.

McIntrye, Joan (1975), *Mind in the Waters: A Book to Celebrate the Consciousness of Whales*, New York: Charles Scribner's Sons.

McKibben, Bill (1989), *The End of Nature*, New York: Random House Trade Paperbacks.

McNeill, John R. (2000), *Something New Under the Sun: An Environmental History of the Twentieth Century*, New York: W.W. Norton & Company, Inc.

Meadows, Donella H., Dennis L. Meadows, Jorgen Randers, and William W. Behrens (1972), *The Limits to Growth: A Report for the Club of Rome's Project on the Predicament of Mankind*, London: Earth Island.

Meadows, Donella H., Dennis L. Meadows, Jorgen Randers, and William W. Behrens (1974), *Limits to Growth: A Report for the Club of Rome's Project on the Predicament of Mankind*, New York: Universe Books.
Mentz, Steve (2015), *Shipwreck Modernity: Ecologies of Globalization, 1550–1719*, Minneapolis: University of Minnesota Press.
Mero, John L. (1965), *The Mineral Resources of the Sea*, New York: Elsevier.
Merz, Alfred (1925), "Die Deutsche Atlantische Expedition auf dem Vermessungs- und Forschungsschiff 'Meteor'," report 1, "Die Atlantische Hydrographie und die Planlegung der Deutschen Atlantischen Expedition," *Sitzungsberichte der Preussischen Akademie der Wissenschaften, Physikalisch-Mathematische Klasse*, 31: 562–86.
Michelet, Jules (1861), *The Sea*, New York: Rudd & Carleton.
Miles, Edward L. (1998), *Global Ocean Politics: The Decision Process at the Third United Nations Conference on the Law of the Sea, 1973–1982*, Cambridge, MA: Kluwer Law International.
Miller, James W. and Ian G. Koblick (1984), *Living and Working in the Sea*, New York: Van Nostrand Reinhold.
Miller, James W. and Ian G. Koblick (1995), *Living and Working in the Sea*, 2nd edn., Plymouth, VT: Five Corners Publications.
Miller, Marc L. (1993), "The Rise of Coastal and Marine Tourism," *Ocean & Coastal Management*, 20 (3): 181–99.
Miller, Michael B. (2012), *Europe and the Maritime World: A Twentieth-Century History*, Cambridge: Cambridge University Press.
Mills, Eric L. (1989), *Biological Oceanography: An Early History, 1870–1960*, Ithaca, NY: Cornell University Press.
Mills, Eric L. (2009), *The Fluid Envelope of Our Planet: How the Study of Ocean Currents Became a Science*, Toronto: University of Toronto Press.
Milner, Harold W. (1953), "Algae as Food," *Scientific American*, 189 (4): 31–5.
Milner, Harold W. (1954), "Food or Fuel from Algae?," *Science Digest*, April: 65–7.
"Miniature Sub" (1950), *Life*, 29 (8) August 21: 75.
Mitchell, Jon (2013), "A Drop in the Ocean: the Sea-Dumping of Chemical Weapons in Okinawa," *Japan Times*, July 27.
Mitman, Gregg (1999), "A Ringside Seat in the Making of a Pet Star," in *Reel Nature: America's Romance with Wildlife on Film*, 157–79, Seattle: University of Washington Press.
Möllers, Nina, Christian Schwägerl, and Helmuth Trischler, eds. (2015), *Welcome to the Anthropocene: The Earth in our Hands*, Munich: Deutsches Museum.
Mondré, Aletta and Annegret Kuhn (2017), "Ocean Governance," *Aus Politik und Zeitgeschichte*, 67 (51–2): 4–9.
Morais, Pedro and Francoise Daverat (2016), "A History of Fish Migration Research," in Pedro Morais and Francoise Daverat (eds.), *An Introduction to Fish Migration Research*, 3–14, Boca Raton: CRC Press.
Morgan, Elaine (1972), *The Descent of Woman*, London: Souvenir Press.
Morgan, Elaine (1982), *The Aquatic Ape: A Theory of Human Evolution*, London: Souvenir Press.
Morison, S.E. ([1963] 2007), *The Two-Ocean War: A Short History of the United States Navy in the Second World War*, Annapolis, MD: Naval Institute Press.
Mückler, Hermann (2000), *Melanesien in der Krise: ethnische Konflikte, Fragmentierung und Neuorientierung*, Wiener Ethnohistorische Blätter 46, Vienna: Institut für Völkerkunde.

Mückler, Hermann (2009a), *Einführung in die Ethnologie Ozeaniens*, Vienna: Facultas.
Mückler, Hermann (2009b), "Einleitung," in Hermann Mückler (ed.), *Ozeanien: 18. bis 20. Jahrhundert, Geschichte und Gesellschaft*, vol. 17, 7–12, world regions edn., Vienna: Promedia.
Mückler, Hermann (2012), *Kolonialismus in Ozeanien*, Vienna: Facultas.
Müller, Simone M. (2016), "'Cut Holes and Sink 'em": Chemical Weapons Disposal and Cold War History as a History of Risk," *Historical Social Research*, 41(1): 263–84.
Müller, Simone M. (2017), "Corporate Behavior and Ecological Disaster: Dow Chemical and the Great Lakes Mercury Crisis, 1970–1972," *Business History*, 60 (3): 399–422.
Müller Simone M. and David Stradling (2019), "Water as the Ultimate Sink: Linking Fresh and Saltwater History," *International Review of Environmental History*, 5 (1): 23–41.
Murphy, Robert Cushman (1947), *Logbook for Grace*, New York: The Macmillan Company.
Mystic Seaport (2019), "The 38th Voyage: Introduction." Available online: https://www.mysticseaport.org/voyage/cwm/ (accessed March 20, 2019).
Naimou, Angela (2015), *Salvage Work: U.S. and Caribbean Literatures amid the Debris of Legal Personhood*, 1st edn., New York: Fordham University Press.
Narvaez, Alfonso A. (1991), "Irving M. Johnson, Who Wrote of Trips at Sea, is Dead at 85," *New York Times*, January 3: 6.
Neeson, Jeanette M. (1995), *Commoners: Common Right, Enclosure and Social Change in England, 1700–1820* (repr.), Cambridge: Cambridge University Press.
Nelson, Derek Lee (2016), "The Ravages of Teredo: The Rise and Fall of Shipworm in US History," *Environmental History*, 21: 100–24.
"New Ways to Go Under" (1953), *Life*, 35 (5) August 3: 70–1.
Newby, Eric (1956), *The Last Grain Race*, New York: Houghton Mifflin.
Niedenthal, Jack (2002), "The Atomic History of Bikini Atoll," the *Guardian*, August 6. Available online: https://www.theguardian.com/travel/2002/aug/06/travelnews.nuclearindustry.environment (accessed March 20, 2019).
Nitzke, Solvejg (2012), "Apokalypse von innen: Die andere Natur-Katastrophe in Frank Schätzings Der Schwarm und Dietmar Daths Die Abschaffung der Arten," in Solvejg Nitzke and Mark Schmitt (eds.), *Katastrophen: Konfrontationen mit dem Realen*, 167–87, Essen: C. A. Bachmann.
Nixon, Rob (2011), *Slow Violence and the Environmentalism of the Poor*, Cambridge, MA: Harvard University Press.
Noble Shor, Elizabeth (1978), *Scripps Institution of Oceanography: Probing the Oceans, 1936 to 1976*, San Diego, CA: Tofua Press.
Norris, Scott (2002), "Creatures of Culture? Making the Case for Cultural Systems in Whales and Dolphins," *BioScience*, 52 (1): 9–14.
Norton, Trevor (1999), *Stars Beneath the Sea: The Pioneers of Diving*, New York: Carroll & Graf Publishers.
Nouvian, Claire (2007), *The Deep: The Extraordinary Creatures of the Abyss*, Chicago: University of Chicago Press.
Nunn, Patrick (2007), *Climate, Environment and Society in the Pacific during the Last Millennium*, Amsterdam: Elsevier.
Nunn, Patrick and James Britton (2001), "Human-Environment Relationships in the Pacific Islands around A.D. 1300," *Environment and History*, 7 (1): 3–22.

Nye, David E. (1994), *The American Technological Sublime*, Cambridge, MA: MIT Press.

Ocean Literacy Network (n.d.). Available online: https://oceanliteracy.unesco.org (accessed November 2, 2020).

O'Connor Tom (2017), "Fukushima's Nuclear Waste will be Dumped in the Ocean, Japanese Plant Owner says," *Newsweek*, July 14.

Ocean Conference (2017), "Factsheet: People and Oceans," New York: United Nations. Available online: https://www.un.org/sustainabledevelopment/wp-content/uploads/2017/05/Ocean-fact-sheet-package.pdf (accessed October 16, 2020).

Ocearch (n.d.), "Tracker." Available online: https://www.ocearch.org/tracker/?list (accessed October 18, 2020).

Oreskes, Naomi (2014a), "Changing the Mission: From the Cold War to Climate Change," in Naomi Oreskes and John Krige (eds.), *Science and Technology in the Global Cold War*, 141–88, Cambridge, MA: MIT Press.

Oreskes, Naomi (2014b), "Scaling Up Our Vision," *Isis*, 105 (2): 379–91.

Ortmayr, Norbert (2009), "Demographischer Wandel Ozeaniens seit dem späten 18. Jahrhundert," in Hermann Mückler (ed.), *Ozeanien: 18. bis 20. Jahrhundert, Geschichte und Gesellschaft*, vol. 17, 190–228, world regions edn., Vienna: Promedia.

Owen, Paula and Tony Rice (1999), *Decommissioning the Brent Spa*, London: CRC Press.

"Pacific Climate Warriors" (n.d.), "350 Pacific." Available online: https://350pacific.org/pacific-climate-warriors/ (accessed December 16, 2018).

Paddock, William and Paul Paddock (1967), *Famine – 1975! America's Decision: Who Will Survive?*, Boston: Little, Brown and Company.

Paine, Lincoln P. (2013), *The Sea and Civilization: A Maritime History of the World*, 1st edn., New York: Alfred A. Knopf.

Pardo, Arvid (1975), *The Common Heritage of Mankind: Selected Papers on Oceans and World Order 1967–1974*, International Ocean Institute Occasional Paper No. 3, Malta: Malta University Press.

Parrott, Daniel S. (2003), *Tall Ships Down: The Last Voyages of the Pamir, Albatross, Marques, Pride of Baltimore, and Maria Asumpta*, Camden, ME: International Marine/McGraw-Hill.

Paskoff, Roland and Robert Petiot (1990), "Coastal Progradation as a By-Product of Human Activity: An Example From Chañaral Bay, Atacama Desert, Chile," *Journal of Coastal Research*, 6 (6): 91–102.

Past, Elena (2009), "Lives Aquatic: Mediterranean Cinema and an Ethics of Underwater Existence," *Cinema Journal*, 48 (3): 52–65.

Patton, Kimberley Christine (2007), *The Sea Can Wash Away All Evils: Modern Marine Pollution and the Ancient Cathartic Ocean*, New York: Columbia University Press.

Pazifik aktuell (2018a), "Protest gegen Atommüll-Endlager auf Runit," September, Nr. 115.

Pazifik aktuell (2018b), "Überwachungssystem auf Moruroa modernisiert," September, Nr. 115.

Penck, Albrecht (1925), "Die Deutsche Atlantische Expedition," *Zeitschrift der Gesellschaft für Erdkunde zu Berlin*, 7–8: 243–51.

Peterkin, Tom (2005), "MoD Dumped Munition in Irish Sea," *The Telegraph*, April 22.

Philander, S. George (2004), *Our Affair with El Niño: How We Transformed an Enchanting Peruvian Current into a Global Climate Hazard*, Princeton, NJ: Princeton University Press.

Phillips, Catherine and Jadeep Sirkar (2012), "The International Conference on Safety of Life at Sea, 1914: The History and the Ongoing Mission," *Coast Guard Journal of Safety & Security at Sea, Proceedings of the Marine Safety & Security Council*, 69 (2): 27–8. Available online: https://uscgproceedings.epubxp.com/i/70722-sum-2012 (accessed March 20, 2019).

Piccard, Jacques and Robert S. Dietz (1961), *Seven Miles Down: The Story of the Bathyscaph Trieste*, New York: G. T. Putnam's Sons.

Plunkett, Geoff (2003a), *Chemical Warfare Agent Sea Dumping off Australia*, Canberra: Department of Defence.

Plunkett, Geoff (2003b), *Sea Dumping in Australia: Historical and Contemporary Aspects*, 1st ed, Canberra: Department of Defence.

Pollnac, Richard, Patrick Christie, Joshua E. Cinner, Tracy Dalton, Tim M. Daw, Graham E. Forrester, and Timothy R. McClanahan (2010), "Marine Reserves as Linked Social–Ecological Systems," *Proceedings of the National Academy of Sciences*, 107 (43): 18262–5.

Polynesian Voyaging Society (2019), "The Story of Hōkūle'a." Available online: http://www.hokulea.com/voyages/our-story/ (accessed March 20, 2019)

Powell, David C. (2001), *A Fascination for Fish: Adventures of an Underwater Pioneer*, Berkeley: University of California Press.

Poyer, Lin (2004), "Dimensions of Hunger in Wartime: Chuuk Lagoon, 1943–1945," *Food and Foodways*, 12 (2–3): 137–64.

Poyer, Lin (2008), "Chuukese Experiences in the Pacific War," *Journal of Pacific History*, 43 (2): 223–38.

Prehoda, Robert W. (1967), *Designing the Future: The Role of Technological Forecasting*, Philadelphia: Chilton Book Company.

Price, Willard (1966), *America's Paradise Lost*, New York: John Day Co.

Quilley, Geoff (2000), "Duty and Mutiny: The Aesthetics of Loyalty and the Representation of the British Sailor c.1789-1800," in Philip Shaw (ed.), *Romantic Wars: Studies in Culture and Conflict, 1793–1822*, 81–109, Aldershot: Ashgate.

"Radioactive Waste was Dumped in Irish Sea," (1997), *The Irish Times*, June 30.

Radkau, Joachim (2011), *Die Ära der Ökologie: Eine Weltgeschichte*, Munich: Beck.

Reeves, Robert W. and Daphne deJersey Gemmill, eds. (2004), *Reflections on 25 Years of Analysis, Diagnosis and Prediction, 1979–2004*, Washington, DC: US Government Printing Office.

Rehling, Andrea (2017), "Materielles Kultur- und Naturerbe als Objekt und Ressource kultureller Souveränitätsansprüche," in Gregor Feindt, Bernhard Gißibl, and Johannes Paulmann (eds.), *Kulturelle Souveränität: Politische Deutungs- und Handlungsmacht jenseits des Staates im 20. Jahrhundert*, 257–84, Göttingen: Vandenhoek & Ruprecht.

Reidy, Michael S., Gary Kroll, and Erik M. Conway (2007), *Exploration and Science: Social Impact and Interaction*, Denver: ABC–CLIO.

Revelle, Roger (1985), "Oceanography from Space," *Science*, 228: 133.

Rheinberger, Hans-Jörg (1998), "From the 'originary phenomenom' to the 'system of pelagic fishery': Johannes Müller (1801–1858) and the Relation between Physiology and Philosophy," in Kurt Bayertz and Roy Porter (eds.), *From Physico-Theology to Bio-Technology: Essays in the Social and Cultural History of Biosciences*, 133–52, Amsterdam: Rodopi.

Rich, Nathaniel (2018), "Losing Earth: The Decade We Almost Stopped Climate Change," *New York Times Magazine*, August 1.

Riedy, Michael S., Gary Kroll, and Erik M. Conway (2007), *Exploration and Science: Social Impact and Interaction*, Santa Barbara, CA: ABC-CLIO.

Rieger, Bernhard (2003), "'Modern Wonders': Technological Innovation and Public Ambivalence in Britain and Germany, 1890s to 1933," *History Workshop Journal*, 55: 153–76.

Roberts, Callum (2007), *The Unnatural History of the Sea*, Washington, DC: Island Press.

Rosenberg, Andrew A. (2003), "Managing to the Margins: The Overexploitation of Fisheries," *Frontiers in Ecology and the Environment*, March: 102–6.

Rothschild de, David (2011), *Plastiki Across the Pacific on Plastic: An Adventure to Save Our Oceans*, San Francisco: Chronicle Books.

Roy, M.K. (1995), *War in the Indian Ocean*, New Delhi: Lancer Publishers.

Royal Society for the Protection of Birds (1922), *Bird Notes and News*, 10, no. 2.

Rozwadowski, Helen M. (2002), *The Sea Knows No Boundaries: A Century of Marine Science Under ICES*, Seattle: University of Washington Press; London: International Council for the Exploration of the Sea.

Rozwadowski, Helen M. (2005), *Fathoming the Ocean: The Discovery and Exploration of the Deep Sea*, Cambridge, MA: Belknap Press of Harvard University Press.

Rozwadowski, Helen M. (2010a), "Ocean's Depths," *Environmental History*, 15 (3): 520–5.

Rozwadowski, Helen M. (2010b), "Playing by – and on and under – the Sea: The Importance of Play for Knowing the Ocean," in Jeremy Vetter (ed.), *Knowing Global Environments: New Historical Perspectives on the Field Sciences*, 162–89, Rutgers: Rutgers University Press.

Rozwadowski, Helen M. (2012) "Arthur C. Clarke and the Limitations of the Ocean as a Frontier," *Environmental History*, 17 (3): 578–602.

Rozwadowski, Helen M. (2013), "From Danger Zone to World of Wonder: The 1950s Transformation of the Ocean's Depths," *Coriolis: Interdisciplinary Journal of Maritime Studies*, 4 (1): 1–20.

Rozwadowski, Helen M. (2016), "Scientists Writing and Knowing the Ocean," in Steve Mentz and Martha Elena Rojas (eds.), *The Sea and Nineteenth-Century Anglophone Literary Culture*, 29–46, London: Routledge.

Rozwadowski, Helen M. (2018), *Vast Expanses: A History of the Oceans*, Chicago: University of Chicago Press.

Rozwadowski, Helen M. and David van Keuren, eds. (2004), *The Machine in Neptune's Garden: Historical Perspectives on Technology and the Marine Environment*, Canton, MA: Science History Publications/USA.

Ruppenthal, Jens (2018), *Raubbau und Meerestechnik: Die Rede von der Unerschöpflichkeit der Meere*, Stuttgart: Franz Steiner Verlag.

Safina, Carl (2002–3), "Launching a Sea Ethic," *Wild Earth*, (Winter): 2–5.

Sail Training International (2019), "Sail Training International: History." Available online: https://sailtraininginternational.org/sailtraining/origins/ (accessed March 20 2019).

Schätzing, Frank (2004), *Der Schwarm*, Cologne: Kiepenheuer & Witsch.

Schmidt, Frithjof (1986), "Brennpunkt Pazifik: Eine politische Skizze der 'pazifischen Herausforderungen,'" in Peter Franke (ed.), *Die Militarisierung des Pazifik*, in Informationszentrum Dritte Welt, Freiburg und der Südostasien-Informationsstelle, Bremen, 13–34, Gießen: Prolit-Vertriebs-GmbH.

Schertow, John Ahni (2008), "Indigenous Communities Oppose Deep Sea Mining," *International Cry*, July 10. Available online: https://intercontinentalcry.org/indigenous-communities-oppose-deep-sea-mining/ (accessed December 15, 2018).

Schott, Gerhard (1926), "Messung der Meerestiefen durch Echolot," *Wissenschaftliche Abhandlungen des 21. Deutschen Geographentages zu Breslau* vom 2. bis 4. Juni 1925, 140–50, Berlin: Dietrich Reimer.

Schrijver, Nico (2010), *Development without Destruction: The UN and Global Resource Management*, Bloomington: Indiana University Press.

Schulz, Matthias (2007), "Netzwerke und Normen in der internationalen Geschichte: Überlegungen zur Einführung," *Historische Mitteilungen*, 17: 1–14.

Schwartz, Stuart B. (2015), *Sea of Storms: A History of Hurricanes in the Greater Caribbean from Columbus to Katrina*, Princeton, NJ: Princeton University Press.

Scott, James C. (1998), *Seeing Like a State: How Certain Schemes to Improve the Human Condition Have Failed*, New Haven, CT: Yale University Press.

Sea Turtle Conservancy (1996–2020), "Sea Turtle Tracking: Active Sea Turtles." Available online: https://conserveturtles.org/sea-turtle-tracking-active-sea-turtles/ (accessed October 18, 2020).

Seavitt Nordenson, Catherine (2014), "The Bottom of the Bay, Or How To Know the Seaweeds," *Harvard Design Magazine*, 39 (Fall/Winter): 6–8.

Sebille, Erik van (2014), "Under the Deep Blue Ocean: The Search for MH370's Black Box," *UNSW Sydney Newsroom*, March 31. Available online: https://newsroom.unsw.edu.au/news/science/under-deep-blue-ocean-search-mh370s-black-box (accessed April 10, 2019).

Sekula, Allan (2002), "Fish Story: Notes on the Work," in Gerti Fietzek, Heike Ander, and Nadja Rottner (eds.), *Documenta 11, Platform 5: Exhibition: Catalogue*, 582–3, Ostfildern-Ruit: Hatje Cantz.

Sekula, Allan, B.H.D. Buchloh, and centrum voor hedendaagse kunst Witte de With (1995), *Fish Story*, Rotterdam: Witte de With, center for contemporary art; Düsseldorf: Richter Verlag.

Sekula, Allan, Noel Burch, Frank van Reemst, Joost Verheij, Vincent Lucassen, Ebba Sinzinger, Menno Boerema, and Allan Sekula (2010), [Video] *The Forgotten Space*, Brooklyn, NY: Icarus Films.

Selin, Henrik and Stacy D. VanDeveer (2013), "Global Climate Change: Beyond Kyoto," in Norman J. Vig (ed.), *Environmental Policy: New Directions for the Twenty-First Century*, 278–98, Thousand Oaks, CA: CQ Press.

Shackelford, Scott J. (2008), "The Tragedy of the Common Heritage of Mankind," *Stanford Environmental Law Journal*, 27: 101–20.

Shapin, Steven (2010), *Never Pure: Historical Studies of Science as if It Was Produced by People with Bodies, Situated in Time, Space, Culture, and Society, and Struggling for Credibility and Authority*, Baltimore: Johns Hopkins University Press.

Shell, Hanna Rose (2005), "Things Under Water: Etienne-Jules Marey's Aquarium Laboratory and Cinema's Assembly," in Bruno Latour and Peter Weibel (eds.), *Dingpolitik: Atmospheres of Democracy*, 326–32, Cambridge, MA: MIT Press.

Sherman, P. (1972), "Acoustic Monitoring of the Sinking of the LeBaron Russell Briggs," in *Ocean 72 – IEEE International Conference on Engineering in the Ocean Environment*, Newport, RI, 286–8. Available online: https://doi.org/10.1109/OCEANS.1972.1161133.

Silverstein, Harvey B. (1978), *Superships and Nation-States: The Transnational Politics of the Intergovernmental Maritime Consultative Organization*, Westview Replica edn., Boulder, CO: Westview Press.

Simcock, Alan (2010), "The United Nations, Oceans Governance and Science," in Geoff Holland and David Pugh (eds.), *Troubled Waters: Ocean Science and Governance*, 28–40, New York: Cambridge University Press.

Simon, Zoltán Boldizsár (2020), "The Limits of Anthropocene Narratives," *European Journal of Social Theory*, 23 (2): 184–99.

Slocum, Joshua (1901), *Sailing Around the World Alone*, New York: The Century Company.

Sluga, Glenda (2010), "UNESCO and the (One) World of Julian Huxley," *Journal of World History*, 21 (3): 393–418.

Sluga, Glenda (2013), *Internationalism in the Age of Nationalism*, Philadelphia: University of Pennsylvania Press.

Smith, Jason W. (2016), "Thou Uncracked Keel: The Many Voyages of the Whaleship *Charles W. Morgan* and the Presence of the American Maritime Past," *New England Quarterly*, 89 (3): 421–56.

SOLAS (International Convention for the Safety of Life at Sea) (1914), "Text of the Convention for the Safety of Life at Sea," HM Stationary Office. Available online: http://www.archive.org/stream/textofconvention00inte#page/n5/mode/2up (accessed March 20, 2019).

Sörlin, Sverker and Paul Warde (2009), "Making the Environment Historical – An Introduction," in Sverker Sörlin and Paul Warde (eds.), *Nature's End: History and the Environment*, 1–19, Basingstoke: Palgrave Macmillan.

Sörlin, Sverker and Nina Wormbs (2018), "Environing Technologies: A Theory of Making Environment," *History and Technology*, 74 (2): 1–25.

Souchen, Alex (2018), "The Dark Side of Disarmament: Ocean Pollution, Peace, and the World Wars," in *ActiveHistory.ca*, December 4. Available online: http://activehistory.ca/2018/12/the-dark-side-of-disarmament-ocean-pollution-peace-and-the-world-wars/ (accessed March 17, 2019).

Sound Experience (2016), "History of Adventuress." Available online: https://www.soundexp.org/about-us/our-ship/history-of-adventuress/ (accessed March 20, 2019).

SoundWaters (2017), "Schooner SoundWaters." Available online: https://soundwaters.org/schooner-soundwaters/ (accessed March 20, 2019).

Sparenberg, Ole (2015a), "Meeresbergbau nach Manganknollen (1965–2014): Aufstieg, Fall und Wiedergeburt?," *Der Anschnitt: Zeitschrift für Kunst und Kultur im Bergbau*, 67 (4–5): 128–45.

Sparenberg, Ole (2015b), "Mining for Manganese Nodules: The Deep Sea as a Contested Space (1960s–1980s)," in Heta Hurskainen and Marta Grzechnik (eds.), *Beyond the Sea: Reviewing the Manifold Dimensions of Water as Barrier and Bridge*, 149–64, Cologne: Böhlau.

Speth, James Gustave and Peter M. Haas (2006), *Global Environmental Governance*, Washington, DC: Island Press.

Staples, Amy L. (2006), *The Birth of Development: How the World Bank, FAO, and WHO changed the world, 1945–1965*, Kent, OH: Kent State University Press.

Starosielski, Nicole (2013), "Beyond Fluidity: A Cultural History of Cinema under Water," in Stephen Rust, Salma Monani, and Sean Cubitt (eds.), *Ecocinema Theory and Practice*, 149–68, New York: Routledge.

Starosielski, Nicole (2015), *The Undersea Network*, Durham, NC: Duke University Press.

Starr, Cindy (2016), "Annual Arctic Sea Ice Minimum 1979–2015, with graph," NASA Scientific Visualization Studio, March 10. Available online: https://svs.gsfc.nasa.gov/4435 (accessed October 9, 2020).

Steffen, Will, Jacques Grinevald, Paul Crutzen, and John McNeill (2011), "The Anthropocene: Conceptual and Historical Perspectives," *Philosophical Transactions of the Royal Society A.*, (369): 843. Available online: https://royalsocietypublishing.org/doi/full/10.1098/rsta.2010.0327 (accessed April 8, 2019).

Steinberg, Philip E. (2001), *The Social Construction of the Ocean*, Cambridge: Cambridge University Press.

Steinberg, Philip E. and Kimberley Peters (2015), "Wet Ontologies, Fluid Spaces: Giving Depth to Volume through Oceanic Thinking," *Environment and Planning D: Society and Space*, 33: 247–64.

Steinberg, Philip E., Jeremy Tasch, and Hannes Gerhardt (2015), *Contesting the Arctic: Politics and Imaginaries in the Circumpolar North*, London: Tauris.

Steinsson, Sverrir (2016), "The Cod Wars: A Re-analysis," *European Security*, 25 (2): 256–75.

Sténuit, Robert (1966), *The Deepest Days*, trans. Morris Kemp, New York: Coward-McCann.

Stimson, Thomas E. (1956), "Algae for Dinner," *Popular Mechanics*, November: 134–6, 262, 264.

Stradling, David and Richard Stradling (2015), *Where the River Burned: Carl Stokes and the Struggle to Save Cleveland*, Ithaca, NY: Cornell University Press.

Strong, A.L., J.J. Cullen, and S.W. Chisholm (2009), "Ocean Fertilization: Science, Policy, and Commerce," *Oceanography*, 22 (3): 236–61.

Suárez, José (1928), report in the League of Nations Archives, C.P.D.I.28, Geneva, January 8.

Suárez-de Vivero, Juan L. and Juan C. Rodríguez Mateos (2017), "Forecasting Geopolitical Risks: Oceans as Source of Instability," *Marine Policy*, 75: 19–28.

Subcommittee on Environmental Pollution (1985), *Ocean Dumping: Hearing before the Subcommittee on Environmental Pollution of the Committee on Environment and Public Works*, Washington, DC: US Government Printing Office.

Subcommittee on Fisheries and Wildlife Conservation, and Subcommittee on Oceanography of the Committee on Merchant Marine and Fisheries (1971), *Ocean Dumping of Waste Materials: Hearings*, Washington, DC: US Government Printing Office.

Subcommittee on Natural Resources, Agriculture Research and Environment (1981), *Environmental Effects of Sewage Sludge Disposal: Hearing before the Subcommittee on Natural Resources, Agriculture Research and Environment of the Committee on Science and Technology*, Washington, DC: US Government Printing Office.

Subcommittee on Oceanography (1970), *Dumping of Nerve Gas Rockets in the Ocean: Hearing*, Washington, DC: Government Printing Office.

Subcommittee on the Environment and the Atmosphere (1975), *The Environmental Effects of Dumping in the Oceans and the Great Lakes: Hearings before the Subcommittee on the Environment and Atmosphere of the Committee on Science and Technology*, Washington, DC: US Government Printing Office.

Suman, Daniel (1991), "Regulation of Ocean Dumping by the European Economic Community," *Ecology Law Quarterly*, 18 (3): 560–618.

Sweeney, John (1955), *The How-To Book of Skin Diving and Exploring Underwater*, New York: McGraw-Hill Book Company.

Symonds, Craig L. (2018), *World War II at Sea: A Global History*, Oxford: Oxford University Press.

Tanner, Ariane (2014), "Utopien aus Biomasse: Plankton als wissenschaftliches und gesellschaftspolitisches Projektionsobjekt," *Geschichte und Gesellschaft*, 40 (3): 323–53.
Tanner, Ariane (2019), "Imaginations of the Perfect Human-Ocean Relation," Lunchtime Colloquium at Rachel Carson Center, YouTube, July 31. Available online: https://www.youtube.com/watch?v=HvhqfUzGgao (accessed October 18, 2020).
Tarr, Joel Arthur (1996), *The Search for the Ultimate Sink: Urban Pollution in Historical Perspective*, Akron, OH: University of Akron Press.
Taves, Brian (1996), "With Williamson beneath the Sea," *Journal of Film Preservation*, 52 (April): 54–61.
Telotte, J.P. (2010), "Science Fiction as 'True-Life Adventure': Disney and the Case of *20,000 Leagues Under the Sea*," *Film & History: An Interdisciplinary Journal*, 40 (2): 66–79.
Thompson, Andrea (2015), "Climate Change Is Increasing Stress on Oceans," Climate Central, July 14. Available online: http://www.climatecentral.org/news/climate-change-increasing-ocean-stress-19240 (accessed October 16, 2020).
The Mission to Seafarers (n.d.), "Shipping Stats: Key Facts and Figures," The Mission to Seafarers Media Centre. Available online: http://staff.missiontoseafarers.org/media-centre/statistics (accessed July 1, 2018).
Thompson, Krista A. (2007), "Through the Looking Glass: Visualizing the Sea as Icon of the Bahamas," in *An Eye for the Tropics: Tourism, Photography, and Framing the Caribbean Picturesque*, 156–203, Durham, NC: Duke University Press.
Thorpe, Andy, Pierre Failler, and Maarten J. Bavinck (2011), "Marine Protected Areas (MPAs)," Special Feature: *Environmental Management*, 47 (4): 519–24.
Tolf, Robert W. (1976), *The Russian Rockefellers: The Saga of the Nobel Family and the Russian Oil Industry*, Stanford, CA: Hoover Press.
Tong, Anote H.E. (2012), "HE Beretitenti Anote Tong's Speech," Yumpu. Available online: https://www.yumpu.com/en/document/view/21070088/he-beretitenti-anote-tongs-speech-on-the-occasion-of-the-opening- (accessed March 20, 2019).
Tong, Chris (2014), "Ecology Without Scale: Unthinking the World Zoom," *Animation: An Interdisciplinary Journal*, 9 (2): 196–211.
Tønnessen, Johan Nicolay and Arne Odd Johnsen (1982), *The History of Modern Whaling*, London: C. Hurst & Co.
Torma, Franziska (2013), "Frontiers of Visibility: On Diving Mobility in Unterwater Films (1920s to 1970s)," *Transfers: Interdisciplinary Journal of Mobility Studies*, 3 (2): 24–46.
Toscano, Alberto (2018), "The Mirror of Circulation: Allan Sekula and the Logistical Image," [blog] *Society & Space*, July 30. Available online: http://societyandspace.org/2018/07/30/the-mirror-of-circulation-allan-sekula-and-the-logistical-image/ (accessed March 20, 2019).
Townsend, Colin R., Michael Begon, and John L. Harper (2009), *Ökologie*, Berlin: Springer-Verlag.
Trischler, Helmuth (2016), "The Anthropocene: A Challenge for the History of Science, Technology, and the Environment," *NTM Zeitschrift für Geschichte der Wissenschaften, Technik und Medizin*, 24 (3): 309–35.
Tuan, Yi-Fu (2010), *Passing Strange and Wonderful: Aesthetics, Nature, and Culture*, Washington, DC: Island Press.

Tuan, Yi-Fu (2013), *Romantic Geography: In Search of the Sublime Landscape*, Madison: University of Wisconsin Press.

Tuten-Puckett, Katharyn and Pacific STAR Center for Young Writers (2004), *"We Drank Our Tears": Memories of the Battles for Saipan and Tinian as Told by Our Elders: In Commemoration of the 60th Anniversary of the WWII Battles for Saipan and Tinian*, Saipan, MP: Pacific STAR Center for Young Writers Foundation.

Tyack, Peter L. (2001), "Cetacean Culture: Humans of the Sea?," *Behavioral and Brain Sciences*, 24 (2): 358–9.

Tyrrell, Toby (2011), "Anthropogenic Modification of the Ocean," *Philosophical Transactions of the Royal Society*, 369: 887–908.

United Nations (UN) (1955), "Report of the International Technical Conference on the Conservation of the Living Resources of the Sea: 18 April to 10 May 1955," Rome: United Nations.

United Nations (UN) (1982), United Nations Convention on the Law of the Sea, Montego Bay, December 10. Available online: www.un.org/Depts/los/convention_agreements/texts/unclos/closindx.htm (accessed December 17, 2018).

United Nations (2006–16), "Human Settlements by the Coast," in *UN Atlas of the Oceans*. Available online: http://www.oceansatlas.org/subtopic/en/c/114/ (accessed December 9, 2018).

United Nations (2017a), "Programme of Side Events," *UN Ocean Conference*, June 7. Available online: https://sustainabledevelopment.un.org/content/documents/14666OC_Side_Program_Web.pdf (accessed December 17, 2018).

United Nations (UN) (2017b), *World Ocean Assessment*, Cambridge: Cambridge University Press.

United Nations (UN), ed. (1950), *Proceedings of the United Nations Scientific Conference on the Conservation and Utilization of Resources*, 8 vols, New York: Department of Economic Affairs.

United Nations Educational, Scientific and Cultural Organization (UNESCO) and International Union for the Protection of Nature (IUPN), eds. (1950), *International Technical Conference on the Protection of Nature: Proceedings and Papers*, Paris: UNESCO Publishing.

US Naval Photographic Center (1970), "Scuttling of the SS LeBaron Russell Briggs," August 18, US National Archives College Park, Department of Defense Collection.

US Army Research, Development and Engineering Command, Historical Research and Response Team (2001), *Off-Shore Disposal of Chemical Agents and Weapons Conducted by the United States*, Aberdeen Proving Ground, MD: US Army.

USCG (n.d.), "USCG Port State Information Exchange," USCG Maritime Information Exchange. Available online: https://cgmix.uscg.mil/PSIX/PSIXSearch.aspx (accessed August 18, 2018).

Van Dover, Cindy (1996), *The Octopus's Garden: Hydrothermal Vents and Other Mysteries of the Deep Sea*, New York: Basic Books.

VanDyke, John (1988), "Ocean Disposal of Nuclear Waste," *Marine Policy*, April: 82–95.

UN Environment Programme (UNEP) (2009), *Towards Sustainable Production and Use of Resources: Assessing Biofuels*. Available online: https://www.unenvironment.org/resources/report/towards-sustainable-production-and-use-resources-assessing-biofuels (accessed November 2, 2020).

UN Environment Programme (UNEP) (n.d.), "Discover the World's Protected Areas." Available online: https://www.protectedplanet.net/en (accessed October 22, 2020).

Vartanov, Raphael and Charles D. Hollister (1997), "Nuclear Legacy of the Cold War: Russian Policy and Ocean Disposal," *Marine Policy*, 21 (1): 1–15.

Verne, Jules ([1870] 2001), *20,000 Leagues Under the Sea*, New York: Penguin Books and Signet Classics.

Vinke, Hermann (1984), *Wir sind wie die Fische im Meer: Mikronesien, verseucht, verplant, verdorben*, Momente, Zurich: Arche.

Virilio, Paul (2007), *The Original Accident*, Cambridge: Polity.

Wahllöf, Niklas (2014), "Flygplanet är berättelsen om hur försvinnande faktiskt är möjligt i vår tid," *Dagens Nyheter*, April 10. Available online: https://www.dn.se/kultur-noje/kronikor/niklas-wahllof-flygplanet-ar-berattelsen-om-hur-forsvinnande-faktiskt-ar-mojligt-i-var-tid/ (accessed April 10, 2019).

Walcott, Derek (2007), "The Sea is History," in *Selcted Poems*, New York: Farrar, Straus and Giroux. Available online: https://poets.org/poem/sea-history (accessed October 9, 2020).

Waldron, T.J. and James Gleeson (1950), *The Frogmen: The Story of Wartime Underwater Operators*, London: Evans Brothers.

Walford, Lionel A. (1958), *Living Resources of the Sea: Opportunities for Research and Expansion*, New York: Ronald Press Company.

Walters, Carl and Jean-Jacques Maguire (1996), "Lessons for Stock Assessment from the Northern Cod Collapse," *Reviews in Fish Biology and Fisheries*, 6 (2) (June): 125–37.

Weigel, Viola (2009), "From the Aquarium to the Video Image: Introductory Remarks on the Works," in Viola Wiegel (ed.), *Under Water above Water: From the Aquarium to the Video Image*, 36–49, Bielefeld: Kerber Verlag.

Weinstein-Bacal, Stuart (1987), "The Ocean Dumping Dilemma," *Lawyers of the Americas*, 10 (3): 868–920.

Weisman, Alan (2007), *The World Without Us*, New York: St. Martin's Press.

Weiss, Francis Joseph (1952), "The Useful Algae," *Scientific American*, 187 (6): 15–17.

Westenhöfer, Max (1942), *Der Eigenweg des Menschen. Dargestellt auf Grund von vergleichend morphologischen Untersuchungen über die Artbildung und Menschwerdung*, Berlin: Verlag der Medizinischen Welt, W. Mannstaedt & Co.

Westwick, Peter and Peter Neushul (2013), *The World in the Curl: An Unconventional History of Surfing*, New York: Crown Publishers.

Wharton, Robert A., David T. Smernoff, and Maurice M. Averner (1988), "Algae in Space," in Carole A. Lembi, and J. Robert Waaland (eds.), *Algae and Human Affairs*, 485–509, New York: Cambridge University Press.

Whitehead, Hal and Luke Rendell (2014), *The Cultural Lives of Whales and Dolphins*, Chicago: University of Chicago Press.

Wikipedia (2020), "Holocene Extinction," October 16. Available online: https://en.wikipedia.org/wiki/Holocene_extinction (accessed October 16, 2020).

Williams, R.J., F.B. Griffiths, E.J. van der Wal, and J. Kelly (1988), "Cargo Vessel Ballast Water as a Vector for the Transport of Non-indigenous Marine Species," *Estuarine, Coastal and Shelf Science*, 26 (4): 409–20.

Witt-Miller, Harriet (1991), "The Soft, Warm, Wet Technology of Native Oceania," *Whole Earth*, 72: 64–9.

Wöbse, Anna-Katharina (2008), "Oil on Troubled Waters? Environmental Diplomacy in the League of Nations," *Diplomatic History*, 32 (4): 519–37.

Wöbse, Anna-Katharina (2011), "'The world after all was one': The International Environmental Network of UNESCO and IUPN, 1945–1950," *Contemporary European History*, 20 (3): 331–48.
Wöbse, Anna-Katharina (2012), *Weltnaturschutz: Umweltdiplomatie in Völkerbund und Vereinten Nationen 1920–1950*, New York: Campus.
Wolf, Klaus-Dieter (1981), *Die dritte Seerechtskonferenz der Vereinten Nationen: Beiträge zur Reform der internationalen Ordnung und Entwicklungstendenzen im Nord-Süd-Verhältnis*, Baden-Baden: Nomos.
Wolf, Mark J.P. (1999), "Subjunctive Documentary: Computer Imaging and Simulation," in Jane Gaines and Michael Renov (eds.), *Collecting Visible Evidence*, 274–92, Minneapolis: University of Minnesota Press.
Wong, Sam (2018), "Blue Planet? It's a Dark, Deep-Ocean World," *New Scientist*, August 11: 34–5.
Woodman, Richard (2010), *More Days, More Dollars: The Universal Bucket Chain, 1885–1920*, A History of the British Merchant Navy 4, San Bernardino, CA: Endeavor Press.
Wooster, Warren S. (1969), "The Ocean and Man," *Scientific American*, 221 (3): 218–38.
Working Group on the "Anthropocene" (n.d.), "Results of Binding Vote by AWG Released 21st May 2019," Subcommission on Quaternary Stratigraphy. Available online: http://quaternary.stratigraphy.org/working-groups/anthropocene/ (accessed October 16, 2020).
Wormbs, Nina (2017) "Satellite Sublime: The Workings of Remote Sensing in Ordering the Planetary," lecture, Deutsches Museum Munich, April 16, 2018.
Zalasiewicz, Jan, et al. (2008), "Are We Now Living in the Anthropocene?," *GSA Today*, 18 (2): 4–8.
Zelko, Frank S. (2013), *Make It A Green Peace: The Rise of Countercultural Environmentalism*, New York: Oxford University Press.
Zelko, Frank S. (2014), *Greenpeace: Von der Hippiebewegung zum Ökokonzern*, Göttingen: Vandenhock & Rupprecht.
Zeppetello, Marc A. (1985), "National and International Regulation of Ocean Dumping: The Mandate to Terminate Marine Disposal of Contaminated Sewage Sludge," *Ecology Law Quarterly*, 12 (3): 619–64.

Filmography

20,000 Leagues under the Sea (1916), [Film] Dir. Stuart Paton, USA: Universal Pictures.
20,000 Leagues under the Sea (1954), [Film] Dir. Richard Fleischer, USA: Walt Disney Productions.
The Abyss (1989), [Film] Dir. James Cameron, USA: 20th Century Fox.
Alien Deep with Bob Ballard (2012), [TV program] National Geographic Television, September 11.
Aliens (1986), [Film] Dir. James Cameron, USA: 20th Century Fox.
Aliens of the Deep (2005), [Film] Dir. James Cameron and Steven Quale, USA: Buena Vista Pictures.
Avatar (2009), [Film] Dir. James Cameron, USA: 20th Century Fox.
The Blue Planet (2001), [TV program] BBC One, September 12.
Blue Planet II (2017–18), [TV program] BBC One, October 29.
Chasing Coral (2017), [Film] Dir. Jeff Orlowski, USA: Netflix.

The Cove (2009), [Film] Dir. Louie Psihoyos, USA: Lionsgate.
Dangerous When Wet (1953), [Film] Dir. Charles Walters, USA: Metro-Goldwyn-Mayer.
Deepsea Challenge 3D (2014), [Film] Dir. John Bruno, Ray Quint, and Andrew Wight, USA: Disruptive LA.
Expedition: Bismarck (2002), [TV movie] Dir. James Cameron and Gary Johnstone, USA: Discovery Channel Pictures, December 8.
The Forgotten Space (2010), [Video] Sekula, Allan, Noel Burch, Frank van Reemst, Joost Verheij, Vincent Lucassen, Ebba Sinzinger, Menno Boerema, and Allan Sekula, Brooklyn, NY: Icarus Films.
Frolicking Fish (1930), [Film] Dir. Burt Gillett, USA: Walt Disney Productions.
Ghosts of the Abyss (2003), [Film] Dir. James Cameron, USA: Buena Vista Pictures.
L'Hippocampe, ou "Cheval marin" (*The Seahorse*) (1934), [Film] Dir. Jean Painlevé, France: Cinégraphie Documentaire.
King Neptune (1932), [Film] Dir. Burt Gillett, USA: Walt Disney Productions.
The Martian (2015), [Film] Dir. Ridley Scott, USA: 20th Century Fox.
Menschen unter Haien (1947), [Film] Dir. Hans Hass, Austria: Hans Hass-Filmproduktion.
Merbabies (1938), [Film] Dir. Rudolf Ising and Vernon Stallings, USA: Walt Disney Productions.
The Mysterious Island (1929), [Film] Dir. Lucien Hubbard, Benjamin Christensen, and Maurice Tourneur, USA: Metro-Goldwyn-Mayer.
Pinocchio (1940), [Film] Dir. Ben Sharpsteen and Hamilton Luske, USA: Walt Disney Productions.
Red Planet (2000), [Film] Dir. Antony Hoffman, USA: Warner Bros. Pictures.
Le Royaume des fées (1903), [Film] Dir. Georges Méliès, France: Star-Film.
Sea Scouts (1939), [Film] Dir. Dick Lundy, USA: Walt Disney Productions.
The Shape of Water (2017), [Film] Dir. Guillermo del Toro, USA: Fox Searchlight Pictures.
La Sirène (1904), [Film] Dir. Georges Méliès, France: Star-Film.
Solaris (1972), [Film] Dir. Andrei Tarkovski, Soviet Union: Mosfilm.
Sonic Sea (2016), [Film] Dir. Michelle Dougherty and Daniel Hinerfeld, USA: Imaginary Forces.
Soylent Green (1973), [Film] Dir. Richard Fleischer, USA: Metro-Goldwyn-Mayer.
The Terminator (1984), [Film] Dir. James Cameron, USA: Orion Pictures.
Terminator 2: Judgment Day (1991), [Film] Dir. James Cameron, USA: Carolco PIctures.
Titanic (1997), [Film] Dir. James Cameron, USA: Paramount Pictures.
The Undersea World of Jacques Cousteau (1966–76), [TV program] ABC, September 5.
Visite sous-marine du Maine (1898), [Film], Dir. Georges Méliès, France: Star-Film.
Volcanoes of the Deep Sea (2003), [Film] Dir. Stephen Low, USA: The Stephen Low Company.
Le Voyage à travers l'impossible (1904), [Film], Dir. Georges Méliès, France: Star-Film.
Le Voyage dans la lune (1902), [Film] Dir. Georges Méliès, France: Star-Film.
Water Babies (1935), [Film] Dir. Wilfred Jackson, USA: Walt Disney Productions.
The Whalers (1938), [Film] Dir. David Hand and Dick Heumer, USA: Walt Disney Productions.
World Without Sun (*Le monde sans soleil*) (1964), [Film] Dir. Jacques Cousteau, France: Orsay Films.

CONTRIBUTORS

Jon Crylen is an independent scholar based in Madison, Wisconsin. He holds a PhD in film studies from the University of Iowa, where his most recent academic appointment was as a visiting assistant professor in the Department of Cinematic Arts; he has also taught film studies and video production at Coe College in Cedar Rapids, Iowa. His work has appeared in *Media Fields Journal*, the *Journal of Cinema and Media Studies*, and *Cinema of Exploration: Essays on an Adventurous Film Practice* (ed. James Leo Cahill and Luca Caminati). He is completing a book manuscript titled *Ocean Movies: Representing the Undersea World in the Anthropocene*.

Colin Dewey is Associate Professor of English and Chair of the Department of Culture and Communication at the California State University Maritime Academy, United States. His career began sailing as able-bodied seaman in tankers, container ships, and offshore tugboats; he holds licenses as Mate (1,600 tons) and Master (200 tons) of motor vessels. Later, he graduated from the University of California, Berkeley, and received his PhD from Cornell University in 2011. His scholarship has been supported by an Andrew W. Mellon graduate fellowship at the Cornell Society for the Humanities, the National Endowment for the Humanities, and research grants from the California State University.

Rebecca Hofmann lectures at the institute for sociology at the University of Education in Freiburg, Germany. Her research spans various dimensions and aspects of mobility with a focus on refugee studies. Much of her anthropological work deals with local perceptions of climate change and climate change related mobilities for which she did extensive empirical field research in Micronesia. Questions of environmental change were also part of her research in Alaska and India. During her work at the Rachel Carson Center for Environment and

Society in Munich, she analyzed archival material and collected local histories on the movement of people due to natural disasters throughout the sixteenth to the twentieth centuries, mainly in the Pacific. Lately, she follows her interest in islands with the exploration of perceptions and experiences of "island time".

Sabine Höhler is Associate Professor of Science and Technology Studies at KTH Royal Institute of Technology in Stockholm, Sweden. She holds a MSc in physics and a PhD in history of science and technology. Her research addresses the earth sciences in the nineteenth and twentieth centuries in a global historical perspective: aviation and atmospheric physics, oceanography and deep-sea exploration, space flight and ecology. Her publications include the coedited volume *Civilizing Nature: National Parks in Global Historical Perspective* (2012) and *Spaceship Earth in the Environmental Age, 1960–1990* (2015) on the spaceship as a key metaphor in the late twentieth-century debate over the world's resources and the future of humankind.

Simone M. Müller is Project Director and Principal Investigator of the DFG Emmy Noether Research Group "Hazardous Travels: Ghost Acres and the Global Waste Economy" at the Rachel Carson Center for Environment and Society, Munich, Germany. She works at the intersection of globalization studies, economic and social history, and environmental humanities. She has received numerous awards and fellowships, among them from the Smithsonian Institution, the Science History Institute, and the University of Pennsylvania. Simone is speaker of the Young ZiF at the University of Bielefeld and was nominated as one of the leading female academics in her field by the German Research Foundation (DFG) and the Bosch Foundation in 2017.

Helen M. Rozwadowski is Professor of History and founder of the Maritime Studies program at the University of Connecticut, Avery Point, United States. Her recent publications include *Vast Expanses: A History of the Oceans* (2018) and *Fathoming the Ocean* (2005), winner of the History of Science Society's Davis Prize for best book directed to a wide public audience. She has also coedited *Soundings and Crossings* (2017) and *Extremes* (2007), amongst others. She was awarded the William E. & Mary B. Ritter Fellowship of the Scripps Institution of Oceanography and has received grants and fellowships from the National Endowment for the Humanities, National Science Foundation, and Smithsonian Institution.

Johanna Sackel is a historian and lecturer at Paderborn University, Germany. Her research focuses on international environmental regimes. In this context, she worked and published on the history of fisheries management. Furthermore her research interests include the history of North–South relations after decolonization as well as maritime history, especially the environmental history of the oceans. Her PhD project connected the Third United Nations Conference on the Law of the Sea with conceptions of marine resources and distributional justice during the global 1970s.

Ariane Tanner is a historian and writer. She holds a PhD in the history of science from ETH Zurich. The related monograph was published in German with Mohr Siebeck in 2017: "The Mathematization of Life." In 2019 she contributed to the "Forum: The Environmental History of Energy Transitions" in *Environmental History*. As a researcher, lecturer, and facilitator of participatory projects, her main topics of interest are the history of ecological and marine sciences, cultures of remembrance, and the Anthropocene. In her journalistic work she writes media reviews and reports on climate issues, and the societal role of science. She is involved in performance art.

Franziska Torma is Research Fellow at the Rachel Carson Center for Environment and Society at Ludwig-Maximilians University, Munich, Germany. She works on the history of marine biology in a project funded by the German Research Foundation (DFG-Eigene Stelle, 2017–21). She was a John F. Kennedy Memorial Fellow at the Minda de Gunzburg Center for European Studies, Harvard University (2012–13). She has held several positions at German universities, including project coordinator of the collaborative research project "The Language of Biofacts" (TU Munich). She has published on the history of mountaineering, animal protection issues in Africa, on Germany and the oceans, and on the broader field of colonialism with special reference to Germany's colonial culture and ideology.

Anna-Katharina Wöbse is an environmental historian and curator at the University of Gießen, Germany. Her PhD dissertation explored the environmental diplomacy of the League of Nations and the early United Nations. Anna has extensively published on the history of international environmental movements and environmental biographies, animal–human relations, and visual history. Her current project focuses on the contemporary European environmental history of bogs, tidal flats, fens, swamps, and mires.

INDEX

Note: Page locators in *italic* refer to figures and tables.

The Abyss 201
acoustic sounding technology 26–32, *27*
   Meteor expedition 28–32, *29*, *32*, *37*
   Second World War 32
aesthetics 47, 49, 165, 174
algae 184, 193
   cultivation for food projects 188–91, 193
   fuel from 193
Aliens of the Deep 161, 175–6, 178
Altman, Rick 165, 169
Alvin (DSV) 175, 208n8
animals 6–7, 19–20, 78
   acoustic sounding devices and harm to 32
   dolphins 6, 32, 156, 158, 178
   evolution of social behavior 156–7
   extinction 74–5, 178–9
   Greenpeace campaigns to protect 89
   introduced species 154–6
   migrating 77, 156
   seals 2, 74, 75, 89
   tracking 156, 157
   travelers 154–9
   (*see also* whales; whaling)
animations 167–8, *168*
Anthropocene 15, 184, 197–8, 202, 203
   culture in 1–3
   oceanic imaginations 198–201
   traces of 3–7
aquanauts 147, 196, 199–200
aquariums, cinematic 163–9

aquatic ape theory 6
Arctic Ocean 38, 102, 115, 195
ASDIC 32
"Atlantic Circulation" 30
Atlantic Ocean
   dumpsite sea anemones 109
   introduced species from 154
   Meteor's mapping of 28–32
   Mid-Atlantic Ridge 37
   waste dumping 99, 100, 101, 102, 111
Attenborough, David 170
Australia 111, 132
autonomous underwater vehicles (AUV) 23, 26–8, 44

ballast water 155
Baltic Sea 99, 100, 103, 110, 111, 112, 113
Bay of Biscay 109
Bazin, André 170
Beaches, Fishing Grounds, and Sea Routes Protection Act 1932 111
Beebe, William 144
Behm, Alexander 28
belonging, sense of 130, 138
Bikini atoll 128–30, *129*, 133, 134
biomass 184, 202
   dystopian 191–2
   as an energy source 193
   food or fuel discussion 193
   imaginary potential 185–8

quantification 187
regulation 187
reproductivity 187
utopia 188–91
Bismarck and Solomon Seas Indigenous Peoples' Council 88
Bjerknes, Jacob 40
Bjerknes, Vilhelm 30
"Blue Marble" 8–10, 18–19, 21, 22, 184, 195–6
Borgese, Elisabeth Mann 84–7, *86*
Boutan, Louis 170
Boyle, T.C. 199
Brent Spar campaign 90
Brown, Charles W. 50
bulk carriers 56, 57, 58–9

Cameron, James 161–2, 174, 175–7, 208n7
cargo
　carrying capacity 49, 56–7
　cults 125
　handling 51, *52*
Carson, Rachel 8, 14, 110, 120, 145, 181–3, *182*
CGI 172–4
Challenger expedition 26, 37
Charles W. Morgan 153
CHASE 95–6, 97, 101, 105, 107, 111, 112
chemical weapons 95–6, 98–9, 101, 105, 107, 109, 111, 115
Chlorella 188–90, *189*
Chuuk Lagoon 122–3, *122*, 126, 134, *135*
circumnavigation 140, 149, 151–2
Clark, Colin 192
Clark, Eugenie 144–5
Clarke, Arthur C. 146, 196
Clearwater 152–3
climate change 4, 6, 196–7, *197*
　Arctic Ocean 38, 195
　global warming 3, 14, 120, 184, 185, 196, 198, 202
　Pacific Islands 134–7, 138
　rising sea levels 4, 14, 117, 134, 196, 200–201
　sea-level rise 13, 134, 162
　"technological fix" to mitigate 198–9
　uneven impact 14
coal-fired ships 54, 56

coastal living 106, 200
cod 6–7, *96*, 154
Cohen, Margaret 48, 110, 165
Cold War 9–10, 37, 194
　ocean dumping 98, 101, 102, 115
　Oceania of strategic interest in 127
colonial networks 34, 47, 49, 52
colonialism 120–1, 125, 127, 128, 132
common heritage of mankind 12, 83, 84, 93
　early concepts 74–9
　sharing knowledge 85–7
　trusteeship 88–9
Conrad, Joseph 45, 46, 50, 69
　Lord Jim 47–9
conservation 6, 89
　marine reserves 6, 14
　networks 73, 80
container ships 58–9, 66, 102
　wrecks 66–7, *67*
continental shelf 35, 36, 37–8, 82
Convention on Safety of Life at Sea (SOLAS) 60–1
Convention on the Law of the Sea (*see* United Nations Convention on the Law of the Sea (UNCLOS))
Corbin, Alain 5, 201–2
Cousteau, Jacques-Yves 110, 142, 146, 162, 166, 170, 171, 174
craft of the mariner 48–9, 205n4
cruises 141, 148–9

Darwin, Charles 6
Davis, Susan G. 163
Davis, W. Jackson 115–16
Davy Jones's Locker 98
de Brum, Tony 134
deep sea 25–32
　mining 73, 81, 84, 87–9
　submersibles 167, 174–7, 208n8
Deepsea Challenge 3D 176–7, 208n8
del Toro, Guillermo 200
DeLoughrey, Elizabeth 129, 133, 134
the deluge 200–201
Demoll, Reinhard 186, 187
depth of oceans and seas 103
depth sounding
　acoustic sounding technology 26–32, *27*
　Challenger expedition 26, 37

"German Atlantic Expedition" 28–32, *29*, *32*, 37
  line-and-lead 25, 26, 30
  Second World War 32
Der Schwarm (The Swarm) 201
Diaz, Vicente 124, 125
digital databases 42, 44
diplomacy, maritime 72, 92–3
  League of Nations 75–9
  Pacem in Maribus 84–7
  United Nations 80–2
diving 5, 15, 142–7, *143*, 148
leisure 142, 143, 148
  Oceania tourist attraction 126–7, *126*
  scuba 143, 144, *145*, 148
  technologies 174–7
documentaries, underwater 169, 170, 171–4
  diving technologies 174–7
dolphins 6, 32, 156, 158, 178
dredge spoils 101–102, 108, 113
dumping, ocean 12–13, 96–102, *108*
  chemical weapons 95–6, 98–9, 101, 105, 107, 109, 111, 115
  dredge spoils 101–102, 108, 113
  industrial waste 101
  lack of knowledge of effects of 103, 106
  military 12–13, 95–6, 98–101, 105, 107, 109, 111, 126–7, *126*
  monitoring of 115
  presumed power of sea to wash away all evils 103–106
  protection of ocean from 96, 97–8, 107, 108, 109–113, *114*, 115
  radioactive waste 102, 108–109, 115, 131–2
  reappearing objects 109–111
  records 106–107, 109
  reports 113
  research 108–109
  sewage sludge 101, 104, 105, 108, 110, 111, 113–15
  and the vast expanse of ocean 103
dystopia 191–2, *192*

Earle, Sylvia 145
earth system science 38
"Earthrise" 8–9, *9*, *195–196*
eco-romantic narrative 8

El Niño 39–40, 42–3
empathy 183, 196, 201
Empire of Ants 110
engineers 50–1
ENSO (El Niño Southern Oscillation") 43
environmental approaches 4–5, 7, 13, 72–3
  Greenpeace 89–91
  international law and 83–4
  resource "turn" 79–82
  shared heritage concept 74–9, 83
environmental awareness 9, 12, 84, 89, 153, 184, 195–6
ESSO (Standard Oil of New Jersey) 61–2
"eternal sea" narrative of 8
Exclusive Economic Zones (EEZs) 35–6
exploitation of resources 4–5, 7, 38, 75, 82–3, 195
extinction of marine life 74–5, 178–9

Farbotko, Carol 136
films 5, 14, 67, 110, 144, 199, 200
  literature review of ocean 162–3
  science fiction 167, *169*, 191–2, *192*, 198, 199, 202
  (*see also* underwater filmmaking)
Fink, Leon 60
First World War 12, 14, 15
  dumping of materials from 98
  Germany after 31
fish
  cod 6–7, 96, 154
  culture 20, 158
fisheries 4, 4–5, 34, 78, 112, 154, 155
fishing
  dumped objects reappearing in nets 110
  expansion of industrial trawler 34, 74, 82
  overfishing 4–5, 7, 75, 195
  rights 35, 76
  setting of quotas and managing stocks 75
  spear fishing 142, 148
flags of convenience 61–2, 63
Fleming, Richard 108–109
Food and Agriculture Organization (FAO) 13, 80, 81, 189
food chain 115, 131, 185, 187, 188, 202
fragility, sense of 9, 12, 14, 184, 195–8
France 130

frontier, ocean as 143, 147, 184, 194, 195
future
    Cold War politics and exploration of 9–10
    geopolitical shift in oceanic imagined 192–5
    imagined food projects 188–91, 192
    MASS and 56–7, 69

George, Rose 68
"German Atlantic Expedition" 28–32, *29, 32, 37*
Gilpatric, Guy 142
global commons 13–14, 72–3, 76, 79, 84, 92, 93
    concept of common heritage and idea of 74, 83, 85
Global South
    climate change and impact in 14
    decolonization 15, 81
    and "ocean engineering" 82
    overfishing and impact on 4–5
    protein gap 13
    sharing knowledge with 85–7
globalization 13, 15, 59
Golding, William 121
Goldman, Francisco 63–5
governance, ocean 12, 13, 34, 75, 77, 80–2, 85, 93, 97
Great Britain
    call for a transnational solution to oil pollution 78, 81
    concerns over US dumping 111
    dumping at sea 100, 102, 104, 105, 107
Greenpeace 73, 89–91, *90*, 132
Grotius, Hugo 34
Guam 121, 123, 124, 125, 133, 138

Haeckel, Ernst 185
Hardin, Garrett 72
Hardy, Alister 188, 200
Hau'ofa, Epeli 138, 151, 203
Hawaii 151–2, *152*
Hayden, Sterling 149
Heezen-Tharp topographical map 36–7, *36*
Helmreich, Stefan 8, 24, 177
Helsinki Convention 113
Hensen, Victor 185, 187
Heyerdahl, Thor 152

history of long twentieth century 10–15
Hōkūle'a 151–2, *152*
Homer, Winslow 103
humpback whales *20*, 156, 158, 167

Iceland 111–12
"imaginary war" 194
imagination
    biomass potential 185–8
    characteristics of oceanic 183–5
    geopolitical shift in oceanic 192–5
    of ocean space 103–104, *104*
    oceanic Anthropocene 198–201
IMAX films 161, *168*, 169, 171–2, 175, 176
imperialism 11, 14
incineration, ocean 111
infrastructure 45
    of ports 51–2
    transported species and damaged 154–5
inner space 9, 147, 194
insurance 60
Intergovernmental Panel on Climate Change (IPCC) 196
International Congress of Geography 33
International Convention for the Prevention of Pollution of the Seas by Oil (OILPOL) 81–2
International Council for the Exploration of the Seas (ICES) 34, 75
International Geophysical Year (IGY) 35, 40
international law of seas (*see* law of the seas)
International Ocean Institute 85
International Polar Year (IPY) 33
International Seabed Authority 91–2
International Union for Conservation of Nature (IUCN) 14, 80
International Whaling Commission 81, 82
internationalisation, ocean 33–6, 46, 74, 77
introduced species 154–6
Irish Sea 99, 107
islands
    in Global Age 117–18
    imaginaries of 117–18, 136, 138
    metaphor of isolation 133
    (*see also* Pacific Islands)

Jameson, Frederic 47, 48
Japan
    dumping waste 104, 131–2
    factory discharges 112
    occupation of Pacific Islands 121, 122
    Pacific War 123–4
Jasanoff, Sheila 184, 195
Jeddah, SS 205n3
Jetnil-Kijiner, Kathy 137
Johnson, Irving 149–50, *150*

Kaldor, Mary 90, 194
killer whales 156
Klose, Alexander 59, 66
Kon-Tiki 152

Latour, Bruno 37, 42, 201
law of the seas 34
    League of Nations expert committee on international 76–9, 77
    (*see also* United Nations Convention on the Law of the Sea (UNCLOS))
League of Nations 12, 14, 73, 75–9, 77, 122
LeBaron Russell Briggs, SS 95–6
Lem, Stanisław 202
Leopold, Aldo 158
leveraged buyouts 58–9
Liberian Flags of Convenience 62, 65, 67
line-and-lead depth sounding 25, 26, 30
logistics 46–7, 48, 56, 59
    as ontology 65–7
London Dumping Convention 96, 97, 108, 109, 112–13
London Protocol 113
Lord Jim 47–9
Lord of the Flies 121
Low, Stephen 172, 175
Lowry, Malcolm 53–5

Maclellan, Nic 128, 130, 132
Malaysia Airlines flight MH370 23, 25, 28
mare liberum 34
Marey, Etienne-Jules 170
Mariana Trench 26, 103, 131, 147
marine artists 103, *104*
marine reserves 6, 14
Marshall Islands 128–30, 133, 134
The Martian 199

Masefield, John 150
MASS (Maritime Autonomous Surface Ship) 46–7, 69
McLean, Malcolm 58–9
Meadows, Donella 7, 87, 196
Melanesia 120–1, 125–6, 173
Merz, Alfred 29
Meteor expedition 28–32, *29*, *32*, 37
Michelet, Jules 74–5
Micronesia 121, 122, 126–30, 132, 134
    Bikini atoll 128–30, *129*, 133, 134
    Chuuk Lagoon 122–3, *122*, 126, 134, *135*
    Compacts of Free Association 128, 133
    Guam 121, 123, 124, 125, 133, 138
    Marshall Islands 128–30, 133, 134
    Palau 132–3
Mid Atlantic Ridge 37
military dumping 12–13, 95–6, 98–101, 105, 107, 109, 111, 126–7, *126*
Mills, Eric 40, 185
mineral resources 4, 13, 15, 73, 82, 96, 147
    mining 87–9
Mission to Planet Earth 39
Morgan, Elaine 6
MSC Napoli, MV 66–7
Murphy, Robert Cushman 150

Naimou, Angela 63, 64
narratives of the sea 7–8, 10
NASA 22, 39, *39*, 41, 42, 195, *197*, 199, *200*
nationalism 11
    ocean 33
navigation
    Pacific 151–2
    (*see also* acoustic sounding technology)
networks 71, 72
    diversification of 84–91
    early concepts of shared heritage 74–9
    institutionalization of 79–82
    maritime economic 88
    Pacific Islanders 88
    web of maritime regimes 91–2, *93*
New York City 60, 101, 104, 105
Newby, Eric 149
non-governmental organizations (NGOs) 72, 78, 81, 89
    Greenpeace and 90, 91

INDEX 247

North Atlantic 99, 100, 101, 111
North Sea 91, 99, 100, 103, 111, 112, 155
Norway 61, 101, 112
nostalgia 67, 68, 150, 152
Nouvian, Claire 207n1
Nuclear Free and Independent Pacific Movement (NFIPM) 132
Nuclear Free Zone Treaty 132
nuclear testing 128–34

ocean-atmosphere circulation 40, 42–3
ocean circulation theory 40
Ocean Conference 2017 93, 117
Ocean Dumping Act 107, 108, 112
ocean engineering 82
ocean internationalisation 33–6, 46, 74, 77
Ocean Literacy 21–2, 42, 43
Ocean Management Incorporation (OMI) 88–9
ocean nationalism 33
Oceania 118–21, 138, 206n2
    climate warriors 134–7
    Cold War 127
    colonialism 120–1, 125, 127, 128, 132
    map *119*
    nuclear programs 128–34
    Second World War 121, 122–4
    Second World War legacies 124–8
    sense of belonging 130, 138
oceanography 23–4, 43–4, 185
    Challenger expedition 26, 37
    continental shelf 35, 36, 37–8
    of deep sea 25–32
    diving and 141, 144
    "German Atlantic Expedition" 28–32, 29, *32*, 37
    Heezen-Tharp topographical map 36–7, *36*
    international communication and exchange 33–6
    Ocean Literacy 21–2, 42, 43
    opacity of sea to 23
    satellite 38–9, 40–3
    search for Malaysia Airlines flight MH370 23, 25, 28
    "technology writ large" 174–7
oil 55–6
    -burning ships 55, 56
    companies 55, 61–2

offshore 35, 82
pollution 73, 76, 78, 80, 81, 92
spills 67, 110
tankers 55–6, 56–7, *57*, 61, 62, 110
OILPOL (International Convention for the Prevention of Pollution of the Seas by Oil) 81–2
Operation Davy Jones's Locker 98
optics, underwater 165–6, 171
The Ordinary Seaman 63–5
Oreskes, Naomi 39, 194, 198
Organisation for Economic Co-operation and Development (OECD) 101, 102
Orlowski, Jeff 171
Oslo Convention 113
outer space 8, 9, 14, 18, 21, 173, 183, 193, 194, 202
overfishing 4–5, 7, 75, 195

Pacem in Maribus 84–7, *86*
Pacific Islands 118, 119
    imaginaries of 117–18, 136, 138
    map *119*
    metaphor of isolation 133
    navigation 151–2
    US Trust Territory 127, 132
    wars on and between 120, 137–8
    (*see also* Melanesia; Micronesia; Oceania)
Pacific navigation 151–2
Pacific Ocean *41*, 103, 118, 201
    dumping ground 100, 101, 102, 126–7, *126*, 132
    El Niño 39–40, 42–3
    Great Garbage Patch 138
    Mariana Trench 26, 103, 131, 147
    a "nuclear cesspool" 131
Pacific War 121, 123–4
Painlevé, Jean 170, 171
painting, marine 103, *104*
Palau 132–3
Panama 61–2
Pardo, Arvid 83, 84
Parry, Zale 144
Pearl Harbor 123, 127
Penck, Albrecht 31
perspective, linear 165
Piccard, August 147
plankton 184, 185, 186, *186*, 187, *197*

    as a carbon carrier 198–9
    cultivation for food 188–91
    decline in 196–7
    dystopian 191–2
plastics 2, 7, 7, 138, 153, 196
Plastiki 22, 40, 153
pollution
    conventions to prevent 112
    dilution of 105
    industrial waste 101
    nuclear testing in Pacific 131
    oil 73, 76, 78, 80, 81, 92
    plastic 2, 7, 7, 138, 153, 196
    washing up on Australian shores 111
    (*see also* dumping, ocean)
Polynesia 151–2
ports 51–2
Price, Willard 127
Pritchard, Zarh H. 165
Project Marina 109
property regulation 35
protection of ocean 13
    from dumping of waste 96, 97–8, 108, 109–113, *114*, 115
    early advocates for 12
    marine reserves 6, 14
    Ocean Conference 2017 93
    sense of fragility and need for 8, 195–8
    (*see also* United Nations Convention on the Law of the Sea (UNCLOS))

RADAR 32
radioactive waste 102, 108–109, 115, 131–2
recreation 139, 141, 142, 143, 148, 153
Red Planet 199
regulation, international marine transport 46, 59–61
Rena, MV 66–7, *67*
resources
    Arctic 38, 195
    exploitation of 4–5, 7, 38, 75, 82–3, 195
    extraction of 34, 35, 87–9, 148, 193–4
    mineral 4, 13, 15, 73, 82, 96, 147
    reservoir 10, 193–4
    rights to 35, 82
    "sovereignty" of 81
    turn from preserving to managing 79–82

romantic
    approach to human connections to the sea 5–6, *5*, 8
    biology 6
Royal Navy 55
Runit Island 130

safety regulations 12, 46
    Safety of Life at Sea (SOLAS) 60–1
Safina, Carl 158
sail training 148–54
sailing ships 49, 50, 51
San Francisco Bay 154–5
Sarasin, Paul 75
satellite oceanography 38–9, 40–3
Schätzing, Frank 201
Schott, Gerhard 27, 28
science fiction
    Red Planet 199
    Solaris 202
    Soylent Green 191–2, *192*, 198
    Twenty Thousand Leagues Under the Sea 25, *167*, 169
Scott, Ridley 199
Scripps Institute of Oceanography 144
scuba diving 143, 144, *145*, 148
sea
    anemones 109
    birds 78, 81, 107
    depth 103
    ethic 158
    floor mapping 31, 33, 36–7, *36*
    levels, rising 4, 14, 117, 134, 196, 200–201
    narratives 7–8, 10
    romantic approach to human connections to 5–6, *5*, 8
    vast expanse of 103
    washing away all evils 103–106
    zones 3–4
Sea Hunt 144
seafarers 46–7, 68–9
    conditions aboard ship 64–5, 69
    craft of 48–9, 205n4
    on margins of representation and society 63
    recruitment 59, 68
    steamships and changing roles of 49–51
    training 69

seals 2, 74, 75, 89
Second World War 12–13, 15, 142
   acoustic sounding technology 32
   changes to maritime industry 56
   dumping of materials from 12–13, 99–100, *99*, *100*
   ending of 128
   legacies in Pacific Islands 124–8
   in Pacific Islands 121, 122–4
   "resource turn" after 79–82
sewage sludge 101, 104, 105, 108, 110, 111, 113–15
The Shape of Water 200
Shell 90–1
shipworms 154, 155
shipwrecks 66–7, *67*, 110
size of ships 56–7, 59
Skagerrak 100, 110
Slocum, Joshua 140–1
Solaris 202
SOLAS (Safety of Life at Sea) 60–1
SONAR 32
"Southern Oscillation El Niño" 40
southern right whales 157, *157*
Soviet Union 102, 115, 127
Soylent Green 191–2, *192*
space exploration 146, 184, 193, 195–6
spear fishing 142, 148
species
   existing in ocean 103
   introduced 154–6
Standard Oil of New Jersey (ESSO) 61–2
Starosielski, Nicole 45, 66, 163, 178
steamships 49–52, *50*, *54*
Suárez, José León 76, 77, *77*, 83, 92
Subcommittee on Fisheries and Wildlife Conservation and Subcommittee on Oceanography 105, 106, 107
submarines 28, 32, 142, 147
submersibles
   deep-sea 167, 174–7, 208n8
   small 147–8, 167
surrealism 165, 170
The Swarm (Der Schwarm) 201

tailings, dumping of 101
Talley, Wilson 98
Teaiwa, Teresia 118
"technological fix" 192, 198–9

telegraph cables 26, 37, 49
The Terranauts 199
Thompson, William 170
tipping point 187, 197, 201, 202
Titanic, RMS 11–12, *11*, 28, 60
Tong, Anote 137
TOPEX/Poseidon Measurement System 39, *39*, 41, *41*, 42
tourism 5, 126
"The Tragedy of the Commons" 72
Trieste 147
Turner, J.M.W. 103, *104*
Twenty thousand Leagues Under the Sea 25, 167, *169*

Ultramarine 53–5
underwater filmmaking 109–110, 144, 161–79
   animation 167–8, *168*
   aquarium aesthetic 163–9
   CGI 172–4
   diving technologies 174–7
   documentaries 169, 170, 171–4
   extinction of marine life 178–9
   IMAX films 161, 168, 169, 171–2, 175, 176
   magnification 171
   microscopic imagery 171
   optics 165–6, 171
   power relations and cultural difference 178
   slow motion 171
   soundtracks 166–7, 207n2
   time lapse 171
   visual uncertainty 166
   walking the seabed 194
   zoom cameras 173
underwater habitats 146–7, 148
United Nations 35, 38, 80–2, 127, 136
United Nations Climate Summit 2014 137
United Nations Committee on the Peaceful Uses of the Sea-Bed 112
United Nations Convention on the Law of the Sea (UNCLOS) 13, 24, 35, 37–8, 83–4
   III 13, 38, 83, 84, 85, 88, 91
United Nations Educational, Scientific and Cultural Organization (UNESCO) 80, 81

United Nations Environment Programme (UNEP) 14, 193
United Nations Scientific Conference on the Conservation and Utilization of Resources (UNSCCUR) 80
United States
  Army-Kwajalein Atoll (USAKA) 131
  dive clubs 144
  Navy 62, 127, 146, 147, 175
  nuclear testing in Pacific 128–34
  ocean dumping 95–6, 97, 101, 104, 105, 107, 108, 111–12
  Ocean Dumping Act 107, 108, 112
  Operation CHASE 95–6, 97, 101, 105, 107, 111, 112
  Pacific War 121, 123–4
  strategic and trading interests in Pacific Islands 127–8
  Trust Territory of Pacific Islands 127, 132
utopia 188–91

VanDyke, John 104, 109, 113, 115–16
Verne, Jules 25, 147, 167
vertical ocean travel 142–8

Volcanoes of the Deep 172, 175
vulnerability, sense of 9, 12, 14, 184, 195–8

Walford, Lionel A. 189
Walker, Gilbert 40
West Germany 111
whales 6–7, *20*, 73, 74, 75, 76
  culture 156, 158
  humpback *20*, 156, 158, 167
  killer 156
  migrating 156
  southern right 157, *157*
whaling 74, 81, 89, 150, 157
  regulation of 75, 78, 81, 82
  ship 153
Williamson, John Ernest 167
Wolf, Mark J.P. 83, 173
World Without Sun 166, 171
writing and voyaging, link between 140, 144

zones of the sea 3–4
zoom, camera 173